Teacher's Book

CW01066655

American Headway

STARTER

Liz and John Soars
Amanda Maris

OXFORD

UNIVERSITY PRESS

OXFORD
UNIVERSITY PRESS

198 Madison Avenue
New York, NY 10016 USA

Great Clarendon Street
Oxford OX2 6DP England

Oxford New York

Auckland Bangkok Buenos Aires Cape Town Chennai
Dar es Salaam Delhi Hong Kong Istanbul Karachi Kolkata
Kuala Lumpur Madrid Melbourne Mexico City Mumbai Nairobi
São Paulo Shanghai Singapore Taipei Tokyo Toronto

with an associated company in Berlin

Oxford is a trademark of Oxford University Press.

ISBN 0-19-435389-3

American Headway Starter Teacher's Book:
Editorial Manager: Nancy Leonhardt
Managing Editor: Jeff Krum
Editor: Pat O'Neill
Production Editor: Arlette Lurie
Art Director: Lynn Luchetti
Designer: Michael Steinhofer
Senior Art Buyer: Jodi Waxman
Art Buyer: Andrea Suffredini
Production Manager: Shanta Persaud
Production Coordinator: Zai Jawat Ali

Printing (last digit): 10 9 8 7 6 5 4 3 2 1

Printed in China.

Acknowledgements

Cover concept by: Rowie Christopher
Cover illustration by: Rowie Christopher and Silver Editions
Illustrations by: Adrian Barclay, Chris Paveley

The publishers would also like to thank the following for their help:
p. 102 "You're My Everything" by Mort Dixon, Harry Warren, and
Joseph Young. Used by permission.
p. 108 "Don't Worry, Be Happy" by Bobby McFerrin. Copyright ©
1988 Prob Noblem Music. Used by permission of Original Artists.

Contents

American Headway

PHOTOCOPIABLE MATERIALS

Extra Ideas

STUDENT BOOK SCOPE AND SEQUENCE

Unit	Grammar

Vocabulary	Skills work	Everyday English

Introduction

American Headway

American Headway is a multilevel, four-skills series for adults and young adults who want to use American English both accurately and fluently. *American Headway* consists of four levels that take students, including true beginners, up through the intermediate levels.

American Headway combines the best of traditional teaching methods with more recent approaches to make the learning of English stimulating, motivating, and effective. *American Headway* enables students to analyze the systems of language in context as it exposes them to a variety of challenging and interesting types of text. Students are encouraged to produce accurate and level-appropriate language, and to bring their own personal experiences and feelings to the learning context.

Each level of *American Headway* contains approximately 80 to 120 hours of classroom material. Teaching time can be extended beyond this by using the extra activities in the Teacher's Book and Teacher's Resource Book and the practice activities in the Workbook.

American Headway Starter

American Headway Starter is for absolute beginners who want the reassurance of a steady, measured approach in the early stages of their language learning. Students are guided through the various exercise types, and there is tight control over the language they are exposed to. Beginning-level students who have studied English in the past can also use *American Headway Starter*, although you may find it more useful to have them begin with *American Headway 1*.

Student Book

The Student Book contains fourteen units. Each unit contains language input (Grammar, Vocabulary, and Everyday English) plus skills development (Reading, Speaking, and Listening). In addition, a complete Tapescript, a point-by-point Grammar Reference, and Word List are at the back of the Student Book.

The audio program for the *Starter Student Book* is contained on a set of two Student Book Cassettes or CDs. These are meant for use in the classroom or in a self-access center. Exercises that have been recorded are clearly labeled (for example, **T 2.1**).

Workbook

The Workbook is mainly for home study, although the exercises can also be used in class to provide extra review and consolidation. The Workbook contains further practice of all the grammar and vocabulary presented in the Student Book. It also contains the writing syllabus.

The audio program for the *Starter Workbook* is contained on a Workbook Cassette or CD, which is designed for use by students on their own. Workbook exercises that have been recorded are clearly labeled (for example, **T 2.1**). However, all of the exercises in the Workbook can still be completed without the cassette/CD.

Teacher's Book

The Teacher's Book details the aims of each unit and provides step-by-step guidance on how to exploit the activities in each section of the unit. The Teacher's Book also contains notes on the language input (including areas of potential confusion), answers to all Student Book exercises, and cultural notes. The Workbook Answer Key and extra photocopiable material, including songs, are at the back of the book. The Teacher's Book also contains Progress Tests, and Stop and Check quizzes.

Teacher's Resource Book

The Teacher's Resource Book contains a wide variety of photocopiable activities, such as role plays, games, vocabulary work, quizzes, discussions, crossword puzzles, and information-gap exercises. These extra activities are designed to review and extend the material in the Student Book by providing additional speaking and listening practice.

Key features of *American Headway*

A balanced approach

American Headway adopts a balanced approach to teaching English by combining the best of traditional methods with current approaches.

A TRADITIONAL APPROACH

- Grammar is given a high profile. It is not disguised. The grammatical systems of English are presented, practiced, tested, and explained.
- Vocabulary acquisition is an important element of every unit.
- There are pre-communicative exercises to provide controlled practice. These boost students' confidence, especially at lower levels.

A CURRENT APPROACH

- Students are guided to work out rules for themselves. They are encouraged to adopt a certain responsibility for their own learning.

- Real-life situations are rehearsed in the classroom, with role plays, situational activities, authentic material, excerpts from newspapers and magazines, and interviews with real people.
- The language is seen as a whole. Learners acquire new language items by seeing them and using them in communicative activities.

EFFECTIVE TEACHING

Teachers will appreciate the comprehensiveness and effectiveness of *American Headway*. It has been designed to meet the practical lesson-to-lesson needs of the teacher. The units provide a balanced, cohesive timetable for the presentation, practice, and personalization of target language in a variety of exercise types, relevant vocabulary work, extensive skills work, and practical everyday situational English.

EFFECTIVE LEARNING

Students will appreciate the accessibility and effectiveness of *American Headway*. The units speak directly to students. The contents page, unit openers, headings, instructions, explanations, and cross-references are designed to guide students through the book with maximum understanding and involvement.

Unit Organization

Each Student Book unit in *American Headway* consists of the following sections:

Starter

The Starter is designed to be a warm-up for the lesson and has a direct link with the unit to come. This link might be topical or grammatical, or it might review input from a previous unit.

Presentation

A Presentation section follows the Starter. It has a personalized heading (for example, *What time do you...?*) followed by a definition of the language item being studied (e.g., Present Simple). Within each Presentation section, a Grammar Spot guides students to an understanding of the target language with questions, charts, and mini-tasks. There is usually a referral to the Grammar Reference at the back of the Student Book. (The Grammar Reference is intended for home study, although teachers might choose to have their students refer to it briefly during class.)

Practice

The Practice section provides a wide variety of engaging exercise types, such as matching, fill-in-the-blank, survey, role play, and information-gap activities. Students' attention is focused directly on the target language and related language areas in exercises such as Check It. *American Headway* features a mix of practice activities, both controlled and free, personal and impersonal.

Skills

Reading and listening are always taught with speaking. Reading and listening texts feature pre-activities to arouse students' interest and curiosity, and to get them thinking and talking about what they might read or listen to. A variety of comprehension activities give students clear reading or listening tasks. Follow-up activities invite students to personalize the topic and can be anything from a short discussion to project work. (Writing is covered in the Workbook.)

Vocabulary

Vocabulary either relates to the topic of the text, or is utilized in the text. A variety of vocabulary exercise types provides lexical input and works on the systems of vocabulary, such as collocations. The vocabulary in *American Headway Starter* is carefully graded and recycled throughout, so that students don't get overloaded.

Everyday English

An Everyday English section finishes off the unit and focuses on high-usage functional, situational, or social language.

The Syllabus

The Syllabus of *American Headway* combines language input (Grammar, Vocabulary, and Everyday English) with skills work (Reading, Speaking, Listening, and Writing).

Grammar

In *American Headway*, the language that students are exposed to and the language that they are invited to produce is very carefully graded. Over the series, the depth of language analysis gradually increases. Students' knowledge is confirmed and extended, and the range of their linguistic abilities widens accordingly.

It is our belief that an understanding of the grammar of English is one of the key enabling skills for language learners.

In *American Headway*, structures that are simpler in form and meaning are taught before approaching more complex ones. An understanding of the basics will help when more difficult items are encountered. This is exemplified by the sequence of presentations of tense forms in *American Headway 1* through *American Headway 3*.

AMERICAN HEADWAY STARTER

- to be
- present simple
- past simple
- present continuous
- present continuous for future

AMERICAN HEADWAY 1

- to be
- present simple
- past simple
- present continuous
- going to future
- present perfect simple

AMERICAN HEADWAY 2

- verb tense review
- extension of the present simple and present continuous
- presentation of the past continuous
- *will* and *going to*
- extension of the present perfect simple
- presentation of the perfect continuous
- presentation of the past perfect

AMERICAN HEADWAY 3

- verb tense review
- extension of the present simple and present continuous with state and event verbs
- comparison and contrast of the past simple, past continuous, and past perfect
- comparison and contrast of *will*, *going to*, and the present continuous for future meaning
- comparison and contrast of the present perfect simple and present perfect continuous

Teachers are constantly consolidating and extending their students' knowledge. Every classroom activity can be seen as a test of the state of the individual student's language abilities. It is our view that learners learn in the context of good teaching, but not necessarily as a direct result of it. A grammatical syllabus enables students to build a view of the structure of English. Over time, recognition of an item raises awareness that in the end leads to automatic production.

Vocabulary

In *American Headway*, vocabulary is developed in its own section. There are several important features about the way vocabulary is handled:

- New words are taught in lexical sets and learned in context.
- Vocabulary learning strategies show students how to begin to assume more responsibility for their own vocabulary acquisition.

- Systems of vocabulary (such as synonyms, antonyms, and compound nouns) help students perceive patterns in the language.
- Collocations (for example, *fly + a plane*, or *tell + a story*) put new vocabulary in context and make it immediately usable.

Everyday English

The Everyday English section at the end of each unit covers three main areas:

- survival skills (e.g., on the phone)
- functions (e.g., social expressions)
- language for special occasions (e.g., saying good-bye)

Skills work

The skills work in *American Headway* is carefully selected according to the level of the students. The ideal task should be realistic within the student's linguistic abilities and should challenge and interest them. Tasks should build confidence in the skill and leave students with a sense of satisfaction and achievement.

READING AND LISTENING

Items come from a wide variety of sources such as newspapers, magazines, short stories, biographies, reference books, real interviews, radio broadcasts, and songs. They are all authentic, but at lower levels we have adapted the language to suit the level.

SPEAKING

American Headway aims to enable students to speak, make conversation, be sociable, and function in the target language. Speaking activities range from totally controlled to totally free. There are many repetition exercises, especially at the lower levels, where students are invited to repeat items simply to show that they can get their mouths around the sounds. Often this is for "display" purposes, so students can have the satisfaction of their teacher's praise when they succeed.

Many speaking activities are personalized. Students are invited to relate the material in the Student Book to themselves, their lives, their family, and experiences. There is a lot of pair and group work to maximize students' contribution to the lesson.

WRITING

The writing syllabus is in the Workbook. In the Writing sections, students complete a number of simple tasks such as completing a family tree and then writing a short paragraph about their family to practice terms of relationships and possessive 's. It is probably the best use of class time to set up the writing exercises in class and then assign the actual writing task as homework.

A note from the authors ...

The concept of combining the best of traditional and more recent approaches has always been at the core of our writing. We write as teachers for the classroom. We have learned that the most important thing is to stay firmly rooted in the reality of the day-to-day teaching situation and not to discard approaches that are tried and tested just because they aren't trendy. We try to keep ourselves fully informed of the latest developments in the profession, but we draw only on what we believe is practically useful and usable in the classroom.

We have written *American Headway* to be a complete and balanced package that includes work with grammar, vocabulary, functions, situations, pronunciation, speaking, listening, reading, and writing. It is our hope that when students finish a unit of *American Headway*, they will feel that they have been challenged and that they have really learned something.

We have also written *American Headway* to be flexible, so that you can adapt the series for yourself, your students, and your teaching situation. You can follow the Student Book exactly as it is, using the notes in this Teacher's Book, or you can supplement the Student Book material with exercises from the Workbook and activities from the Teacher's Resource Book. You can also change the order of activities and use *American Headway* as a springboard for your own ideas. Remember, you are in control of the book, not the other way around.

We hope that you and your students enjoy using *American Headway* and have success with the books.

John and Liz Soars

A step-by-step approach

Beginners require a very careful, staged approach with plenty of repetition, practice, and review to help them internalize new language and to give them confidence. Suggested stages are as follows:

STARTER

This short warm-up to the lesson should not go on too long. Generally speaking, five minutes is the maximum.

PRESENTATION OF LANGUAGE POINT

You can vary the presentations if you like. Sometimes it is useful to play a recording first while the students look at the picture with the text covered. Then, after that, they can read and listen. This method may be helpful for students who are not very familiar with the Roman alphabet.

LISTENING AND REPEATING (DRILLING)

When introducing a new item of language, stop and practice pronunciation when students have grasped the meaning. You can use the recording as a model, or provide the model yourself. There are short pauses on the recording; you will need to stop the tape/CD to give students time to repeat at an appropriate pace. Allow students to listen to the word, phrase, or sentence two or three times before you ask them to repeat it. For example, to drill the sentence *How are you?* Play the recording and/or model the sentence yourself two or three times using the same pronunciation and intonation, then ask the students as a class to repeat the phrase, i.e., *choral drilling*. Don't say it with them, but instead listen to what they are saying. Say *Again* for them to repeat a second time. If it sounds as if they have it right, ask one or two students individually to say it again for you to check, i.e., *individual drilling*. If the choral repetition *doesn't* sound right, remodel the phrase for students to listen to again, then have them repeat chorally again, before moving on to individual drilling.

PRACTICE

Move carefully from controlled to freer practice. Beginners require plenty of practice in order both to get their mouths around new language and vocabulary, and also to internalize and remember it. Be sure to provide adequate practice and review, but at the same time do not spend too long on any one thing, or the students may get bored and switch off. You can always come back later and do more work on it.

The following techniques ensure enough practice as well as variety.

Pair work

A lot of work can be done in pairs. Open and closed pair work are often referred to in the teaching notes.

Open pair work

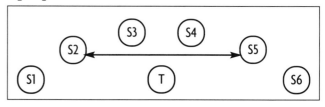

As a stage after drilling and before closed pair work, you can call on two students at a time to practice the lines of a conversation, ask and answer a question, etc., across the room, with the rest of the class listening.

Do open pair work:
- to set up and demonstrate a closed pair work activity
- to check understanding of a task
- to check students' grammar, pronunciation, and intonation before they go on to closed pair work
- after a closed pair work activity or a written exercise to check performance of the task.

Don't call on the whole class to perform open pair work. Two or three pairs of students, each performing one or two exchanges, should be sufficient to check language. More than this may make the activity drag and become boring.

Closed pair work

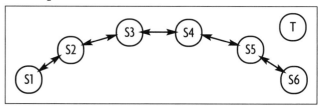

With closed pair work, students talk and listen only to each other. This gives them more speaking time and a chance to practice with a peer without having to "perform" in front of you and the class. It is important, though, for you to monitor students' performances unobtrusively. This will help you to identify persistent errors and misunderstandings. Do not interrupt and correct students while you monitor unless absolutely necessary, as this inhibits fluency. Instead, make a note of persistent errors and put some of them on the board for students to correct afterward. (It is probably not necessary to identify the culprits!)

Chain practice

This is a good way of using flash cards in a practice speaking activity. It offers variety, a change of pace, and a lot of speaking practice of the language point without becoming boring. The following example describes a way of using flash cards of famous people.

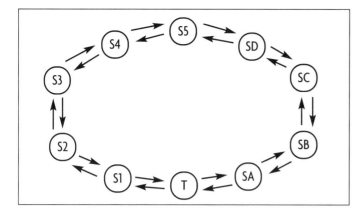

1 Stand in a circle with the students, with the flash cards in your hands.
2 Turn to S1 on your left, show the first card, and ask a question, e.g., *What's his/her name?* S1 answers, and receives the flash card from you.
3 S1 then turns to S2 and asks the same question. S2 answers, and receives the card.
4 While S1 is asking S2, turn to SA on your right, show the second card, and ask the question *What's his/her name?* SA answers, receives the card, and turns to ask SB.
5 While SA is asking SB, turn back to S1 with the third flash card, and ask the same question.
6 Continue the process until all the flash cards are in circulation and the students are asking and answering. There will be a bottleneck when the student across from you starts getting questions from both sides at once, but that's part of the fun. Eventually the flash cards should all come back to you. This practice game can get fast and furious!

Classroom practices

Whether you have a monolingual or a multilingual class, it will save a great deal of time and effort if, at the beginning, you set up clear classroom practices and establish familiar routines. This will quickly provide comfort and reassurance for beginners who can find it nerve-racking to deal with a new and alien language. Also, many complete beginners are adults who haven't been in a classroom for a long time, and whose previous experience of learning a language was probably very different.

CLASSROOM LANGUAGE

Numbers 1–30 and the alphabet will have been introduced by Unit 4 so that you can refer students to page and exercise numbers in English, and spell words for them. You should also spend a little time at the beginning pre-teaching some useful classroom language, e.g., *Sorry, I don't understand.*, *Can you spell it, please?* and instructions, e.g., *Work with a partner*, *Read*, *Listen*, *Repeat*, *All together*, *Again*, *Homework*, etc. All of this will enable you to keep an "English" atmosphere.

When having to give instructions for an activity, rehearse them beforehand so that they are simple, clear, and concise, and *demonstrate* rather than explain wherever possible. Avoid repeating yourself or over-explaining, as it tends only to create further confusion.

EXPLAINING NEW VOCABULARY

Explanation of new vocabulary to beginners can be problematic, particularly in multilingual classes, and/or where you have no knowledge of the students' mother tongue. Make sure that students have a simple bilingual dictionary. Use pictures and/or draw on the board whenever possible. Do not worry if you are not a great artist—simple line drawings are very quick and effective. Start collecting flash cards, posters, photos, etc., to help you.

Example sentences with the new word in context are often better than explanations. Giving a similar word or the opposite can also be useful, e.g., *finish = stop*, *get up ≠ go to bed*.

PRONUNCIATION OF NEW VOCABULARY

When you introduce new vocabulary, make sure you drill the pronunciation of the words as well. This should be done after the meaning has been established so that students are not mouthing words they do not understand. It is also a good idea to get yourself into the habit of highlighting and marking up on the board the main stress of new words, and having students copy this down, e.g., *teacher* or *teacher*.

USE OF MOTHER TONGUE

There can be no doubt that it is useful to *know* the students' own language (L1), especially if you have a monolingual class. How much you *use* it is another matter. It is probably best to use it sparingly:
- Perhaps in the first class talk to students in L1 about the course, how they will work, etc., and explain that you will be using English with them.
- Perhaps use L1 to check instructions for a new and unfamiliar activity, or to check understanding of a new language point, but only after using English.
- You can use L1 for translation of new vocabulary (where there is a one-to-one direct translation) and to deal with students' queries, particularly when it would waste a lot of time trying to explain in English.

Otherwise, you may find that if beginners feel that it is acceptable to use their own language freely in the classroom, they are inhibited from taking the plunge and speaking English to you and to each other, and it becomes more difficult for them to make that important leap.

am/are/is, my/your • This is…

How are you? • What's this in English?

Numbers 1–10 • Plurals

Hi!

Introduction to the unit

As you begin Unit 1 of *American Headway Starter* you are probably beginning a new class with a new group of students. The title of Unit 1 is "Hi!" and one goal is to let the students get to know each other and you, and for you to get to know them. The context of greetings and introductions in different settings allows students to do this and shows them how they can communicate in English in a meaningful way with even quite basic language.

Key language aims are fulfilled with the introduction of parts of the verb *to be,* the introduction of some basic vocabulary, numbers 1–10, and the plural endings *-s/-es.*

Language aims

Grammar—*am/are/is*   The verb *to be* is introduced in the singular with the subjects *I, you, this,* and *it* (*he/she/they* are introduced in Unit 2). The focus is on affirmative statements and questions with the question words *what* and *how*. (The question words are introduced through the functions of meeting people and greetings: *What's your name?, How are you?*; and talking about objects: *What's this in English?* Other question words are introduced and reviewed systematically throughout the text.)

Possessive adjectives   *My* and *your* are introduced in this unit; other possessive adjectives are presented over the first four units of the book.

Vocabulary   A set of key everyday words is introduced, some of which are international words, e.g., *camera*. There is an opportunity to extend this basic set via the classroom context.

Everyday English   Numbers 1–10 and *-s/-es* noun plurals are introduced and practiced. Students are introduced to the pronunciation of the *-s/-es* plural endings:

/s/	/z/	/ɪz/
books	cars	houses

Workbook   *To be* and *my/your* are consolidated through further practice with greetings and introductions. Key vocabulary, numbers 1–10, and *-s/-es* plurals are also practiced.

Notes on the unit

STARTER (SB p. 2)

T 1.1   Smile, greet the class, and say your own name: *Hi, I'm (Liz).* Point to yourself to make the meaning clear. Point to the speech bubbles and play the recording.

Invite students to say their own name, including the greeting *Hi.* If you have a very large group, you could ask a few students to say their names and then get students to continue in pairs. Keep this stage brief as students will have the opportunity to introduce themselves and each other in the next section.

WHAT'S YOUR NAME? (SB p. 2)

am/are/is, my/your

1 **T 1.2** Focus attention on the photo of Sandra and Kazu. Point to the conversation on p. 2 and ask students to read and listen. Play the recording through once.

Play the recording twice more, first pausing at the end of each line and getting the students to repeat as a class. Students then repeat lines individually before practicing the conversation in open and then in closed pairs (see Teaching Beginners—Tips and Techniques, TB p. xii). Encourage an accurate voice range—the amount by which the pitch of the voice changes. (Many languages do not use such a wide voice range as English so this needs to be actively encouraged.) Also make sure students can accurately reproduce the contracted forms *I'm* and *name's*. If necessary, model the sentences again yourself to help emphasize the pronunciation in a visual way.

> **GRAMMAR SPOT (SB p. 2)**
>
> Focus attention on the contractions. Ask students to circle the contracted forms in Exercise 1. Demonstrate this by writing the conversation on the board and putting a circle around the first contraction *I'm*.

2 This is a mingle activity. Demonstrate the conversation with one student for the rest of the class. Then ask another two students to repeat the conversation in open pairs (see Teaching Beginners Tips and Techniques, TB p. xii). Demonstrate the meaning of *stand up* and get the students to move around the class, practicing the conversation. You may want to encourage them to shake hands as they introduce themselves, particularly if they don't know each other. Monitor and check for pronunciation.

This is…

3 This section focuses on introducing people in a slightly more formal context, giving last names as well as first names. Say your first name again: *I'm Liz.* Write it on the board and say: *Liz is my first name.* Then say your last name and write it on the board: *My last name is Brown.* Repeat *I'm Liz Brown. Liz is my **first** name, Brown is my **last** name.* Then ask a student whose first name you know: *Mayumi—Mayumi is your first name, what's your last name?* Elicit last names from other students.

T 1.3 Focus attention on the photo of John, Sandra, and Kazu on p. 3. Point to the conversation and ask students to read and listen. Play the recording through once. Play the recording again and get students to point to the correct characters as they are referred to in the conversation.

Play the recording twice more, first pausing at the end of each line and getting the students to repeat as a class. Students then repeat lines individually before practicing the conversation in open and then in closed pairs.

Encourage accurate pronunciation of the short sound /ɪ/ and of the linking:

/ɪ/ /ɪ/
this is John Clark

4 Point to the speech bubbles. Choose two confident students to demonstrate the conversation with you for the rest of the class. Introduce the students to each other and encourage them to shake hands when they say *Hi.* Choose two more groups of three to practice the conversation in front of the class.

Divide the class into groups of three and get each student to take a turn introducing the other two. Monitor and check for pronunciation and intonation. Depending on the class, when the activity is over, you may want to ask one or two groups to perform the conversation again while the whole class listens.

> **SUGGESTION**
>
> If appropriate, you can play a memory game based on the students' names. Ask one student to go around the class saying everyone's name while the other students help if necessary. Encourage students in a multilingual group to pronounce everyone's name as accurately as possible. (You might want to do the memory game yourself, too, to make sure you have remembered all the students' names!)

How are you?

5 **T 1.4** Focus attention on the photo of Sandra and John on p. 4. Check that students can remember the names of the characters by asking *Who's this?* Point to the speech bubbles in the photo and ask students to read and listen. Play the recording through once. Play the recording twice more, first pausing at the end of each line and getting the students to repeat as a class. Students then repeat lines individually before practicing the conversation in open and then in closed pairs. Encourage accurate stress and intonation on the questions:

How are you?

And you?

6 **T 1.5** Focus attention on the photo of John and Kazu on p. 4. Check that students can remember the names of the characters. Follow the same procedure as for Exercise 5.

7 Focus attention on the speech bubbles. If necessary, check comprehension of *OK, fine, good* with simple board drawings of faces—a straight face for *OK* ☺, a half smile for *fine* ☺, and a full smile for *good* ☻. Ask individual students *How are you?* to elicit the answer F*ine,/Good, thanks. And you?* Reply to each student in turn. Make sure students realize that *And you?* requires an answer *Fine,/Good, thanks.*

Then get students to ask you in open pairs around the class. It may be helpful to gesture to your partner when you say *And you?* to aid comprehension.

8 This is another mingle activity. (You might want to develop a gesture that means "mingle.") Demonstrate the complete conversation from Exercise 7 with one student for the rest of the class. Then ask another two students to repeat the conversation in open pairs. Get the students to move around the class practicing the conversation. Monitor and check for pronunciation and intonation.

GRAMMAR SPOT (SB p. 4)

Focus attention on the sentences. Elicit the word to complete the first sentence with the whole class as an example *(am)*. Then ask students to complete the other sentences.

> **Answers**
> I **am** Sandra.
> How **are** you?
> This **is** John.

Read Grammar Reference 1.1 and 1.2 on p. 124 together in class, and/or ask students to read it at home. Encourage them to ask you questions about it, in L1 if appropriate.

PRACTICE (SB p. 5)

Introductions

1 Focus attention on the photos and conversations. Give students 30 seconds to read. Hold up the book so the class can see the photos. Read the first line of the first conversation aloud and point to the female character in the photo. Ask *Anna or Ben?* Point to the male and ask *Who's this?* Elicit the identities of Carla and Dennis for the second photo.

It is a good idea to write the first fill-in-the-blank conversation on the board and do it with the whole class, as students may not be familiar with this kind of exercise. Write students' suggestions (right or wrong) in the blanks.

T 1.6 Play the conversations for students to listen and check. See if they can hear and correct any mistakes

themselves before you offer correction. Then check the answers with the whole class.

> **Answers and tapescript**
> 1. **A** Hello. **My** name's Anna. **What's** your name?
>   **B** Ben.
> 2. **C** Hi. My **name's** Carla. What's **your** name?
>   **D My** name's Dennis.

Get students to practice the conversations first in open pairs and then in closed pairs. Monitor and check for accurate pronunciation. If necessary, model the conversations again, either yourself or from the recording, and get students to practice again.

2 If students had few problems filling in the blanks in Exercise 1, you could put them in pairs to try to complete the conversations in Exercise 2 together. Circulate and monitor, but don't correct any mistakes yet.

T 1.7 Play the conversations for students to listen and check their answers before checking them with the whole class.

> **Answers and tapescript**
> 1. **B Hi,** Anna. **How** are you?
>   **A** Fine, thanks, Ben. **And you?**
>   **B Good,** thanks.
> 2. **D** Hi, Carla. **How are** you?
>   **C Fine,** thanks. **And you?**
>   **D** OK, **thanks.**

Get students to practice the conversations first in open pairs and then in closed pairs. Monitor and check for accurate pronunciation. If necessary, model the conversations again, either yourself or from the recording, and get students to practice again.

3 **T 1.8** Focus attention on the conversation and play the recording. Make it clear that students should just listen the first few times and not try to fill in the answers. Play the recording twice more, then write the first line on the board and elicit what the second should be. Get students to fill in the number *2* next to the correct line in their books, then finish the exercise individually or in pairs. Play the recording again for them to check their answers. Elicit the whole conversation in the correct order from the class and put it on the board for the practice stage which follows.

As this is a longer conversation than the students have practiced up to now, play the recording two or three times and have them repeat chorally and individually. Then get them to continue in groups of three. (If appropriate, get them to stand up as this encourages a more dynamic performance!) Let students refer to the correct order on the board, but discourage them from reading it word for word, as they will lose the correct intonation and not make eye contact with the other students. Monitor and check for accurate pronunciation and intonation. If you think more practice is needed at this stage, get students to repeat the conversation using their own names.

> **Answers and tapescript**
> M = Mary   P = Pam   T = Tina
> **P** Hi. My name's Pam. What's your name?
> **T** I'm Tina, and this is Mary.
> **P** Hi, Tina. Hi, Mary.
> **M** Hi, Pam. How are you?
> **P** I'm OK, thanks. And you?
> **M** Fine, thanks.

Refer students to Grammar Referance 1.3 on p. 124.

ADDITIONAL MATERIAL

Workbook Unit 1
Exercises 1–4   These exercises provide further practice of greetings and introductions.

VOCABULARY (SB p. 6)

What's this in English?

1   Many of the words in the lexical set may be known to the students as they are "international" words or may be similar in their own language. Focus on the example and then get students to work individually or in pairs to match the rest of the words with the photos. Monitor and check for correct spelling.

Check the answers with the whole class.

> **Answers**
>   2. a camera
>   3. a television
>   4. a sandwich
>   5. a hamburger
>   6. a book
>   7. a computer
>   8. a bag
>   9. a house
> 10. a car

2   **T 1.9**   Play the recording and get students to listen and repeat the words. Check for accurate word stress and, if necessary, explain the system of stress marks used in *American Headway* by writing the words with more than one syllable on the board and highlighting the stress:

•
photograph

•
camera

•
television

•
sandwich

•
hamburger

•
computer

3   **T 1.10**   Focus attention on the speech bubbles. Demonstrate the conversation by pointing to the example in Exercise 1 and asking *What's this in English?* Elicit the reply *It's a photograph.* Play the recording and get students to repeat. Point to different pictures on p. 6 and get students to ask and answer in open pairs. Check for accurate pronunciation of *It's a* and, if students produce **Is a,* repeat the drill.

Students then continue asking and answering about the objects in Exercise 1, working in closed pairs.

> **GRAMMAR SPOT** (SB p.6)
>
> Focus attention on the contracted form. Ask students to circle the same form in the conversation.

4   Pick up a book and ask *What's this in English?* Elicit the reply *It's a book.* Pick up another object that students don't know how to say in English and elicit the question *What's this in English?* Give the answer *It's a (dictionary).* Students then continue picking up or going to objects in the classroom and asking and answering. Write the words on the board and highlight the word stress if necessary. (Avoid words beginning with a vowel and the need for students to use *an.* Also, try to limit students' questions to vocabulary that will be useful to them at this stage in their learning, e.g., *pen, dictionary.* Try not to let the activity go on too long!)

> **SUGGESTION**
> You can ask students for more examples of "international" words or cognates with the students' own language (e.g., *supermarket, hospital, telephone, video, cassette, radio, tennis, golf, football*). Write the words on the board and practice the pronunciation.

ADDITIONAL MATERIAL

Workbook Unit 1
Exercise 5   provides more practice of vocabulary.
Exercise 6   In this exercise, students translate sentences containing the main grammar points presented in the unit.

Numbers 1–10 and plurals

> **SUGGESTION**
>
> Students need a lot of practice with numbers, so from now on, use numbers as much as possible when referring to pages and exercises. Continue to do quick number reviews in future classes, especially as more numbers are introduced. This can include number dictations, either with you dictating or with the students working in pairs.
>
> **Teacher dictation:** Say numbers at random, writing them down yourself so that you have a way of checking. Students write the numerals, not the words, as you say them. Have one student read his or her list of numbers aloud to check.
>
> **Pairs dictation:** Students prepare a list of random numbers to dictate to their partner. They take turns dictating their lists. The student who is writing down the dictated numbers writes the numerals, not the words, and then reads the list back to his/her partner to check the answers.
>
> Make sure you limit the range of numbers to those covered at any stage in the book, e.g., Unit 1: numbers 1–10.

1 **T 1.11** Play the recording once and get students to read and listen to the numbers. Write *two* and *eight* on the board and put a line through the *w* and the *gh* to show that they are silent. Play the recording again and get students to repeat. Get students to say the numbers around the class, starting again at *one* once they reach *ten*. You can also get students to say the numbers in reverse order if appropriate. If students need more practice, write figures at random on the board and get students to say the numbers as you write.

ADDITIONAL MATERIAL

Workbook Unit 1
Exercises 7 and 8   These exercises provide further practice with numbers.

2 This exercise presents and practices formation of plurals with *-s/-es,* and reviews the vocabulary from this unit and numbers 1–10. Focus attention on the pictures and get students to count the objects/people and say the correct number, e.g., *a. ten.*

Look at the example with the whole class. Then get students to complete the rest of the exercise, referring back to the list of numerals and words at the top of the page. Monitor and check for correct spelling.

T 1.12 Play the recording and get students to check their answers. Get students to write the words on the board as a final check.

> **Answers and tapescript**
> a. **ten** sandwiches
> b. **two** books
> c. **six** bags
> d. **five** computers
> e. **four** houses
> f. **seven** hamburgers
> g. **eight** cameras
> h. **nine** photographs
> i. **three** cars
> j. **ten** students

> **GRAMMAR SPOT** (SB p. 7)
>
> Focus attention on the singular nouns and the plural noun endings. Ask students to underline the plural endings in Exercise 2.
> Refer students to Grammar Reference 1.4 on p. 124.

3 **T 1.13** Play the recording through once and let students just listen. Play the recording again and get the students to repeat chorally and individually. Focus attention on the symbols at the top of each column of words. Explain to students that these symbols represent the pronunciation of the plural endings *-s/-es.* These symbols will be used throughout *American Headway.*

Refer students to Grammar Reference 1.4 on p. 124 and highlight the use of the *-ies* plural, e.g., *city – cities.*

ADDITIONAL MATERIAL

Workbook Unit 1
Exercises 9 and 10   These exercises provide further practice of plurals. Exercise 10 recycles numbers.

Don't forget!

Word List   Ask the students to turn to SB p. 131 and look at the word list for Unit 1. Explain that this contains important words from the unit. Go through the words in class and ask students to learn them for homework. Test them on a few of the words in the following class.

2

Countries

Where are you from? • *he/she/they*

his/her • Numbers 11–30

Your world

Introduction to the unit

The title of Unit 2 is "Your world" and it focuses on countries and cities, and talking about where people are from. The characters introduced in Unit 1 are shown again in a different context. *Wh*-question words are reviewed and extended, and students continue with numbers 11–30. In terms of skills, students meet their first unseen listening task as well as a short reading text. These are important first steps in developing listening and reading skills and help to prepare students for handling progressively longer listening and reading texts throughout the book.

Language aims

Grammar—Where are you from?; *he/she/they* Students build on the *Wh*-questions introduced in Unit 1 with the introduction of *Where are you from?* The verb *to be* with *I* and *you* is consolidated and extended to include *he/she/they.*

Possessive adjectives *His* and *her* are introduced and *my* and *your* are reviewed from Unit 1.

Vocabulary Names of common cities and countries are introduced.

Everyday English Numbers are extended to cover 11–30.

Workbook The key lexical set of countries and cities is reviewed, including work on spelling and pronunciation.

He/she and *his/her* are consolidated through fill-in-the-blank activities.

Talking about where people are from is further practiced through fill-in-the-blank activities and a reading task.

Numbers 11–30 are practiced in a range of activities.

POSSIBLE PROBLEMS
- Beginners often make mistakes with *he/she* and *his/her* (especially if subject pronouns are not used and/or if the possessives are expressed differently in their own language). The text provides a lot of practice on this possible area of confusion, but be prepared to monitor and check the use of *he/she* and *his/her* and to go over these points whenever problems occur. Further confusion is possible with the contracted form *he's.* It's worth taking the time to drill the pronunciation of *his* /hɪz/ and *he's* /hiz/ to help students perceive and produce the difference.
- Students often have problems distinguishing teen numbers (*13–19*) from ten numbers (*30, 40, 50,* etc.). Highlight the different word stress:

    ●   ●   ●   ●

  thirteen   *thirty*   *fourteen*   *forty*

Notes on the unit

SUGGESTION
Take the opportunity to review the greetings covered in Unit 1 at the beginning of each class. Greet each student as they arrive in class and ask how they are. Encourage students to greet one another in English so that they get into the habit of using the language they have learned in a meaningful way.

STARTER (SB p. 8)

1 Focus attention on the place names in the box and on the map on p. 9. Demonstrate the activity by getting students to locate Australia on the map. Students continue locating the other places in Exercise 1 on the map, working in pairs. If there is any disagreement, check the answers with the whole class.

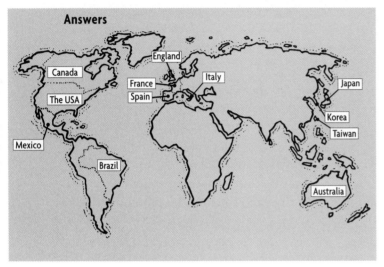

Answers

Get students to write their own country on the map. Remind them of the question *What's … in English?* from Unit 1 so that they can ask you for the name of their country, e.g., *What's (Nippon) in English?* (If you do not recognize the name of the country in the students' mother tongue, then ask them to point it out on the map.) Write the names of the countries on the board and drill the pronunciation as necessary.

2 **T 2.1** Play the recording and get the students to repeat chorally and individually. Pay particular attention to stress. If you have a lot of students from other countries, get them to say the name of their country and check the pronunciation.

WHERE ARE YOU FROM? (SB p. 8)

he/she, his/her

1 **T 2.2** This conversation introduces the second-person question form. Focus attention on the photos of Sandra and Kazu, who appeared in Unit 1. Point to the conversation and ask students to read and listen. Play the recording through once. Play the recording again and then ask *Where's Mexico? Where's Japan?* Get students to point to the correct part of the map.

Play the recording again, pausing at the end of each line and getting the students to repeat as a class. They then repeat lines individually before practicing the conversation in open and then in closed pairs. Encourage accurate reproduction of the contrastive stress in the questions, and of the falling intonation:

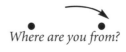

Where are you from?

Where are you from?

2 This is a mingle activity. If you have a multilingual class, make sure that all the students' countries are written on the board and practiced beforehand. If you have a monolingual class, you might want to teach them *I'm from (town/city) in (country)* to vary the answers. Demonstrate the conversation with one student for the rest of the class. Then ask another two students to repeat the conversation in open pairs. Get students to move around the class practicing the conversation. Monitor and check for pronunciation.

3 **T 2.3** Focus attention on the photos of Kazu and Sandra. Point to the sentences and ask students to read and listen. Play the recording through once. Play the recording again and get students to repeat. Encourage students to reproduce the long and short sounds in *his* and *he's*:

/ɪ/   /i/
His name's Kazu. He's from Japan.

Write the sentences about Kazu on the board. Circle *his* and *he*. Repeat **His** name's Kazu, **he's** from Japan. and model the sentence on another male class member: **His** name's Waleed, **he's** from Lebanon. Now contrast with a female student: **Her** name's Mei-ling, **she's** from China. Write the sentences about Sandra on the board and circle *Her* and *She*. Elicit more examples from the class to consolidate the use of *he/she* and *his/her*.

GRAMMAR SPOT (SB p. 8)

Focus attention on the contractions. Ask students to circle the contracted forms in Exercise 3. Read Grammar Reference 2.1 and 2.2 on p. 124 together in class, and/or ask students to read it at home. Encourage them to ask you questions about it.

4 Focus attention on the photos on p. 9. Read number 1 (about Jenny) with the whole class. Students continue working individually and then check their answers in pairs.

T 2.4 Play the recording through once and let students check their answers. Play the recording again and get students to repeat chorally and individually.

ADDITIONAL MATERIAL

Workbook Unit 2
Exercises 1–3   These exercises provide further practice of the countries introduced in the Student Book including pronunciation work.

Questions

5 **T 2.5** This exercise introduces third-person question forms. Play the recording and get the students to repeat chorally and individually. Check that students can reproduce the falling intonation of the *Wh-* questions.

GRAMMAR SPOT (SB p. 9)

1 Focus attention on the contraction *Where's*. Ask students to circle the contraction *Where's* in Exercise 5. Check that students recognize *What's* in Exercise 5 as the contraction of *What is*.
2 Focus attention on the sentences. Complete the first sentence with the whole class as an example *(is)*. Then ask students to complete the other sentences.

Answers
Where **is** she from?
Where **is** he from?
Where **are** you from?

Refer students to Grammar Reference 2.3 on p. 124.

6 Go through the activity with the whole class first before letting students do it in pairs. Focus attention on the photos on p. 8. Ask *What's his/her name?* and *Where's he/she from?* to elicit the answers. Monitor and check for correct use of *he/she* and *his/her*.

SUGGESTIONS

- If students need further practice with *I/you, my/your, he/she,* and *his/her,* make a photocopy of TB p. 99 and cut out the role cards. This exercise provides further practice by giving students a new name and country. The cards provide a male and a female name from each of the countries in the Student Book.
- Review the exchanges *What's your name? My name's (Robert). Where are you from? I'm from (the United States),* writing them on the board if necessary. Also

review when to use *he/she.* Pass out the role cards to the students, telling them this is their new name and country. Ask students to stand up and go around the class, asking and answering the question. Tell them they must try to remember everyone's new name and where they are from.

- When they have finished, point to various students and ask the class *What's his/her name?* and *Where's he/she from?* If the class is good, you can also check with the student in question whether the class has remembered correctly, asking *Is that right?*, and having him/her answer *Yes* or *No.*
- Alternatively, or in addition to the above suggestion, you could bring in pictures of famous people for more practice. You can use them for open pair work, or you could try a question-and-answer chain as follows:

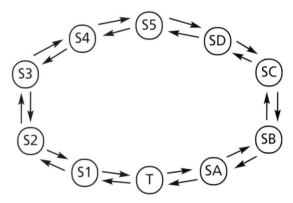

1 Stand in a circle with the students, holding the pictures in your hand.
2 Turn to S1 on your left, show the first card, and ask *What's his/her name?* and *Where's he/she from?* S1 answers and receives the picture from you.
3 S1 then turns to S2 and asks the same question. S2 answers and receives the picture.
4 While S1 is asking S2, turn to SA on your right, show the second picture, and ask the question *What's his/her name?* and *Where's he/she from?* SA answers, receives the picture, and turns and asks SB.
5 While SA is asking SB, turn back to S1 again with the third picture and ask the question.
6 Continue the process until all the pictures are in circulation and the students are asking and answering. There will probably be a bottleneck when the student across from you starts getting questions from both sides at once, but that's part of the fun. Eventually the pictures should all come back to you.

ADDITIONAL MATERIAL

Workbook Unit 2
Exercise 5   consolidates *he/she* and *his/her.*
Exercise 6   focuses on *Where are you from?* and also reviews the greetings from Unit 1.

Cities and countries

1 Focus attention on the names of the cities on p. 10 and drill the pronunciation chorally and individually. Model the conversation and get students to repeat chorally. Students repeat the conversation with a different city, e.g., *Boston,* in open pairs. Students continue working in closed pairs.

   T 2.6 Play the recording and let students check their answers.

Answers and tapescript	
Where's Tokyo?	It's in Japan.
Where's Seoul?	It's in Korea.
Where's Toronto?	It's in Canada.
Where's Rio de Janeiro?	It's in Brazil.
Where's London?	It's in England.
Where's Boston?	It's in the United States.
Where's Sydney?	It's in Australia.
Where's Mexico City?	It's in Mexico.

2 This is the first information-gap exercise that students have encountered in the book; it therefore needs to be set up carefully. Make sure students understand that they shouldn't look at each other's pages until the end of the activity. Each student has the name plus the city and country of four of the eight people in the photos. The aim is for each student to find out about the other four by asking their partner. If necessary, explain this using the students' own language and demonstrate a couple of question-and-answer exchanges with a good student first. Remind students of the forms they will need to talk about the men and women in the photos (*What's his/her name?* and *Where's he/she from?*). Drill all four questions again if necessary.

   Divide the class into pairs and make sure students know if they are Student A or B. Student A should look at p. 10 in the unit and Student B at p. 108 at the back of the book. Students can refer to each photo by saying the number. They should write their answers in the spaces provided.

   While students are asking and answering about the people in the photos, go around monitoring and helping out. If the names cause problems, get students to write them on a separate piece of paper and show it to their partner. When they have finished, you can check by asking individual students to tell you about one of the people in the photos. Say *Tell me about number one,* etc.

Answers
1. Her name's Mayumi. She's from Tokyo.
2. Her name's Carol. She's from London.
3. His name's Young-soo. He's from Seoul.
4. Her name's Paula. She's from Rio de Janeiro.

5. His name's Adam. He's from Sydney.
6. Her name's Rosa. She's from Mexico City.
7. His name's Ted. He's from Boston.
8. His name's Doug. He's from Toronto.

Talking about you

3 Point to a few students and ask the class *What's his/her name?* and *Where's he/she from?* Focus attention on the speech bubbles and get students to practice the questions and answers in open pairs across the class. Then get students to replace the examples in Exercise 3 with students' names and countries and to include the name of a city or town if appropriate. Students continue working in closed pairs.

ADDITIONAL MATERIAL

Workbook Unit 2
Exercise 4   reviews cities and countries.

Questions and answers

4 **T 2.7** Focus attention on the photo of Sandra and Luis on p. 11. Ask students *What's her name?* about Sandra and elicit the answer. Ask *What's his name?* about Luis and use the opportunity to elicit/teach *I don't know.*

   Play the conversation through once and get students to fill in as many blanks as possible. (With a weaker group, you may want to let them listen through once before they fill in the blanks.) Play the conversation again and get students to complete their answers. Check the answers with the whole class.

Answers and tapescript
S Hi, I'm Sandra. What's **your** name?
L **My** name's Luis.
S Hi, Luis. Where are you **from**?
L **I'm** from Mexico. Where are *you* from?
S Oh, I'm from Mexico, too. **I'm** from Mexico City.

Play the recording again, pausing at the end of each line and getting the students to repeat as a class. Have a couple of pairs of students practice the conversation in open pairs; then have the class continue in closed pairs.

> **SUGGESTION**
> If you have pictures of famous people of different nationalities, you can use these for additional practice. If not, you can write on the board the names of some famous people whose nationalities students will know, for more question and answer practice.

5 **T 2.8** This exercise consists of three short conversations with people from different countries and it is the students' first unseen listening. They should be well

prepared for the language by now, but some students tend to panic without the support of the written word. Explain that they only have to listen for two countries in conversations 1 and 2, and one country in conversation 3. Tell them not to worry if they don't understand every word!

Play the first conversation and elicit where Gabriel is from (Brazil). Play the rest of the recording and let students compare their answers in pairs. Play the recording again as many times as is necessary to let students complete their answers.

Answers
1. Gabriel: **Brazil**
   Akemi: **Japan**
2. Charles: **England**
   Mike: **the United States**
3. Loretta and Jason: **Australia**

T 2.8
1. **G** Hello, I'm Gabriel. I'm from Brazil.
   A Hello, Gabriel. I'm Akemi from Japan.
2. **C** Hello. My name's Charles. What's your name?
   M Hi, Charles. I'm Mike. I'm from the United States.
      Where are *you* from?
   C I'm from London, in England.
   M Oh, yeah? I'm from Chicago.
3. **L** Hi, I'm Loretta. I'm from Sydney, Australia.
   J Hi, Loretta. I'm Jason. I'm from Australia, too.
   L Wow! Are you from Sydney?
   J No. I'm from Melbourne.

SUGGESTION
Allowing students to tell you other details that they have understood from a listening can help build their confidence, so you can ask extra questions within the students' language range, e.g., *What's his/her name? Where in (England)?*

6 Look at the example with the whole class. Elicit the match for question 2 (*Her name's Amina*); then have students continue working individually before checking their answers in pairs.

T 2.9 Play the recording and let students check their answers.

Answers and tapescript
1. Where are you from? I'm from Brazil.
2. What's her name? Her name's Amina.
3. What's his name? His name's Luis.
4. Where's he from? He's from Mexico City.
5. What's this in English? It's a computer.
6. How are you? Fine, thanks.
7. Where's Toronto? It's in Canada.

Check it

7 Focus attention on the first pair of sentences as an example. Check that students understand the convention of putting a check mark (✔) to indicate that something is correct. Students continue working individually to choose the correct sentence.

Get students to check their answers in pairs before checking them with the whole class.

Answers
2. What's his name?
3. "What's his name?" "Luis."
4. He's from Mexico.
5. Where's she from?
6. What's her name?

READING AND LISTENING (SB p. 12)

Where are they from?

1 This is the first reading text that students have encountered in the book. It presents the subject pronoun *they*. Focus attention on the photo and get students to guess where Miguel and Angela are from. Get students to read through the text quickly and check (*Miguel—Brazil, Angela—Canada*). Check comprehension of *Canada* and *Brazil* by getting students to locate them on the map on p. 9.

T 2.10 Play the recording and ask students to read and listen. Then explain any new words. Words and phrases not previously introduced are *married, doctor, hospital, teacher, school,* and *in the center of. Married* can be explained by referring to a famous married couple. To explain *doctor,* you can turn to p. 14 of the Student Book (the start of Unit 3), where there is a picture of a doctor. Ask students *Where?* about the doctor to elicit/explain *hospital. Teacher* and *school* should be easy to explain in the context of the classroom. *In the center of* can be illustrated on the board.

GRAMMAR SPOT (SB p. 12)

Focus attention on the sentences. Complete the first sentence with the whole class as an example (*is*). Then ask students to complete the other sentences.

Answers
He **is** a doctor.
She **is** a teacher.
They **are** from Brazil.

If necessary, highlight the use of *he/she/they,* by pointing to a male student and saying *he,* a female

student and saying *she*, a pair of students and a group of students and saying *they*.
Refer students to Grammar Reference 2.4 on p. 124.

2 Students work in pairs to complete the sentences about the text. Make sure they understand that they can give the country or city as the answer to number 1. Go over the answers by asking individual students to read out their completed sentences.

> **Answers**
> 1. Miguel is from **Brazil/Rio (de Janeiro)**.
> 2. He's a **doctor**.
> 3. His hospital is in the **center** of Rio.
> 4. Angela is from **Toronto** in Canada.
> 5. She's a **teacher**.
> 6. Her **school** is in the center of Rio.
> 7. They **are** in New York.
> 8. They are **married**.

3 Focus attention on the questions in the speech bubbles in Exercise 3. Highlight the use of the contraction: *'s*. Get students to ask and answer in open pairs. Students then work individually to write questions about Miguel and Angela, using the prompts. Then get students to write other questions using *What …?* and *Where …?* Monitor and help as necessary. Students ask and answer in closed pairs. Monitor and check for correct use of *he/she* and *his/her*, and for falling intonation on the *Wh-* questions.

ADDITIONAL MATERIAL

Workbook Unit 2
Exercises 7 and 8   provide further reading and sentence completion practice.
Exercise 9   This is an exercise to practice *his/her*.
Exercise 12   In this exercise, students translate sentences containing the main grammar points presented in the unit.

EVERYDAY ENGLISH (SB p. 13)

Numbers 11–30

1 Get students to say the numbers 1–10 around the class, repeating as many times as necessary until students can say them without hesitation.

2 **T 2.11** Focus attention on the numbers 11–20. Remind students of the system used in the book for highlighting word stress. Play the recording and get students to listen, read, and repeat chorally. Play the recording again and get students to repeat individually. If necessary, remind students that the *gh* in *eighteen* is silent by writing the word on the board and crossing out the letters.

Get students to say the numbers 1–20 around the class. Again, get them to repeat as many times as necessary until they can say the numbers without hesitation.

> **SUGGESTION**
> Give students a number dictation. (See the *Everyday English* Suggestion on TB p. 6 of Unit 1.) Then write a random selection of numbers 1–20 (as figures) on the board and get students to say the numbers first chorally, then individually.

3 Focus attention on the example. Then get students to continue matching in pairs.

T 2.12 Play the recording through once and have students just listen. Have students check their answers in pairs. Play the recording again and get them to repeat, first chorally then individually. Check that students can distinguish the word stress on *thirteen* and *thirty*:

●   ●
thirteen   thirty

Get students to say numbers 1–30 around the class. Get them to repeat as many times as necessary until they can say the numbers without hesitation.

4 **T 2.13** Focus attention on the rows of numbers in Exercise 4. Play the first one as an example and focus on the answer *(12)*. Play the recording through once and get students to check (✔) the numbers. Let students compare their answers in pairs and then play the recording again if necessary. Review the answers with the whole class.

> **Answers and tapescript**
> 1. 12
> 2. 16
> 3. 21
> 4. 17
> 5. 30

5 Get students to do a number dictation in pairs using numbers 1–30 (See the *Everyday English* Suggestion on TB p. 6 of Unit 1). Student A should say the numbers and Student B should write. Then get students to change roles. Monitor and check for accurate pronunciation and comprehension of the numbers. Note any common errors, and drill and practice the numbers again in the next class.

ADDITIONAL MATERIAL

Workbook Unit 2
Exercises 10 and 11   review and consolidate numbers 11–30.

Don't forget!

Word List   Ask the students to turn to SB p. 131 and go through the words with them. Ask them to learn the words for homework, and test them on a few in the next class.

3

Jobs

am/are/is—negatives and questions

Address, phone number • Social expressions

Personal information

Introduction to the unit

The title of Unit 3 is "Personal information" and the main aim of the unit is to allow students to exchange more information about themselves. This includes job, age, address, phone number, and whether or not students are married. The grammar of the verb *to be* is recycled and extended to include the *we* form, negatives, *Wh-* and Yes/No questions, and short answers. In terms of skills, students get practice in listening and speaking, and reading and speaking.

Language aims

Grammar—*am/are/is*   The verb *to be* is recycled and extended to include the subject pronoun *we* in the negative and affirmative; negative forms *'m not, isn't;* questions with question words including *How old* and *Who;* Yes/No questions and short answers.

Possessive adjectives   *My, your, his,* and *her* are reviewed from Units 1 and 2.

Vocabulary   A set of common jobs is presented and there is an opportunity to extend this set with students' own jobs.

Everyday English   This section focuses on social expressions including greetings at different parts of the day (*Good morning, Good night,* etc.), and key situational language like *Excuse me, Sorry,* etc.

Workbook   The lexical set of jobs is recycled.

The forms of *to be* are fully reviewed with exercises on the negative, questions, and short answers.

Students are given extra practice in reading.

There is an exercise on word stress.

The social expressions from *Everyday English* are reviewed.

Notes on the unit

STARTER (SB p. 14)

> **NOTE**
> In this section, students are asked to give their own job. If you have a multilingual group or you don't speak the students' own language, ask them to look up the name of their job in a dictionary before class. Briefly check the pronunciation with the students so that they are prepared for Exercise 2.

1   This section introduces some job vocabulary and practices the question *What's your job?* Students will already be familiar with *doctor* and *teacher* from the *Reading* in Unit 2, so use these as examples to demonstrate the activity.

If you think students might know some of the jobs, put them in pairs and ask them to match any jobs they know and guess the others. Then check answers with the class. If you think students won't know any of the vocabulary or won't want to guess the answers, then do the matching activity as a whole-class exercise.

T 3.1 Play the recording and get students to listen and repeat the words, first chorally and then individually. Concentrate on correct pronunciation and word stress. Make sure students don't get confused by the spelling of *nurse* and *businessman* and pronounce the *u* incorrectly:

nurse /nərs/

businessman /ˈbɪznəsmæn/

2 Focus attention on the speech bubbles. Write the sentences on the board and circle the *a* in each answer to emphasize that we use an article before job titles. Drill the question and answers chorally and individually. Quickly check if students have jobs that are different from those in the Student Book. If students want to use a job beginning with a vowel, e.g., *engineer*, point out that they will have to use *an*—*I'm an engineer.*

WHAT'S HER JOB? (SB p. 14)

Negatives—*isn't*

1 **T 3.2** Briefly review *his* and *her* by pointing to a man and a woman in the *Starter* pictures and eliciting *What's his job?* and *What's her job?* Play the recording, pausing at the end of each line and getting the students to repeat chorally and individually. Make sure students include the article *a* each time. Students practice talking about the people in the pictures in open and then in closed pairs. Monitor and check for correct intonation and use of *his/her* and *a.*

> **SUGGESTION**
>
> If you think students need more practice, you can use flash cards of the same jobs that appear in the Student Book. Get students to ask and answer *What's his/her job?* in pairs, swapping the flash cards as they finish with them.

2 Point to the teacher in the Student Book and say *He isn't a student. He's a teacher.* Shake your head as you say the negative sentence to make the meaning clear. Point to the doctor and say *She isn't a nurse. She's a doctor.*

GRAMMAR SPOT (SB p. 14)

Focus attention on the negative sentence and what the contracted form is in full. Make sure students understand that the sentence is negative. Ask students to circle the negative forms in Exercise 2.

T 3.3 Play the recording, pausing at the end of each line and getting the students to repeat chorally and individually. Make sure students can reproduce the negative form correctly and that they include the article *a* each time.

Write the following cues on the board to demonstrate the activity:

Number 2   *He / sales assistant* ✗ */ taxi driver* ✔
Number 3   *She / teacher* ✗ */ police officer* ✔

Get students to give the above sentences in full (*He isn't a sales assistant. He's a taxi driver.* and *She isn't a teacher. She's a police officer.*). Students then continue talking about the pictures in closed pairs. Monitor and check for correct intonation, pronunciation of *isn't*, and use of *a.*

> **SUGGESTION**
>
> If you think students need more practice with *is/isn't*, you can get them to produce sentences with information about each other. You can talk about jobs and also review the language from Unit 2, e.g.:
> *Ana isn't a student. She's a teacher.*
> *Luis isn't a teacher. He's a doctor.*
> *Yoshi isn't from Tokyo. He's from Osaka.*
> *Her name isn't Helen. It's Helena.*

ADDITIONAL MATERIAL

Workbook Unit 3
Exercises 1–3   These exercises review jobs, the question *What's his/her job?*, and *is/isn't.*

Questions and short answers

3 Focus attention on the computer screen details. Read through the information with the class. Check comprehension of *address, phone number,* and *age* and drill the pronunciation of these words. Remind students of *married* from the *Reading* in Unit 2.

4 Focus attention on the example in number 1. Put students into pairs to complete the questions and answers. Note that students will have to generate the question *Where's she from?* for the *Country* category on the screen. This question should not be a problem for them, as they have already practiced it several times. The question *How old is she?* is new and is given in full so that students can familiarize themselves with it before they practice it. The short answer *No, she isn't.* is included in

this exercise. Again, students will be able to generate the question *(Is she married?)* for this answer, and Yes/No questions and short answers are covered in the following exercise. (With a weaker group, you could complete the questions and answers with the whole class first and use the "Listen and check" phase for repetition.)

T 3.4 Play the recording, pausing after each question and answer so that students can check their answers.

Answers and tapescript
1. What's her **name**?   Amy Roberts.
2. Where's she **from**?   The United States.
3. What's her **address**?   18 Cedar Street, Chicago.
4. What's her **phone number**?   It's (773) 726-6049.
5. How old is she?   She's **20**.
6. What's **her job**?   **She's a student.**
7. Is she **married**?   No, she isn't.

Play the recording again and get students to repeat all the questions and answers. Do this chorally and individually. Point out that in English we usually give our phone numbers using single figures 0–9, and the *0* is often pronounced "oh." Get students to ask and answer about Amy, working in open and then in closed pairs.

SUGGESTION

For further practice, cut out a picture of a man from a magazine (or draw one on the board) and provide similar ID information about him. Students then practice asking and answering the questions with *he/him*.

GRAMMAR SPOT (SB p. 15)

Focus attention on the questions and short answers. Make sure students understand that we don't repeat the key word from the question in the short answer. Ask students to circle the short answer in Exercise 4.

5 Yes/No questions and short answers, which appeared in Exercise 4, are covered in full here.

T 3.5 Focus attention on the speech bubbles. Ask students to read and listen. Play the recording through once. Play the recording again, pausing at the end of each line and getting the students to repeat as a class. Check for accurate reproduction of the rising intonation on the question and falling intonation on the answer:

Is Amy from England? No, she isn't.

Focus attention on the question cues in number 1 and demonstrate the first question-and-answer exchange with a confident student: *Is she from Portland? No, she isn't.* Students continue asking and answering about the other cities in question 1, working in open pairs. They

then continue asking and answering the other questions in closed pairs. Monitor and check for correct intonation and correct use of short answers.

Answers
1. Is she from Portland?   No, she isn't.
   Is she from Dallas?   No, she isn't.
   Is she from Chicago?   Yes, she is.
2. Is she 16?   No, she isn't.
   Is she 18?   No, she isn't.
   Is she 20?   Yes, she is.
3. Is she a teacher?   No, she isn't.
   Is she a nurse?   No, she isn't.
   Is she a student?   Yes, she is.
4. Is she married?   No, she isn't.

6 This exercise practices the affirmative and negative forms in sentences. Focus attention on the two examples in number 1. Students complete the sentences with the information about Amy. Get students to check their answers in pairs before checking them with the whole class.

Answers
2. Her phone number **isn't** (763) 726-6049. It's (773) 726-6049.
3. She **isn't** 18. She's 20.
4. She **isn't** married.

ADDITIONAL MATERIAL

Workbook Unit 3
Exercise 4   uses an ID card to practice personal information.
Exercise 5   A third-person question formation exercise.
Exercise 6   An exercise to practice third-person short answers.

WHAT'S YOUR JOB? (SB p. 16)

Negatives and short answers

1 Yes/No questions in the second person and short answers in the first person are presented here. Focus attention on the information about Jeff in the Visitor Record. Give students time to read it.

T 3.6 Play the recording through once and ask students just to listen. Play the recording again and get students to complete as many questions and answers as they can while they listen. Get them to compare their answers in pairs and help each other to complete the conversation, using the information about Jeff.

Play the recording again and get students to check their answers and/or complete any they missed. Check the answers with the whole class.

Answers and tapescript
A Is **your name** Jeff?
B Yes, it is.
A **Are you** from England, Jeff?
B No, I'm not from England. I'm from Houston, Texas.
A **Are you** a police officer?
B Yes, I am.
A **Are you** 23?
B No, **I'm not.** I'm 25.
A **Are you** married?
B Yes, **I am.**

GRAMMAR SPOT (SB p. 16)

1 Focus attention on the negative sentence and what the contracted form is in full. Make sure students understand that the sentence is negative. Ask students to circle the negative forms in Exercise 1.

2 Focus attention on the short answers. Make sure students understand that we use the full form in the third-person affirmative—*Yes, it is,* not **it's,* and that we cannot say **I amn't* for the first-person negative. Ask students to circle the short answers in Exercise 1.

Read Grammar Reference 3.1 on p. 125 together in class, and/or ask students to read it at home. Encourage them to ask you questions about it.

2 This is a "listen-and-answer" exercise where students reply to your questions. Focus attention on the speech bubbles. Ask the question to a number of students and elicit true short answers *Yes, I am* or *No, I'm not.* Drill the pronunciation of the short answers. Then ask the students further questions to generate a range of true short answers. These can include:

Name: *Are you (Yoshi)?*
Country: *Are you from (Brazil)?*
City: *Are you from (Taipei)?*
Job: *Are you a (teacher)?*
Age: *Are you (28)?*
Married: *Are you married?*

3 In this exercise, students mingle and ask each other Yes/No questions. Focus attention on the speech bubbles and get students to ask and answer in open pairs. It's a good idea to give students time to prepare their questions before they mingle, especially with a weaker group. Get students to write five questions using those in the book as a model and substituting information where possible.

Get students to stand up and do the activity. Monitor and check for correct intonation and use of short answers.

ADDITIONAL MATERIAL

Workbook Unit 3
Exercise 7 This exercise provides practice of the first-person short answers.
Exercise 8 A second-person question formation exercise.
Exercise 9 This exercise provides practice of first-person answers to questions with question words.

PRACTICE (SB p. 17)

Listening and speaking

1 Focus attention on the photos of Sang-hoon and Diana. Get students to read through the information in the chart so that they know what they have to listen for. Explain that they are going to hear two conversations, one with Sang-hoon and one with Diana. These are a little longer than in previous units, but reassure students that they only need to complete the information in the chart, and they don't have to understand every word.

T 3.7 Ask students to listen for the country Sang-hoon is from. Check the answer *(Korea).* Play the recording again from the beginning and get students to complete the information about Sang-hoon. Pause before moving on to conversation 2.

Play conversation 2 through once and get students to complete the information about Diana. Get students to compare their answers in pairs. Play the conversations again, pausing after conversation 1 and get students to complete/check their answers.

Check the answers with the whole class.

Answers

Name:	Sang-hoon Pak	Diana Black
Country:	Korea	**the United States**
City/town:	**Seoul**	**New York**
Phone number:	**(822) 773-3862**	(646) 463-9145
Age:	23	**29**
Job:	**Businessman**	Sales assistant
Married?	No	**Yes**

T 3.7

I = Interviewer   S = Sang-hoon   D = Diana
1. **I** Good morning.
   S Hi.
   I What's your name, please?
   S My name's Sang-hoon Pak.
   I Thank you. And where are you from, Sang-hoon?
   S I'm from Seoul, in Korea.
   I Thank you. And your telephone number, please?
   S It's (822) 773-3862.
   I How old are you, Sang-hoon?
   S I'm 23.

I And... what's your job?
S I'm a businessman.
I And... are you married?
S No, I'm not.
I Thank you very much.

2. I Hello.
D Hi.
I What's your name, please?
D Diana Black.
I And where are you from?
D From New York.
I Ah! So you're from the United States?
D Yes, I am.
I What's your phone number?
D It's (646) 463-9145.
I Thank you. How old are you?
D I'm 29.
I What's your job, Ms. Black?
D I'm a sales assistant.
I Are you married?
D Yes, I am.
I OK. Thank you very much.

2 Demonstrate the activity by asking a confident student the first question. Students continue asking and answering in closed pairs. Monitor and check. If students have problems with intonation or with the short answers, drill the questions and answers across the class and get students to repeat.

Check the answers with the whole class.

Answers

Yes, he is.	Yes, she is
No, he isn't.	No, she isn't.
Yes, it is.	Yes, she is.

SUGGESTION

If students need more practice, get them to ask and answer more Yes/No questions with the information about Sang-hoon and Diana, e.g.:
Is Sang-hoon from Korea?
Is Diana from Chicago?
Is he a teacher?
Is he 23?
Is her phone number (646) 463-9145?
Is she a sales assistant?
Is he married?
Is she married?

Talking about you

3 Focus attention on the example. Tell students they need a question word, e.g., *Where* or *What*, in all the questions except number 6. Get students to complete the questions in pairs. Check the answers with the whole class.

Answers

2. **Where are** you from?
3. **What's your** phone number?
4. How old **are you?**
5. **What's your** job?
6. **Are you** married?

Check the pronunciation of the questions. Make sure students use a falling intonation on the *Wh-* questions and a rising intonation on the Yes/No question (number 6). Divide the class into groups of three and get students to interview each other, using the questions. Get students to write down information about one student to use in Exercise 4.

4 Get students to use the information they found in Exercise 3 to write a short description. This can be done in class or for homework.

Check it

5 Focus attention on the first pair of sentences as an example. Remind students of the convention of putting a check mark to indicate that something is correct. Students continue working individually to choose the correct sentence.

Get students to check their answers in pairs before checking them with the whole class.

Answers

1. Her name's Soraya.
2. She's a teacher.
3. Are you from Brazil?
4. His phone number is 796-5242.
5. How old is she?
6. She isn't married.
7. "Are you married?" "Yes, I am."

ADDITIONAL MATERIAL

Workbook Unit 3
Exercise 12 This exercise provides further practice of questions and short-answer forms.

READING AND SPEAKING (SB p. 18)

A pop group

1 Check comprehension of the title "A pop group" by asking students to give names of groups they know. Focus attention on the photo and make sure students understand that it shows a pop group called 4 x 4 (said "four by four"). Pre-teach/check *on tour, great,* and *who?* The text also introduces the subject pronoun *we* and the preposition *at.* Students should understand these from context, but be prepared to explain if necessary.

Ask students to read through the text fairly quickly.

2 Focus attention on the answer in number 1 *(is 4 x 4)*. Students complete the rest of the sentences, working in pairs. Check the answers with the whole class.

> **Answers**
> 1. The name of the group **is 4 x 4.**
> 2. **Melanie Ryan is** from Australia.
> 3. Jennifer and Jason Walters **are from** the United States.
> 4. **Robert Lacoste is from** Canada.
> 5. "We**'re** on tour in the United States."

3 **T 3.8** Get students to read the questions through before they listen. If necessary, review the numbers 11–30 to help students when picking out the ages of the characters.

Play the first eight lines of the conversation (to "I'm 22.") and elicit the answer to question 1 *(Melanie is 22)*. Play the rest of the conversation and get students to listen for the answers to 2–4. If necessary, refer them back to the text so that they can remember the names of the characters.

Play the recording through again and get students to check/complete their answers.

Check the answers with the whole class.

> **Answers and tapescript**
> 1. Melanie is 22.
> 2. Jennifer is 21 and Jason is 20.
> 3. Robert is 19.
> 4. Melanie is married. Robert, Jennifer, and Jason aren't married.
>
> **T 3.8**
> **I = Interviewer   M = Melanie   Jas = Jason**
> **Jen = Jennifer   R = Robert**
> **I**   Hi!
> **All**   Hi!
> **I**   Now, you're Melanie, right?
> **M**   That's right.
> **I**   And you're from Australia?
> **M**   Uh-huh.
> **I**   How old are you, Melanie?
> **M**   I'm 22.
> **I**   And Jason and Jennifer. You're from England, right?
> **Jas**   No, no. We aren't from England. We're from the United States.
> **I**   The United States. Sorry. How old are you both?
> **Jen**   I'm 21 and Jason is 20.
> **R**   And I'm 19.
> **I**   Thanks. Now, who's married in 4 x 4?
> **R**   Well, I'm not married.
> **Jen and Jas**   We aren't married!
> **I**   Melanie, are you married?
> **M**   Yes, I am!
> **I**   Well, thank you, 4 x 4. Welcome to New York!
> **All**   It's great here. Thanks!

Check students understand *we* by gesturing to yourself and another student. Focus attention on the affirmative sentence and the contracted form *We're*. Make sure students understand what the contracted form is in full. Ask students to circle the examples of *we're* in the reading text.

Focus attention on the negative sentence and the contracted form *aren't*. Make sure students understand what the contracted form is in full and that the sentence is negative. Ask students to circle the examples of *aren't* in the reading text.

Refer students to Grammar Reference 3.2 on p. 125.

4 Tell students that they are going to invent a musical group. Focus attention on the questions in Exercise 4. Check students understand *Where are you now?* by asking the same question about the classroom situation. Divide the class into groups of four. Try to get a mixture of males and females in each group. Give students time to invent their imaginary identities and write down the details. Demonstrate the questions and answers with a confident group. For the answer to *What are your names?*, encourage students to use *I'm …*, and *This is …* to avoid the need for *our*, which is presented in Unit 4.

Then get the groups of students to ask and answer about their pop groups. Monitor and check. Get one or two groups to describe themselves to the rest of the class.

ADDITIONAL MATERIAL

Workbook Unit 3
Exercise 13   This exercise provides further reading practice.

EVERYDAY ENGLISH (SB p. 19)

Social expressions

1 Focus attention on the conversations and the expressions in the box. Focus attention on conversation 1 and elicit the second part of the answer *(Good morning)*. Students continue completing the conversations in pairs, using the pictures to help.

> **Answers and tapescript**
> 1. **Good morning.**
>   **Good morning,** Mr. Brown.
> 2. **Good afternoon.** The Grand Hotel.
>   **Good afternoon.**
> 3. **Good night.**
>   **Good night,** Peter.
> 4. **Good-bye!**
>   **Good-bye!** Have a good trip!

T 3.9 Play the recording and get students to check their answers. Students then practice the conversations in open and closed pairs.

NOTE

Exercise 2 contains examples of the Present Simple (*I don't know* and *I don't understand*). At this stage, it's best to treat these as useful expressions rather than explain the grammar behind the use of the Present Simple. This will be covered in Units 5 and 6.

---

2 **T 3.10** Focus attention on the first photo and on the fill-in-the-blank conversation. Play the first conversation as an example and review the answer *(I don't know)*. Play the rest of the recording, pausing at the end of each conversation. Students complete their answers using the words given.

If necessary, play the recording again to allow students to check/complete their answers before checking them with the whole class.

Answers and tapescript
1. **A** What's this in English?
   B I don't know.
   A It's a dictionary.
2. **A** *Hogy hívnak?*
   B Sorry. I don't understand.
   A What's your name?
   B My name's Manuel. I'm from Venezuela.
3. **A** The homework is on page … of the Workbook.
   B Excuse me?
   A The homework is on page *30* of the Workbook.
   B Thank you.

3 If necessary, play the recording again and get students to repeat. Students then practice the conversations in open and closed pairs.

ADDITIONAL MATERIAL

Workbook Unit 3
Exercises 14–16 These exercises review and consolidate the social expressions from the *Everyday English* section.

Don't forget!

Workbook Unit 3
Exercise 10 In this exercise, students translate sentences containing the main grammar points presented in the unit.
Exercise 11 is a word-stress exercise.
Word List Ask students to turn to SB p. 131 and go through the words with them. Ask them to learn the words for homework, and test them on a few in the following class.
Stop and Check 1 There is a Stop and Check quiz for Units 1–3 on p. 108 of the Teacher's Book.

our/their • Possessive *'s*

Family relations • *has/have*

The alphabet • On the phone

Family and friends

Introduction to the unit

The title of this unit is "Family and friends" and one goal is to extend the range of personal information students can give. The unit introduces the possessive *'s* with family vocabulary, *has/have*, and irregular plurals. Students get practice in all four skills with listening and speaking tasks, reading texts on family and friends, and a guided writing task.

The lexical set of family is presented and another important communicative tool—the alphabet—is introduced in *Everyday English*. This section also covers telephone language.

Language aims

Grammar—possessive *'s* The possessive *'s* is introduced via the context of family. The way of expressing possession in English is different from many other languages so students may initially have problems with this. Students are given lots of controlled practice in the Student Book and Workbook, and the *Grammar Spot* highlights possible confusion with *'s* as a contraction of *is*.

has/have *Has/have* are introduced in the affirmative. Apart from the third person singular affirmative, *have* operates like all the other verbs presented in the Present Simple so students won't be overloaded by new language.

Irregular plurals These are introduced as part of the presentation on families and are covered in Grammar Reference 4.3.

Possessive adjectives *Our* and *their* are introduced in this unit, and there is a review of all possessive adjectives and subject pronouns.

Vocabulary The lexical set of the family is introduced and practiced. There is also a focus on the language of describing a friend. Basic adjective + noun combinations are introduced via the reading texts, e.g., *a good job*.

Everyday English The alphabet is introduced and practiced and there is also a focus on telephone language.

Workbook The lexical set of the family is recycled.

Possessive *'s* is consolidated. There are exercises to help with potential confusion between both the possessive *'s* and the contracted form of *is*, and plurals.

Possessive adjectives and subject pronouns are consolidated.

Has/have are reviewed and consolidated.

There is a vocabulary categorizing exercise to review vocabulary from Units 1–4.

Students are given extra reading practice.

There is an exercise on word stress.

The alphabet and phone language from *Everyday English* are reviewed.

Notes on the unit

STARTER (SB p. 20)

1 **T 4.1** This section reviews all the possessive adjectives students have seen in Units 1–3 and also presents *our* and *their*. Focus students' attention on the subject pronoun column and briefly review *I*, *you*, etc., by pointing to yourself and students and eliciting the correct pronoun. Focus attention on the examples in the chart. Get students to continue completing the chart, working in pairs. Play the recording and let students check their answers.

Play it again and get them to repeat chorally and individually. Make sure they can distinguish *you/your*, *they/their*, and that they can pronounce *our* correctly.

Answers and tapescript

Subject pronoun	I	you	he	she	we	they
Possessive adjective	my	your	his	her	our	their

2 Focus attention on the examples in the speech bubbles. Say the sentences, pointing to relevant objects and getting students to repeat. Elicit more examples by pointing to objects that belong to the students and objects in the classroom.

PATTY'S FAMILY (SB p. 20)

Possessive *'s*—family relations

1 Focus attention on the photographs.

T 4.2 Play the recording and ask students to follow the text in their books. Check comprehension of *husband*, *bank manager*, *children*, and *school*.

Point to one member of the family and ask *Who's this?* to elicit the person's name. Take the opportunity to further practice *How old is…?* and *(I think) She's…* by asking *How old is (Patty)?*, and so on, to elicit possible ages.

GRAMMAR SPOT (SB p. 21)

1 Focus attention on the examples. Make sure that students understand that *'s* is the contracted form of *is*.

2 Review the use of *her* and then focus attention on the use of possessive *'s*. Make sure students understand that we use this form to express possession.

3 Review the use of *his* and then focus attention on the other examples with possessive *'s*. Ask students to circle the examples of possessive *'s* in the text about Patty. Make sure students don't confuse the contracted form of *is* with possessive *'s*.

Read Grammar Reference 4.1 and 4.2 on p. 126 together in class, and/or ask students to read it at home. Encourage them to ask you questions about it. Grammar Reference 4.3 on p. 126 focuses on irregular plurals. Read it together in class, and/or ask students to read it at home. Ask students to find an irregular plural in the text about Patty on p. 20 *(children)*.

2 Elicit the answers to questions 1 and 2 *(Yes, she is.* and *It's in San Diego.)*. Get students to continue answering the questions in pairs.

Answers and tapescript

1. Is Patty married?
   Yes, she is.
2. Where's their house?
   It's in San Diego.
3. What is Patty's job?
   She's a teacher.
4. Where's her school?
   It's in the center of town.
5. What is Tom's job?
   He's a bank manager.
6. Where's his bank?
   It's in the center of town.
7. Are their children doctors?
   No, they aren't. They're students.

T 4.3 Play the recording and get students to check their answers.

3 **T 4.4** Focus attention on the words in the chart. Play the recording and get students to repeat as a class.

4 **T 4.5** Focus attention on the family tree. Ask *Who's Patty?* and get students to point to the correct person in the photo on p. 20. Now focus attention on the example and play sentence 1 on the recording. Continue playing the sentences, pausing at the end of each one and getting students to write the correct words. Play the recording again and get students to check their answers.

Answers and tapescript

1. Patty is Tom's **wife.**
2. Tom is Patty's **husband.**
3. Kayla is Patty and Tom's **daughter.**
4. Nick is their **son.**
5. Patty is Nick's **mother.**
6. Tom is Kayla's **father.**
7. Kayla is Nick's **sister.**
8. Nick is Kayla's **brother.**
9. Patty and Tom are Kayla and Nick's **parents.**
10. Kayla and Nick are Tom and Patty's **children.**

Play the recording through again, pausing after each sentence and getting students to repeat chorally and individually. Make sure they reproduce the possessive *'s* accurately.

SUGGESTION

With a weaker group, use the family tree in a teacher-lead presentation, e.g., point to Patty and then to Tom and say *wife. Patty is Tom's wife.* Have students repeat the word in isolation first, then the whole sentence chorally and individually. Make sure that they pronounce the possessive *'s*. Students can then listen to the recording and write the words down as reinforcement.

5 Write the following on the board to reinforce the use of possessive *'s*:

Who(*'s*)Nick?   *'s* = *is*

He's Kayla(*'s*)brother   *'s* = *possessive, not is*

Drill the question and answers in open pairs. Then drill a plural example, e.g., *Who are Tom and Patty? They're Nick's parents.* Get students to continue asking and answering about Patty's family in open pairs. Make sure they give all possible answers about the different relationships and that they include plural examples, too. Students continue asking and answering in pairs. Monitor and check for correct use of possessive *'s* and *is/are*.

SUGGESTION

You can give students further practice on families and possessive *'s* by referring to famous people. Draw the family tree of a famous family, e.g., the Kennedys or some other famous family students will know, and get students to ask and answer questions with *Who?* Alternatively, you can prepare true/false statements about the family relationships.
You can also try a quiz based on famous people. Prepare questions based on relationships that your students will know. You can include movie stars, musicians, politicians, and athletes, e.g.:
Who's Laura Bush? (*She's George W. Bush's wife.*)
Who's Guy Ritchie? (*He's Madonna's husband.*)
Who's Kiefer Sutherland? (*He's Donald Sutherland's son.*)
Who's Stella McCartney? (*She's Paul McCartney's daughter.*)
Be prepared to modify the questions to suit the age and experience of individual groups.

ADDITIONAL MATERIAL

Workbook Unit 4
Exercises 1 and 2   provide further practice of family vocabulary.

PRACTICE (SB p. 22)

The family

1 Focus attention on the photo of Rachel Choi's family and on the names. Ask some general questions about the family: *Where are they from? What are their names?* Focus attention on the chart and make sure students understand what information they have to listen for by eliciting possible answers for each category, e.g.: name *(Joe)*, age *(16)*, job *(student)*.

T 4.6 Play the first part of the recording as far as *He's a student in high school.* Elicit the answers about Rachel's brother *(Steve, 15, student)*. Play the rest of the recording and get students to complete the chart.

Check the answers with the whole class.

Answers and tapescript

	Name	Age	Job
Rachel's brother	Steve	15	student
Rachel's mother	Grace	42	doctor
Rachel's father	Joe	44	businessman

T 4.6
Hi! My name's Rachel, and I'm from the United States. This is a photo of my family. Our house is in San Diego. This is my brother. His name is Steve, and he's 15. He's a student in high school. This is my mother. Her name's Grace. She's 42, and she's a doctor. And this man is my father, Joe. He's 44, and he's a businessman.

As a follow-up, point to each of Rachel's relations and get students to give a brief description, e.g., *This is Steve. He's Rachel's brother. He's 15, and he's a student.*

2 Focus attention on the example and then get students to complete the sentences in pairs.

Check the answers with the whole class, making sure students have included possessive *'s* where necessary.

Answers
2. Her **mother's** name is Grace.
3. Grace is Joe's **wife.**
4. "What's **his** job?" "He's a businessman."
5. "Where's **their** house?" "It's in San Diego."

3 Demonstrate the activity by writing the names of your own family on the board and talking about them. Give the information quite slowly but naturally and then ask a few questions to check understanding, e.g., *Who's this?, What's her job?*, etc.

SUGGESTION

If possible, it's a nice idea to base family descriptions on real photos. Bring in pictures of your family and ask students to do the same. If you have a small enough class, sit them around you and talk about the pictures slowly but naturally and pass them around. Encourage students to ask questions, following the models in Exercise 3 on p. 22.
Get students to draw their own family tree (and have their family photos ready if relevant). Divide the class into pairs and get students to ask about each other's family. Monitor and check for correct use of *he/she, his/her,* and *a* + job.
Ask a few students to choose someone in a family tree or in a photo and give a brief description of him/her. The person can be from their own or their partner's family.

Workbook Unit 4
Exercise 3   provides practice of possessive *'s*.
Exercises 4 and 5   help with potential confusion between possessive *'s* and the contracted form of *is;* and possessive *'s*, the contracted form of *is*, and plural *-s*.

my/our/your ...

4   This section consolidates the possessive adjectives covered in the *Starter* section. Focus attention on the example and then get students to complete the sentences. Ask students to check their answers in pairs before checking them with the whole class.

Answers
2. "What are **your** names?" "Our names are Kayla and Nick."
3. Daniel and Marta are students. **Their** school is in Mexico City.
4. "My sister's married." "What's **her** husband's name?"
5. "My brother's office is in New York." "What's **his** job?"
6. We are in **our** English class.
7. "Mom and Dad are in Seattle." "What's **their** phone number?"

ADDITIONAL MATERIAL

Workbook Unit 4
Exercises 6 and 7   provide further practice of possessive adjectives.

PATTY'S BROTHER (SB p. 23)

has/have

1   This section recycles family vocabulary, possessive *'s*, and possessive adjectives, and also presents *has/have*. Point to the picture of Patty on p. 20 and ask *Who's this?* Elicit the answer *It's Patty Milton.* Tell students they are going to read about Patty's brother.

T 4.7   Focus attention on the photograph of David and his son and play the first line of the recording as an introduction. Play the rest of the recording through to the end. Check comprehension of *farm* and *dogs* by pointing to the photo, and check students understand that *child* is the singular of *children*.

2   Elicit the answer to sentence 1 with the whole class as an example *(true)*. Then get students to complete the exercise working alone.

Get students to check their answers in pairs before checking them with the whole class.

Answers
1. ✔   2. ✔   3. ✘   4. ✘   5. ✘   6. ✘

GRAMMAR SPOT (SB p. 23)

Focus attention on the chart and the examples. Students complete the chart with the other forms of *have*.

Answers
I **have**
You **have**
He **has**
She **has**
We **have**
They **have**

Ask students to circle the examples of *has* and *have* in the reading text. Refer students to Grammar Reference 4.4 on p. 126.

3   **T 4.8**   This is a dictation activity. Each sentence is recorded twice, once at normal speed and once more with time for students to write. Demonstrate the activity by playing the first sentence and getting students to listen only, then play it again and get them to write it down. Tell students there are seven sentences in total. Play the rest of the sentences in the same way.

Write the sentences on the board and get students to check their answers.

Answers and tapescript
1. I have a small farm in Vermont.
2. My wife has a job in town.
3. We have one son.
4. We have two dogs.
5. My sister and her husband have a house in Los Angeles.
6. He has a very good job.
7. They have a son and a daughter.

Play the recording again, pausing at the end of each sentence and getting the students to repeat as a class. Students then repeat the lines individually.

4   In this exercise students write about themselves. Focus attention on the examples in the speech bubbles. Write a few more examples about yourself on the board and list the categories students can write about: brothers/ sisters, children, home, job, animals. Go around helping and checking.

Then ask a few students to tell the rest of the class about themselves and their family.

PRACTICE (SB p. 24)

has/have

1   Focus attention on the example. Students then complete the exercise working alone.

Get students to check their answers in pairs before checking them with the whole class.

2 Focus attention on the examples in the speech bubbles. Drill the sentences chorally and individually. List the categories students can talk about on the board: number of teachers / students / classrooms; size of school; equipment at your school (e.g., TV, VCR, CD player, computer). You will need to modify the examples to include equipment that students know you have at your school so that they only generate affirmative sentences.

Divide the class into pairs and get students to talk about their school. Monitor and check for correct use of *has/have*.

ADDITIONAL MATERIAL

Workbook Unit 4
Exercises 12 and 13   provide further practice of *has* and *have*.

Questions and answers

3 This exercise reviews the question words students have covered to date and also includes a Yes/No question. Focus attention on the example and then get students to match the other questions and answers.

T 4.9   Play the recording and get students to check their answers. Then let them practice the questions and answers in pairs.

Answers and tapescript
1. How is your mother?
   She's fine, thank you.
2. What's your sister's job?
   She's a nurse.
3. How old are your brothers?
   They're ten and thirteen.
4. Who is Patty?
   She's David's sister.
5. Where's your office?
   It's in the center of town.
6. Are you and your husband from Peru?
   Yes, we are.

Check it

4 Focus attention on the first pair of sentences as an example. Remind students of the convention of putting

a check mark to indicate that something is correct. Students continue working individually to choose the correct sentence.

Get students to check their answers in pairs before checking them with the whole class.

Answers
1. Mary's children are married.
2. What's your daughter's name?
3. What's his job?
4. They're from Thailand.
5. Their parents have a house in Bangkok.
6. My brother has a good job.
7. Our house is in the center of town.

ADDITIONAL MATERIAL

Workbook Unit 4
Exercises 8 and 9   provide more practice with family vocabulary.
Exercise 10   is a vocabulary categorizing exercise that reviews words from Units 1–4.
Exercise 11   is a word-stress exercise.
Exercise 14   In this exercise, students translate sentences containing the main grammar points presented in the unit.

READING AND WRITING (SB p. 24)

My best friend

> **NOTE**
> Students need access to dictionaries to check the new words in the reading text. If students don't usually bring dictionaries to class or if there isn't a class set of dictionaries available, ask them to check the new words (in **bold**) in the text for homework before the reading lesson.

1 Working alone or in pairs, students read the text and check the new words (in **bold** in the text). (If students have done the dictionary work for homework before class, ask them to do the reading and matching right away.)

2 Demonstrate the activity by eliciting the photo that goes with paragraph **a** *(Photo 1)*. Students continue to match the other photos and paragraphs, and say who they think the people in the photos are. Check the answers with the whole class.

Answers
Photo 1   paragraph a (Andy and Carrie)
Photo 2   paragraph d
Photo 3   paragraph c (Andy's sisters, Allison and Mary Ann)
Photo 4   paragraph b (Andy's parents)

3 Focus attention on the example sentence. Students complete the activity working individually and then check their answers in pairs. Check the answers with the whole class.

4 Focus attention on the speech bubble and then get students to give more information about Andy. Divide the class into pairs and get students to take turns talking about Andy, using the information they underlined in Exercise 3. Monitor and check for correct use of *is/are, has/have, he/she/they, his/her/their,* and possessive *'s.*

5 Prepare students for the writing phase by eliciting what kind of information can complete each sentence. If you have time, build up a connected description on the board of an imaginary person to provide the students with a model. Get the students to write their description in class or for homework.

> **SUGGESTION**
> It's a good idea to let students look at each other's written work to help correct it. When you correct the work, make a note of the most common mistakes in recent target language and get students to correct them as a class activity before you hand back individual work.

ADDITIONAL MATERIAL

Workbook Unit 4
Exercise 15 is a short reading to provide further practice of family vocabulary, possessive *'s,* and *have.*

EVERYDAY ENGLISH (SB p. 26)

The alphabet

This section covers the alphabet and spelling. Once students have learned the alphabet, take the opportunity whenever possible to spell new words to the students and to get them to spell words in class.

1 **T 4.10** Tell students they are going to practice the alphabet in English. Play the recording, pausing after each letter and getting the students to repeat as a class. Review any letters that students find confusing and drill these thoroughly, for example:

e, i, y

g, j

p, b

u, w

2 The letters in this exercise are arranged according to sound. Demonstrate this by reading the first group of letters /eɪ/. Say these letters again and get students to repeat as a class. Repeat for the other groups of letters and then get individual students to read different letter groups aloud.

Write different letters on the board at random and elicit them from the students. Pay special attention to the vowels as these often cause problems. Then put some known words on the board and elicit the spelling. (You could teach *How do you spell ...?* at this point.)

3 **T 4.11** Check comprehension of *first name* and *last name* and tell students they are going to hear five people spelling their names. Play the recording of the first name as an example. Then play the other names, pausing at the end of each last name. Students write the names and then check their answers in pairs. Check the answers with the whole class by writing the names on the board and getting students to spell them aloud.

4 Focus attention on the examples in the speech bubbles and drill the exchanges chorally and individually. Students practice spelling their own names in open and closed pairs.

5 Focus attention on the examples in the speech bubbles in Exercise 5. Drill the exchange chorally and individually. Students practice the exchange with different words from the text, working in open pairs. Students continue working in closed pairs. Monitor and check for accurate pronunciation of the letters.

6 Focus attention on the example. Students continue with the other countries. Then they check their answers in pairs before checking with the whole class. Get the students to give the spelling of each country, rather than just the name.

SUGGESTIONS

1 You can use anagrams such as the ones in Exercise 6 to review vocabulary at any stage. Write the jumbled letters on the board and ask students to figure out the word in pairs or teams. Always get the class to give the spelling letter-by-letter to review the alphabet as often as possible.

2 This is a spelling game called "Hangman." You can use it at the beginning of classes as a warm-up or as a filler to review vocabulary. You can put students into two or three teams for this, or play as a class.

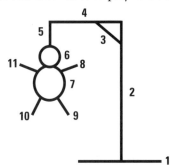

Choose a word and indicate on the board the number of letters it has, using a dash for each letter (i.e., if your word is *doctor*, write _ _ _ _ _ _). One team (or the class) suggests a letter. If the letter appears in your word, write it in the correct place on the dashes, as many times as it appears (i.e., if the letter suggested is *o*, you should write _ *o* _ _ *o* _ for the word doctor). If the letter doesn't appear in your word, write the letter in that team's column at the side of the board with a line through it, and draw one line of the gallows. Then the second team suggests a letter, and so on.

If you are playing in teams, the winning team is the one that guesses the final letter to complete the word or that guesses the whole word at an earlier point. If you complete the drawing of the gallows before the teams/the class guess the word, then you win and they lose.

ADDITIONAL MATERIAL

Workbook Unit 4
Exercise 16 provides further practice of the alphabet.

On the phone

7 **T 4.12** Focus attention on the first business card and ask *What's his name?, Where's his company?,* and *What's his phone number?* Play the recording through once and get students to follow in their books. Make sure students understand that *Who's calling, please?* is a polite way of asking *What's your name?* over the phone.

Play the recording again, pausing at the end of each line and getting students to repeat chorally and individually. Students practice the conversation in closed pairs. Repeat the above procedure for the second conversation, but use the feminine forms *What's her name?, Where's her company?,* and *What's her phone number?* about the second business card.

8 Ask students to write their own information on the blank business card. They should include first name, last name, address, and phone number and they can invent a company name if they like.

Get students to practice conversations 1 and 2 in open pairs, using their own information. Students continue working in closed pairs.

ADDITIONAL MATERIAL

Workbook Unit 4
Exercise 17 provides further practice of the phone language from the *Everyday English* section.

Don't forget!

Word List Ask the students to turn to SB p. 132 and go through the words with them. Ask them to learn the words for homework, and test them on a few in the following class.

> **EXTRA IDEAS UNITS 1–4**
> On TB p. 100, there are additional photocopiable activities to review the language from Units 1–4. There is a reading text with tasks, a question-formation exercise, and a matching activity on everyday English.

Sports, food, and drinks • Present Simple—*I/you/they*

a/an • Languages and nationalities • Numbers and prices

It's my life!

Introduction to the unit

This unit introduces the Present Simple with *I, you,* and *they* in statement forms. *Wh-* questions, and Yes/No questions and short answers are also practiced. At this point the Present Simple is used with a limited range of verbs so that students can become familiar with the new tense. Students get skills practice with reading and listening, and listening and speaking tasks.

Sports, food, and drink vocabulary is introduced in the context of likes and dislikes. The lexical sets of languages and nationalities are also presented. The *Everyday English* section extends numbers from 31–100 and also focuses on prices.

Language aims

Grammar—Present Simple 1   The Present Simple is the most used tense in the English language and it is therefore important to introduce it to beginners in an accessible way. In *American Headway Starter*, the tense is presented over two units, starting in this unit with the subjects *I, you,* and *they*. The affirmative and negative forms are covered along with *Wh-* and Yes/No questions. The third person singular forms are covered in Unit 6.

a/an   Students have met *a/an* + job in Unit 3 and the indefinite article is extended here to cover *a/an* + adjective and noun.

Vocabulary   Students practice the vocabulary of sports, food, and drinks in the context of likes and dislikes. Countries are recycled and languages and nationalities are introduced.

Everyday English   Numbers 31–100 and prices are introduced and practiced.

Workbook   The vocabulary of sports, food, and drinks is recycled.

The Present Simple with *I, you, they* is further practiced along with exercises on question formation.

Languages and nationalities are consolidated in a vocabulary and pronunciation section.

Students are given extra practice in reading.

Numbers and prices from the *Everyday English* section are reviewed.

Notes on the unit

STARTER (SB p. 28)

1   Focus attention on the photos. Demonstrate the activity by matching the first word in each category to the appropriate picture *(1—tennis, 13—Italian food, 4—tea)*. Students match as many words as possible, working individually or in pairs. Encourage them to guess if they are not sure. Ask them to compare their answers before checking them with the whole class.

Answers and tapescript

Sports	Food	Drinks
1 tennis	13 Italian food	4 tea
8 basketball	11 Chinese food	10 coffee
14 swimming	2 pizza	12 soda
7 skiing	3 hamburgers	9 juice
	15 oranges	6 water
	5 ice cream	

T 5.1 Play the recording and get students to repeat chorally and individually. Consolidate the vocabulary by holding up the book and pointing to the pictures. (Alternatively, hold up flash cards if these are available.) Ask *What's this?/What are these?* and elicit replies about three or four examples. Get students to continue asking and answering in pairs.

2 Write on the board three or four things that you like from Exercise 1. Put a check mark (✔) next to them and show by your expression that you like them. Get students to check the things they like in Exercise 1.

Repeat the above procedure for the negative, writing an ✗ next to the things you don't like and getting students to do the same.

THINGS I LIKE (SB p. 29)

Present Simple–*I/you*

1 **T 5.2** Focus attention on the speech bubbles and pictures. Play the recording once or twice before you ask students to repeat. Play the recording again and get students to repeat chorally and individually.

> ### GRAMMAR SPOT (SB p. 29)
>
> Focus attention on the examples. Make sure students understand that *don't* is the contraction of *do not*. If students ask what *do* means, you can explain simply (in the students' own language if possible) that it helps to make negatives and questions. However, do not give a detailed grammatical explanation at this stage.

2 **T 5.3** Focus attention on the photo of Bill and ask students to guess what he likes from the lists in *Starter* Exercise 1. Play the recording once and get students to check their predictions. Focus on the example and play the first line of the recording again. Play the rest of the recording and get students to write their answers. Students check in pairs. Then check the answers with the whole class.

> **Answers and tapescript**
> Well, I like **swimming** and **basketball**. I don't like **tennis**. Mmm... yeah, hamburgers and pizza—I like **hamburgers** and **pizza**. And **Chinese food**, I like Chinese food a lot—but not Italian food. I don't like **Italian food** and I don't like **tea**, but I like **coffee** and **soda**.

3 Drill the example in the speech bubble chorally and individually. Make sure students can reproduce the sentence stress accurately:

● ● ● ●
I like tennis, but I don't like basketball.

Demonstrate the activity by giving examples of what you like and don't like, using the vocabulary from *Starter* Exercise 1. Ask students to write down sentences with their likes and dislikes. Then, in pairs, students take turns talking to each other about their likes and dislikes. Ask a few students to read their sentences to the class.

ADDITIONAL MATERIAL

Workbook Unit 5
Exercises 1 and 2 provide further practice of key vocabulary and the verb *like*.

Questions

4 **T 5.4** The question form *Do you like ...?* is introduced here. Play the recording a couple of times and let students listen before you ask them to repeat line-by-line, chorally and individually. Make sure students can reproduce the pronunciation of *do you* /dyu/ and the rising intonation on the Yes/No questions.

> ### GRAMMAR SPOT (SB p. 29)
>
> Focus attention on the examples. Make sure students understand that we do not use *like* in short answers, i.e., you cannot say *Yes, I like or *No, I don't like. Again, it is probably best not to explain the function of *do* at this stage.

5 Focus attention on the examples in the speech bubbles. Get students to ask you the questions, drilling the pronunciation and intonation again if necessary. Students continue asking about the other items in *Starter* Exercise 1.

6 Focus attention on the examples in the speech bubbles. Drill the intonation, making sure students can reproduce the contrastive stress in the second question:

●
Yes, I do. Do you like tennis?

ADDITIONAL MATERIAL

Workbook Unit 5
Exercises 3 and 4 provide further practice of the Present Simple with *I/you* and short answers.

PRACTICE (SB p. 30)

Reading and listening

1 **T 5.5** Here students are introduced to more Present Simple verbs: *come from, live, work, eat, drink, play, speak,* and *want. Have* is also recycled from Unit 4. Other new words are *waiter, drama, restaurant, language,* and *actor.* The languages/nationalities *Spanish, English, French,* and *German* are also introduced in context.

Students read the text and listen to the recording once or twice. Try to get students to understand the new vocabulary in context and get them to refer to the information in the photos for help. Check comprehension of *live* and *work* by making sentences about yourself, e.g., *I live in (town, country), I work in (this school)*, etc. *Eat, drink, play,* and *speak* should be understandable from the context, but if students need help, mime the actions. (It is probably not worth going into the fact that *drink* is a verb here but a noun on p. 28.) Students should be able to understand *waiter, drama, restaurant,* and *actor* from the photos. If they query *language* and *Spanish, English, French,* and *German,* write the corresponding countries on the board and link them to the languages. You may need to translate *want to* if students query this. If students query the pronoun *it* in *I don't like it,* check that they understand what noun it refers back to *(tea).* (Object pronouns *it* and *them* are presented in full in Unit 7.)

GRAMMAR SPOT (SB p. 30)

Focus attention on the examples. Make sure students understand that we use *an* before a vowel—*a, e, i, o,* and *u.* Point out that this can be a noun, e.g., *an actor,* or an adjective, *an Italian restaurant.*

Refer students to Grammar Reference 5.2 and 5.3 on p. 126.

---

2 **T 5.6** Play the recording, pausing at the end of each question and getting students to repeat chorally and individually.

T 5.7 Get students to complete Brad's answers. Then play the recording and check the answers with the whole class.

Answers and tapescript

1. Do you come from Ohio? Yes, I **do.**
2. Do you live in Cleveland? No, I **don't.** I **live** in New York.
3. Do you live in an apartment? Yes, I **do.** I **live** in an apartment downtown.
4. Do you work in a Chinese restaurant? No, I **don't.** I **work** in an Italian restaurant.
5. Do you like Italian food? Yes, I **do.** I **like** it a lot.
6. Do you like your job? No, I **don't.** I want to be **an actor.**
7. Do you drink tea? No, I **don't.** I **don't** like it.
8. Do you speak Spanish and German? I **speak** Spanish, but I **don't** speak German.

---

3 Before putting students into pairs, demonstrate by asking individual students the questions from Exercise 2. Make sure they answer with information about themselves. Get individual students to ask you the questions and answer with true information. Students continue asking and answering in open pairs. If necessary, drill the pronunciation and intonation of the

questions again before getting students to continue in closed pairs. Monitor and check for correct use of the Present Simple.

Talking about you

4 This exercise introduces the Present Simple in *Wh-* questions. Briefly review the question words *where, what,* and *how many* by giving short answers and eliciting the appropriate question word, e.g.:

a dictionary/an actor   *What?*
Australia/in a hospital   *Where?*
three sisters/ten books   *How many?*

T 5.8 Play the recording, pausing at the end of each line and getting the students to repeat as a class. Students then repeat the questions individually. Make sure they can reproduce the falling intonation on the *Wh-* questions.

Demonstrate the activity by giving the answer to the first question yourself. Get students to write their own answers to each question, using the language in *Starter* Exercise 1 where appropriate. If students need extra vocabulary (e.g., languages), be prepared to supply these words.

Demonstrate the question and answer phase with a confident student by asking and answering the first two questions. Students continue in open and then in closed pairs. Monitor and check for accurate use of the Present Simple.

Role play

5 This is an information-gap activity. There is a male and a female role for Student A and for Student B. Divide the class into pairs, making sure everyone has the correct role in terms of gender. Focus attention on the chart on pp. 109 and 110 and elicit the questions students will need to ask:

What's your name? How do you spell it?
Where do you live?
Do you live in a house or an apartment?
What do you do?
Where do you work?
How many languages do you speak?
What sports do you like?

Drill the questions, making sure students can reproduce the falling intonation.

Ask a confident pair of students to demonstrate the activity in open pairs. Students then continue in closed pairs, completing their charts in the Student Book with information about their partner's character. If possible, get students to stand up to do the role play as if they were at a party. Students can then compare roles to check they have the correct information.

Check it

6 Focus attention on the first pair of sentences as an example. Remind students of the convention of putting a check mark (✔) to indicate that something is correct. Students continue working individually to choose the correct sentence.

Get students to check their answers in pairs before checking them with the whole class.

Answers

1. Do you live in Osaka?
2. Where do you come from?
3. Do you speak Chinese?
4. I don't speak Chinese.
5. "Do you like basketball?" "Yes, I do."
6. "Are you married?" "No, I'm not."
7. He's an actor.

VOCABULARY AND PRONUNCIATION (SB p. 32)

Languages and nationalities

1 Check comprehension of *Italy, Spain, China,* and *France* by referring students back to the map on p. 9. Focus attention on the example. Students continue the matching activity, working individually.

T 5.9 Play the recording through once and let students check their answers.

Answers and tapescript

England	English
Italy	Italian
Spain	Spanish
Mexico	Mexican
Brazil	Brazilian
Japan	Japanese
China	Chinese
France	French
the United States	American
Korea	Korean

Remind students of the system used in *American Headway* to highlight word stress. Play the recording again and get students to repeat the pairs of words as a class. Make sure they can reproduce the change of stress from the country to the nationality/language:

●   ●
Italy   *Italian*

  ●   ●
Japan   *Japanese*

  ●   ●
China   *Chinese*

Play the recording through again and get students to repeat individually.

2 Focus attention on the photos and on the examples in the speech bubbles. Point to the photo of the cheerleaders (photo 2) and drill the examples chorally and individually. Elicit another pair of examples about different people in the photos. Students continue talking about the people in pairs.

3 This exercise includes the *they* form of the Present Simple with the verb *speak*. Students shouldn't have any difficulty with this form, as it's the same as the *I* form they have already practiced.

Check comprehension of *Portuguese*. Focus attention on the example. Students continue making sentences working individually.

T 5.10 Play the recording and get students to check their answers.

Answers and tapescript

1. In Brazil they speak Portuguese.
2. In Canada they speak English and French.
3. In France they speak French.
4. In England they speak English.
5. In Italy they speak Italian.
6. In Japan they speak Japanese.
7. In Mexico they speak Spanish.
8. In Taiwan they speak Chinese.
9. In Spain they speak Spanish.
10. In Korea they speak Korean.
11. In the United States they speak English.

4 Drill the question form in the speech bubbles. Then get students to practice a few examples in open pairs. Students continue in closed pairs, taking turns to ask each other about the places in Exercise 3. Monitor and check for correct use of the question form and for pronunciation of the countries and languages.

5 This exercise consolidates the nationalities and also highlights adjective + noun word order. Focus attention on the photos and the examples. Students complete the exercise by writing the correct nationalities.

T 5.11 Play the recording and get students to check their answers.

Answers and tapescript

1. an **American** car
2. a **Korean** TV
3. **Spanish** oranges
4. a **Japanese** camera
5. **Mexican** food
6. an **English** dictionary
7. an **Italian** bag
8. **Brazilian** coffee
9. **Chinese** tea

Refer students to Grammar Reference 5.3 on p. 126.

6 This exercise gives students the opportunity to practice the Present Simple, nationalities, and noun + adjective word order in a personalized way.

Write the verbs *have, eat,* and *drink* on the board and elicit adjectives and nouns that can go with each verb, e.g.:

have *a/an Japanese/American/Korean/Italian car*
an Italian/American bag
a Japanese camera
an English dictionary

eat *Chinese/Italian/Japanese/Mexican food*
Mexican/American oranges
American/Italian ice cream

drink *Brazilian coffee*
Chinese tea

Give examples of your own with *have, eat,* and *drink.* Try to highlight the use of *a/an,* e.g., *I have **a** Japanese camera. I don't have **an** Italian car.* Then get students to write their own examples. Monitor and help. Check for accurate use of *a/an* and correct adjective + noun word order.

7 Focus attention on the example questions in the speech bubbles. Give students time to write at least four questions of their own using *have, eat,* and *drink.* Monitor and help.

Drill the questions and answers in the speech bubbles. Get students to practice in open pairs across the class and then in closed pairs. Monitor and check for correct use of the Present Simple, *a/an,* and adjective + noun word order.

SUGGESTION

You can bring in advertisements from magazines to give students further practice with nationality adjectives and nouns. Select pictures of cars, cameras, computers, TVs, food, and drinks. Elicit simple adjective + noun phrases, e.g., *an American computer, English tea,* etc., and then get students to use the pictures to practice *Do you have/eat/drink/like ...?* and short answers *Yes, I do./No, I don't.* If pairs of students interview other pairs, you can also practice the *they* form. (If students try to generate *he/she* forms, tell them these are different and that they will practice them in Unit 6.)

ADDITIONAL MATERIAL

Workbook Unit 5

Exercise 5 is a reading text to practice the Present Simple with *they.*

Exercises 6–8 practice *Wh-* questions and answers, and Yes/No questions.

Exercise 13 provides further practice of languages and nationalities.

Exercise 14 provides further practice of *like* and nationality adjectives + nouns.

LISTENING AND SPEAKING (SB p. 34)

At a party

1 This is a fairly long, though fairly simple, unseen listening. Set the scene by pointing to Alessandra and Justin in the illustration. Get students to say what nationality they think they are (*I think he's/she's ...*).

T 5.12 Play the recording through once and let students check their predictions (*Alessandra is Brazilian and Justin is American.*).

Give students time to read the pairs of sentences 1–6. Check pronunciation of *Seattle* /si'ætəl/ in number 1 and *Tacoma* /tə'koʊmə/ in number 2, also check comprehension of *love* in number 5 and *a lot* in number 6. Play the first part of the recording again, and focus attention on the example. Make sure students understand they have to focus on what Justin says. Play the rest of the recording and get students to select the correct sentence from each pair.

Get students to check their answers in pairs before checking them with the whole class. Go over the answers by playing the conversation again and pausing the recording after each correct answer.

Answers and tapescript
1. I work in Seattle.
2. I live in Tacoma.
3. I'm an actor.
4. You speak English very well.
5. I love Brazil.
6. I like the people and the food very much.

T 5.12
A = Alessandra   J = Justin
A Hello. I'm Alessandra.
J Hi, Alessandra. I'm Justin. Justin Bates.
A Do you live here in Seattle, Justin?
J No, I don't. I work in Seattle, but I live in Tacoma.
A What do you do?
J I'm an actor. What do you do?
A I work in a hotel.
J You aren't American, but you speak English very well. Where do you come from?
A I'm Brazilian. I come from Rio.
J Oh, I love Brazil.
A Really?
J Oh, yes. I like the people and the food a lot.

---

2 Turn to the tapescript on p. 118 and get students to practice the conversation in pairs.

Role play

3 Tell students to imagine they are at a party in Seattle. Explain that they have to invent a new identity. Give an example by copying the role card onto the board and writing the information for your new identity. Ask students to complete the role card with their new details. Demonstrate the activity with a confident student, starting with the language in the speech bubbles. Build up a list of possible questions on the board that students could ask each other.

4 Get the class to stand up and complete the role play. Monitor but do not expect perfect accuracy or pronunciation. Make notes of major errors to review later, but try not to spoil students' enjoyment of the role play. If some pairs do well, you could ask them to act it out in front of the class.

ADDITIONAL MATERIAL

Workbook Unit 5
Exercise 10 Students fill in the blanks in a conversation at a party.
Exercise 11 Students match questions with answers.

EVERYDAY ENGLISH (SB p. 35)

Numbers and prices

1 Review numbers 1–30 by getting students to count around the class. Repeat until they can say the numbers accurately without hesitation.

2 **T 5.13** Focus attention on numbers 10–100. Play the recording and get students to repeat chorally and individually. Get students to count to 100 in tens around the class.

3 This is a pairs number dictation. (See the *Everyday English* Suggestion on TB p. 6 of Unit 1 for instructions for this task.)

4 **T 5.14** This exercise presents prices under and over one dollar in English. Play the recording and let students read and listen. Focus attention on the use of ¢ /sɛnts/ for prices under a dollar. Also point out the plural *dollars*, and that we do not always say *dollars* and *cents* in the same price, i.e., we do not always say *one dollar and sixty cents*, but sometimes simply *a dollar sixty*.

Play the recording again and gets students to repeat chorally and individually.

5 Demonstrate the activity by getting students to say the first two prices aloud (*60 cents, 97 cents*). Students then continue saying the prices in closed pairs. Monitor and check students can distinguish the stress on:

●　　　　　●
seventeen dollars and *seventy dollars*

T 5.15 Play the recording and get students to check their answers. If students had problems with pronunciation, play the recording again and get them to repeat. (With a weaker group, you could say the prices as a class activity, drilling the pronunciation as you go along, and then play the recording for reinforcement.)

6 This is a discrimination exercise that gets students to distinguish between prices that sound similar. Focus attention on the objects and prices. (With a weaker group, you could elicit the prices for each object orally first and then get students to listen and check.)

T 5.16 Play the recording through once and get students to check the prices they hear. Play it through a second time so that students can check their answers. Get them to check in pairs before checking with the whole class.

Answers and tapescript
1. The chicken sandwich is $3.90.
2. The baseball is $14.
3. The camera is $90.99.
4. The water is $1.50.
5. The chocolate is 60¢.
6. The cell phone is $24.74.
7. The dictionary is $16.95.
8. The bag is $30.99.

7 Focus attention on the speech bubbles. Drill the question and answer chorally and individually. (If students query the use of *How much ...?*, explain that this is the question we use to ask about prices. Do not go into an explanation of the difference between *How much* and *How many* at this stage.)

Practice two or three exchanges in open pairs. Then get the students to continue in closed pairs. Monitor and check for correct numbers and prices.

SUGGESTION
You can give students extra practice with numbers and prices by bringing in advertisements, leaflets, and menus that show prices and getting students to practice *How much is ...?* Make sure you select the items carefully so that they show objects students know (or ones that you can teach that are in the post-beginner range). If you choose images that show plural objects, you will need to pre-teach/check: *How much are ...?*

ADDITIONAL MATERIAL

Workbook Unit 5
Exercises 15–17 consolidate numbers and prices.

Don't forget!

Workbook Unit 5

Exercise 9   is a review of *is, are,* and *do.*

Exercise 12   In this exercise, students translate sentences containing the main grammar points presented in the unit.

Word List   Ask the students to turn to SB p. 132 and go through the words with them. Ask them to learn the words for homework, and test them on a few in the following class.

Progress Test 1   There is a Progress Test for Units 1–5 on p. 135 of the Teacher's Book.

The time • Present Simple—*he/she/it*

usually/sometimes/never • Questions and negatives

Words that go together • Days of the week

Every day

Introduction to the unit

The title of this unit is "Every day" and it covers the language of daily routines. It presents the third person singular form of the Present Simple and so follows on from the language covered in Unit 5. Basic frequency adverbs, telling the time, and days of the week are also introduced.

The vocabulary syllabus is extended with a focus on an important aspect of English—collocation. The vocabulary includes daily routine verbs that allow students to talk about their own routine and ask about other people's.

Language aims

The time   The unit opens with a section on telling the time in English. This is done with digital time so that students can use the numbers they already know to tell the time, e.g., *five fifteen,* and not have to worry about *a quarter to/after, twenty after (five)*, etc.

Grammar—Present Simple 2   The *I* and *you* forms are reviewed and the presentation of the Present Simple is completed with *he/she/it* in the affirmative, negative, and question forms (both *Wh-* and Yes/No questions). The third person singular form is the one that causes most problems for students so it is divided out into a section of its own for the initial presentation. All forms of the Present Simple are reviewed and recycled throughout the text so that students can deal with the differences in the *I/you/we/they* and *he/she/it* forms.

Frequency adverbs   *Usually, sometimes,* and *never* are introduced and practiced as part of the function of talking about routines.

Vocabulary   The vocabulary section focuses on words that go together thereby introducing an important aspect of English—collocation. The section includes words that go with common verbs to produce a useful lexical set for talking about routines.

Everyday English   Days of the week and prepositions of time are presented and practiced.

Workbook   The time is reviewed in a range of exercises.

The *he/she/it* forms of the Present Simple affirmative are reviewed along with the frequency adverbs from the unit. Students are also given the opportunity to personalize the adverbs and review the *I* form.

Students practice third person singular Present Simple negative and questions, and also review the use of the auxiliary verbs *do/does/don't/doesn't* in all forms.

Vocabulary from the units covered to date is consolidated in a crossword.

Students get skills practice with a guided writing task.

The days of the week and prepositions from *Everyday English* are reviewed and consolidated.

POSSIBLE PROBLEMS
- The Present Simple has very few inflections when compared with equivalent structures in other languages. The addition of the third person singular *-s* is the only change in the affirmative so students often forget to include it. Be prepared to give lots of practice with the *he/she/it* forms!
- The use of *does/doesn't* is an added complication which students often confuse with *do/don't.* Again, regular review and practice will help students produce the forms accurately.

- The third person singular -s can be pronounced in three ways:

works	/wərks/
lives	/lɪvz/
watches	/watʃɪz/

Students also need help in distinguishing and producing these endings.

Notes on the unit

STARTER (SB p. 36)

> **NOTE**
> It is useful to have a cardboard clock with movable hands for this lesson and for subsequent review of telling the time. If you do not have one in your school, it is quite easy to make one.

The Student Book presents digital times so that students can tell the time with the numbers they already know, without having to deal with *a quarter after/to*. The section includes times on the hour, half hour, and quarter hour. The other times, e.g., *9:05*, *11:25*, etc., are covered in an information-gap activity on SB pp. 109–110.

1 **T 6.1** Focus attention on the clocks. Play the recording of the first five times, pausing after each one and getting students to repeat chorally and individually. Highlight the use of *o'clock* for times on the hour, and make sure students can pronounce it accurately.

Get students to complete the remaining five times, following the examples given in 1–5. Play the recording of numbers 6–10 and get students to check their answers. Play the recording again, getting students to repeat chorally and individually.

> **Answers and tapescript**
> 1. It's nine o'clock.
> 2. It's nine thirty.
> 3. It's nine forty-five.
> 4. It's ten o'clock.
> 5. It's ten fifteen.
> 6. It's **two o'clock**.
> 7. It's **two thirty**.
> 8. It's **two forty-five**.
> 9. It's **three o'clock**.
> 10. It's **three fifteen**.

2 **T 6.2** Focus attention on the conversation. Play the recording once and get students to listen and read. Play the recording again, and get students to repeat chorally and individually. Demonstrate the pair work with one student. Ask students to give two or three more examples in open pairs before continuing in closed pairs.

WHAT TIME DO YOU ...? (SB p. 37)

Present Simple—*I/you*

1 This section presents daily routine verbs. Focus attention on the pictures. Elicit some basic information about the character: *What's her name? (Lena). How old is she, do you think? (She's about 16.)*

Explain that students are going to hear Lena talking about her weekday. Review telling the time by getting students to read the pairs of times aloud. (The *Starter* section didn't present *8:40*, which appears in number 3, but students should be able to read the time as they already know the numbers.)

T 6.3 Focus attention on the example and play the first line of the recording. Play the recording to the end and get students to continue circling the correct times. Get them to check their answers in pairs. Play the recording again and get students to confirm/amend their answers. Then check the answers with the whole class.

> **Answers and tapescript**
> 1. 7:45   4. 12:15   6. 4:30
> 2. 8:00   5. 3:30   7. 11:00
> 3. 8:30
>
> **T 6.3**
> Well, on weekdays I get up at seven forty-five. I have breakfast at eight and I go to school at eight thirty. I have lunch in school with my friends, that's at twelve fifteen—it's early in our school. I leave school at three thirty in the afternoon and I walk home with my friends. I get home at four thirty. I go to bed at eleven o'clock on weekdays but not on the weekend.

Say the sentences aloud or play the recording again and get students to repeat chorally and individually. Make sure students aren't confused by the spelling of *breakfast* and pronounce it correctly /ˈbrɛkfəst/. Students practice the sentences in closed pairs.

2 Demonstrate the activity by telling students about your day, giving the same information as in the pictures. Do this in a natural way, but do not add in any new language. Focus attention on the example in the speech bubble and elicit a few single sentences from students about their day with the verbs from Exercise 1. Students continue talking about their day, working in pairs. Monitor and check for correct use of the Present Simple and the times.

3 **T 6.4** This exercise practices *What time ...?* with the Present Simple. Focus attention on the questions and get students to listen and repeat chorally and individually. Make sure they can reproduce the pronunciation of *do you* /dyu/ and the falling intonation on the *Wh-* questions.

Drill the question and answer in the speech bubbles and elicit the other questions students can ask. If students need help, write the verbs on the board: *get up, have breakfast, go to work, have lunch, leave work, get home, go to bed.*

Get students to practice the questions in open pairs. Students continue in closed pairs, working with a different partner from Exercise 2. Monitor and check for correct use of the Present Simple and the times.

ADDITIONAL MATERIAL

Workbook Unit 6
Exercises 1 and 2   practice the time.
Exercise 3   provides practice of the third person singular of the Present Simple and the time.

KEN'S DAY (SB p. 38)

Present Simple—*he/she/it, usually/sometimes/never*

1 This section presents the *he/she/it* affirmative forms of the Present Simple. Focus attention on the photos of Ken and get students to read the description of him. Check comprehension of *millionaire, director, 24-hour, shopping site,* and *Internet.* (You might want to note that *24–7* in the web address means "24 hours a day, 7 days a week.")

Focus attention on the pictures of Ken's day and check comprehension of *take a shower, work late, buy,* and *go out.* Focus attention on the example sentence. Get students to continue writing the times, working individually.

Ask students to check their answers in pairs before checking with the whole class.

Answers
2. six forty-five
3. seven fifteen
4. one o'clock
5. eight o'clock
6. nine fifteen
7. nine thirty, eleven thirty
8. eleven forty-five

1 Focus attention on the examples of third person singular forms *gets up* and *takes.* Have students underline the verbs in sentences 2–8. Check the answers with the class.

Answers
2. has
3. leaves, goes
4. has
5. works, leaves
6. buys, eats, gets
7. goes, works
8. goes

Elicit the key last letter in each of the verbs: *s.*

T 6.5 Play the recording and get students to repeat chorally and individually. Make sure they can distinguish the /s/ endings, e.g., *gets* /gɛts/ from the /z/ endings, e.g., *has* /hæz/. (The tapescript gives the complete verb forms including nouns and particles.)

Tapescript
1. gets up
   takes a shower
2. has breakfast
3. leaves home
   goes to work
4. has lunch
5. works late
   leaves work
6. buys
   eats
   gets home
7. goes out
   works
8. goes to bed

2 Focus attention on the adverbs of frequency and their meaning. Make sure students understand that *usually* and *sometimes* are not fixed references and the actual number of times that they refer to can vary.
Ask students to underline the examples of *usually, sometimes,* and *never* in the sentences about Ken.

T 6.6 Play the recording and get students to repeat chorally and individually. Make sure students reproduce the third person singular ending and encourage them to reproduce the linking in the following sentences:

He sometimes buys a pizza.

He never goes out in the evening.

Tapescript
He usually works late.
He sometimes buys a pizza.
He never goes out in the evening.

Read Grammar Reference 6.1–6.3 on p. 127 together in class, and/or ask students to read it at home. Highlight the use of the *-es* ending, e.g., *go—goes.* Encourage students to ask you questions about it. If appropriate, point out that the frequency adverbs can be used with *to be,* but that they usually come after the verb, e.g., *I am* **never** *at home in the morning.*

Workbook Unit 6
Exercises 4 and 5 practice the Present Simple and frequency adverbs *usually/sometimes/never*.

Questions and negatives

2 This section introduces *does/doesn't* in the question and negative forms. Both *Wh-* and Yes/No questions are presented at the same time, as students are dealing with the third person singular form only at this stage, and they have already had a lot of practice of the individual question types.

T 6.7 Refer students back to the pictures of Ken. Read question 1 aloud (*What time does he get up?*), and elicit the answer (*gets*). Students continue completing the answers, working individually. Get them to check in pairs before playing the questions and answers on the recording. Play the recording through once and let students check their answers.

Play the recording again, pausing after each question-and-answer exchange, and get the students to repeat chorally and individually. Make sure they can reproduce the falling intonation on the *Wh-* questions and the rising intonation on the Yes/No questions. Students practice the questions and answers in open and then in closed pairs.

Answers and tapescript
1. What time does he get up? He **gets** up at six o'clock.
2. When does he go to bed? He **goes** to bed at eleven forty-five.
3. Does he go to work by taxi? **Yes,** he does.
4. Does he have lunch in a restaurant? **No,** he doesn't.
5. Does he go out in the evening? No, he **doesn't**.

GRAMMAR SPOT (SB p. 39)

1 Focus attention on the example sentences. Make sure students understand that the *-s* is on the verb in the affirmative form and on *does* in the question and negative. Highlight *doesn't* as the contracted form of *does not*.

2 Ask students to circle the *-s* ending and the use of *does/doesn't* in the questions and answers in Exercise 2.

3 Focus attention on the language in the speech bubbles. Drill the question and answer. Elicit two or three more examples with students working in open pairs. Students continue asking and answering in closed pairs. Monitor and check for correct use of third person *-s* and of *does/doesn't* in the questions and negatives.

T 6.8 Play the recording and get students to check their answers. If students had difficulties with questions and answers 1–7, drill the questions and answers and get students to practice them in pairs again.

Answers and tapescript
1. What time does he have breakfast? He has breakfast at six forty-five.
2. When does he leave home? He leaves home at seven fifteen.
3. Does he go to work by bus? No, he doesn't. He goes to work by taxi.
4. Where does he have lunch? He has lunch in his office.
5. Does he usually work late? Yes, he does.
6. Does he eat in a restaurant? No, he doesn't. He sometimes buys a pizza and eats it at home.
7. What does he do in the evening? He works on his computer.

GRAMMAR SPOT (SB p. 39)

1 Focus attention on the chart. Elicit the forms for *you* (*work* and *don't work*), and then get students to complete the rest of the chart. Check the answers with the whole class.

Answers

	Affirmative	Negative
I	work	don't work
You	**work**	**don't work**
He	**works**	**doesn't work**
She	works	doesn't work
We	**work**	**don't work**
They	**work**	**don't work**

Highlight again that the *he/she* form is the only one that is different.

2 Get students to complete the *Wh-* questions. Then check the answers with the class.

Answers
1. When **do** you get up?
2. When **does** he get up?

Highlight the use of *does* in the second question. Refer students to Grammar Reference 6.4 on p. 127. Make sure students understand that we repeat *do/does* or *don't/doesn't* in the short answers rather than the main verb, i.e., we cannot say: *Do you get up at 7:30? *Yes, I get up.*

4 This is an information-gap activity which reviews and extends the language of telling the time in the context of daily routine. The activity covers the times students haven't met yet so you will need to pre-teach/check these first. Write the following times on the board:

11:05, 1:10, 7:20, 9:25, 8:40, 6:50, 12:55

Remind students of the use of *oh* /oʊ/, which they met in phone numbers, for *11:05*. Get students to say the times aloud, reading them as digital times, e.g., *one ten*.

Explain that each student has three times and three empty clocks and that the student has to ask *What time does he ... ?* to complete the clocks. Divide the class into pairs and make sure students know if they are Student A or Student B. Students A should look at page 109, and Students B should look at page 110. Focus attention on the conversation. Demonstrate the activity with one student before getting the class to complete the task. Students should complete the clock faces with the correct time. While they are asking and answering about the times, go around monitoring and checking that students are using the times and the question form correctly. Students check their answers by comparing their completed clocks.

PRACTICE (SB p. 40)

Katya's day

1 Remind students of Ken from the previous section. Point to the photos of Katya and ask *Who is she? (She's Ken's sister.)* Pre-teach/check *artist, country, early, toast, go for a walk, paint, studio, cook,* and *play the piano.*

Read the heading of the text aloud. Ask *How old is Katya?* and *What does she do? (She's 25. She's an artist.)* Focus attention on the example. Elicit the second verb *(gets up)* and then have students complete the text, working individually.

T 6.9 Get students to check their answers in pairs. Then play the recording and get them to check/amend their answers.

Answers and tapescript

Katya is 25. She's an artist. She **lives** in a small house in the country. She usually **gets up** at ten o'clock in the morning. She never **gets up** early. She **has** coffee and toast for breakfast and then she **goes** for a walk with her dog. She **gets** home at eleven o'clock and she **paints** in her studio until seven o'clock in the evening. Then she **cooks** dinner and **drinks** a cup of tea. After dinner, she sometimes **listens to** music and she sometimes **plays** the piano. She usually **goes** to bed very late, at one or two o'clock in the morning.

2 Focus attention on the two examples. Make sure students realize that *he* refers to Ken and *she* to Katya. Get students to complete the sentences and then check their answers in pairs. Check the answers with the whole class.

Answers

3. She	5. He	7. She	9. She
4. He	6. She	8. He	10. He

Ask a few students to read the sentences aloud. Then get students to practice the sentences in pairs. If they have serious problems with pronunciation, drill the sentences with the whole class and get them to repeat.

Negatives and pronunciation

3 This exercise practices the negative form and also highlights the importance of contrastive stress when correcting or disagreeing with a statement. Focus attention on the example and ask *Affirmative or negative?* about each sentence in the answer *(first sentence—negative, second sentence—affirmative)*. Explain that the dots indicate where the main stress falls in each sentence.

Pre-teach *stay home* for sentence 8. Elicit the answer to sentence 2 *(He doesn't get up at ten o'clock. He gets up at six o'clock.)*. Tell students to continue correcting the sentences, referring back to the information about Ken and Katya on pages 38 and 40. (With a weaker group, you could do this as a class activity on the board and then play the recording for reinforcement.) Tell them not to worry about the stress in the sentences at this stage.

T 6.10 Play the recording through once, getting students to check their sentences for grammatical accuracy. Then write the pairs of sentences for numbers 2 and 3 and elicit where the main stress falls with the whole class. Remind students that the stress helps to indicate the main difference in the information in the pairs of sentences, and so falls on the key words.

Get students to work in pairs and mark where they think the main stress falls in the rest of the pairs of sentences. Play the recording again and get students to check their answers. Also, check the answers orally with the whole class in case students have problems hearing the main stress.

Play the recording again and get students to repeat chorally and individually.

Answers and tapescript

1. She doesn't live in the city. She lives in the country.
2. He doesn't get up at ten o'clock. He gets up at six o'clock.
3. She doesn't have a big breakfast. She has coffee and toast.
4. He doesn't have a dog. She has a dog.
5. She doesn't work in an office. She works at home.
6. He doesn't cook dinner in the evening. He buys a pizza.
7. She doesn't go to bed early. She goes to bed late.
8. They don't go out in the evening. They stay home.

Talking about you

4 Demonstrate the activity by writing the names of two people (one male, one female) from your family on the board. Get students to ask you questions about them, using the language in the speech bubbles and the cues in the Student Book. If students have problems switching from questions with *be* to the Present Simple questions, drill the language as a class.

Get students to write the name of two family members on a piece of paper. Remind them to choose one male and one female. Students work in pairs and ask and answer about the family members. Monitor and check for correct use of *he/she*, *his/her*, and the third person singular Present Simple forms.

> **SUGGESTION**
> You could ask students to bring in family photos for the above activity.

Check it

5 This exercise consolidates the auxiliary forms *do/don't* and *does/doesn't* in Present Simple questions and short answers. Focus attention on number 1 and elicit the answers *(Do, do)*. Students continue completing the questions and answers, working individually.

Ask students to check their answers in pairs. Then check the answers with the whole class.

> **Answers**
> 1. "**Do** you like ice cream?" "Yes, I **do**."
> 2. "**Does** she work in Dallas?" "Yes, she **does**."
> 3. "Where **does** he work?" "In a bank."
> 4. "**Do** you go to work by bus?" "No, I **don't**."
> 5. "**Does** she go to bed early?" "No, she **doesn't**."
> 6. "**Do** they have a dog?" "Yes, they **do**."
> 7. "**Does** he speak Japanese?" "No, he **doesn't**."
> 8. "**Do** they live in England?" "No, they **don't**."

ADDITIONAL MATERIAL

Workbook Unit 6
Exercise 6 practices word order in *he/she/it* forms of Present Simple *Wh-* questions.
Exercises 7 and 8 provide a reading task to consolidate Present Simple *he/she/it* forms.
Exercise 9 practices Present Simple *he/she/it* forms in the negative.
Exercise 10 practices the *he/she/it* forms of Present Simple Yes/No questions.
Exercise 11 is a review of *do/does/don't/doesn't*.

VOCABULARY AND SPEAKING (SB p. 42)
Words that go together

1 Check comprehension of *shopping*. Focus attention on the examples. Students continue working in pairs to match the verbs and nouns/phrases.

T 6.11 Play the recording and get students to check their answers.

> **Answers and tapescript**
>
> | | |
> |---|---|
> | get up early | go shopping |
> | go to bed late | take a shower |
> | listen to music | eat in restaurants |
> | watch TV | drink water |
> | cook dinner | play the piano |
> | work in an office | stay home |

2 This is a questionnaire activity to practice Yes/No questions. As a variation, students use *Yes, usually.*, *Yes, sometimes.*, and *No, never.* in their answers, rather than *Yes, I do./No, I don't*. This allows them to practice the frequency adverbs in a simple but meaningful way.

T 6.12 Focus attention on the questionnaire. Play the recording and get students to repeat chorally and individually.

3 Focus attention on the language in the speech bubbles. Drill the question and three possible answers. Get students to ask you a few of the questions and give true answers. Demonstrate how to record the answers by putting the three adverbs on the board and putting a check mark (✔) under the appropriate one.

Students then work in closed pairs, asking and answering the questions, and filling in their partner's answers.

4 This follow-up phase allows students to talk about themselves and their partner and to get practice in switching from first to third person. Focus attention on the example; then elicit more information from individual students about themselves and their partner.

ADDITIONAL MATERIAL

Workbook Unit 6
Exercises 13 is a crossword to review vocabulary covered in Units 1–6.

EVERYDAY ENGLISH (SB p. 43)
Days of the week

1 **T 6.13** Explain to students that they are going to learn the days of the week in English. Play the recording and get them to write the days in the correct order. Play the

recording again and get students to repeat chorally and individually. Make sure they can distinguish *Tuesday* and *Thursday* and that they only produce two syllables in *Wednesday* /'wɛnzdeɪ/.

Answers and tapescript
1. Monday
2. **Tuesday**
3. **Wednesday**
4. **Thursday**
5. **Friday**
6. **Saturday**
7. Sunday

Have students practice the days again with each student saying one day of the week in the correct order.

2 Elicit the answer to question 1 as an example. Students do the exercise in pairs. Have a brief feedback session by getting students to give their answers to individual questions.

3 Here students learn which prepositions are used with the days, parts of the day, and times. Elicit the answer for times (*at*) and then get students to write the correct preposition for the other phrases.

T 6.14 Play the recording and get students to check their answers. Highlight the difference between **in** *the evening* but **on** *Saturday evening*, **in** *the afternoon* but **on** *Friday afternoon*, etc.

Answers and tapescript
on Sunday
on Monday
on Saturday evening
on Thursday morning
on Friday afternoon
on the weekend (**at** the weekend in UK English)
at nine o'clock
at ten thirty
at twelve fifteen
in the morning
in the afternoon
in the evening

---

4 Elicit the answer to number 1 (*at*) and then get students to complete the other sentences with either *in, on,* or *at.* Check the answers.

Answers
1. at   2. on   3. in   4. on   5. on

Focus attention on the example answers in the speech bubbles. Get students to practice asking and answering questions 1–5 in closed pairs. This allows them to practice the *we* form of the Present Simple. Get them to complete the sentences in writing about when they do have English class. Encourage them to include the day, part of the day, and time, e.g.: *We have English class on (Monday evening) at (seven thirty).*

5 Students complete the questions with the correct preposition, then ask and answer the questions in closed pairs. Monitor and check for correct question formation, use of short answers, and prepositions of time. If you have time, conduct a brief feedback session to allow students to talk about their partner and so practice the third person singular.

ADDITIONAL MATERIAL

Workbook Unit 6
Exercises 16 and 17   practice the days of the week.
Exercise 18   practices prepositions of time *in/on/at.*

Don't forget!

Workbook Unit 6
Exercise 12   In this exercise, students translate sentences containing the main grammar points presented in the unit.
Exercise 14   provides further writing practice.
Exercise 15   is a guided writing task to consolidate the language of routines.
Word List   Ask the students to turn to SB p. 133 and go through the words with them. Ask them to learn the words for homework, and test them on a few in the next class.
Stop and Check 2   There is a Stop and Check quiz for Units 4–6 on p. 108 of the Teacher's Book.

Question words • *it/them*
this/that • Adjectives
Can I ...?

Places I like

Introduction to the unit

The title of this unit is "Places I like" and it provides practice in describing places. The grammar input includes a review and extension of question words, the introduction of object pronouns, and the demonstratives *this* and *that*. Students get skills practice with a reading and writing section linked to the focus on places.

Useful adjectives and their opposites are introduced and practiced. Making requests with *Can I ...?* is the focus of the *Everyday English* section.

Language aims

Question words   The question words introduced in previous units are reviewed and *how* to refer to manner and *why* are introduced. *Who* in subject questions is also included for recognition.

Object pronouns   Subject pronouns (*I, you, he*, etc.) are reviewed and object pronouns (*me, you, him*, etc.) are introduced. Grammar Reference 7.2 also lists possessive adjectives so that students can see potential areas of confusion.

this/that   This and *that* are introduced in the context of asking about objects: *What's this/that?*

Vocabulary   A set of key everyday adjectives and their opposites is introduced. This gives an opportunity to review objects introduced in earlier units. Students also review the use of *a/an* + adjective + noun.

Everyday English   Requests with *Can I ...?* are introduced and practiced in a variety of situations.

Workbook   There are exercises to practice object pronouns and to help students with potential confusion with subject pronouns and possessive adjectives.

This, that, and objects are consolidated.

Students practice question words in matching and word-order exercises. Students are given an opportunity to give their own answers to questions. There is an exercise to practice the newly introduced question word *why* and answers with *because*.

The adjectives from the unit are consolidated in a variety of exercises.

Students get skills practice with a reading task.

Requests with *Can I ...?* from *Everyday English* are reviewed and consolidated.

> **POSSIBLE PROBLEMS**
> The similarity between subject and object pronouns, and possessive adjectives often present problems for students. The Student Book and Workbook give practice to help students with these areas, but be prepared to monitor these areas during pair work and review as necessary.

Notes on the unit

STARTER (SB p. 44)

> **NOTE**
> *How much?* and *How many?* are reviewed together in this exercise. Students have used *How much?* to talk about prices and *How many?* to talk about numbers, so they should not have any problem with the matching exercise.

It is not advisable at this stage to present the use of *much/many* with count and noncount nouns. This is covered in *American Headway 1*. Similarly, at this stage, don't explain the use of *Who lives ...?* in the subject question in number 7 or contrast it with the object question form *Who does ...?* Just let students recognize which answer goes with *Who?*

1 Focus attention on the example to demonstrate the activity. Students continue to match the questions and answers, working in pairs.

T 7.1 Play the recording and get students to check their answers.

Answers and tapescript
1. What is the capital of Australia?
   Canberra.
2. How old are the Pyramids?
   4,500 years old.
3. What time do Mexican people have dinner?
   Late. At 9:00 in the evening.
4. Where does the American president live?
   In the White House.
5. How many floors does the Empire State Building have?
   Eighty-six.
6. How much is a hamburger in the US?
   $3.50.
7. Who lives in Buckingham Palace?
   The queen of England.

If you feel students need practice with the intonation of *Wh-* questions, play the recording and get them to repeat the questions and answers chorally and individually.

SUGGESTION
To give more practice with question words, you can have a quiz in which the students generate the questions. You can give different groups sets of answers and get them to write the questions. You will need to choose answers that can only generate one question and only focus on the present tense at this stage. Check the questions with each group and then divide the students into pairs so that each student has a different set of questions. Students ask and answer in pairs, scoring a point for each correct answer.

2 Give an example by talking about your favorite town or city. Include known adjectives, e.g., *big, small, beautiful,* etc., and information about what the place has, e.g., *restaurants, hotels,* etc. Take the opportunity to pre-teach *why* and *because,* which will be used in the next section. Check the pronunciation of *because* /bɪˈkɔz/.

Elicit another example from a confident student. Students then continue in pairs. Monitor and check, but only

provide feedback on major errors. Let students have the opportunity to say what they can in a relatively free way.

I LOVE IT HERE! (SB p. 44)

it/them, this/that

1 This exercise reviews questions and answers, including *why* and *because*. Review these words but don't pre-teach all the new vocabulary unless you feel students will have difficulty understanding from context. If this is the case or if you have a weak group, you can pre-teach/check the following by referring to a movie star students will know: *famous, movie star, journalist, fantastic, nice, first, movie, visit* (verb), *vacation, wedding, happy, together.*

Focus attention on the photo of Celine. Ask questions to get students to predict information about her, e.g., *What does she do? Where is she from? Where is she now? Is she married? Does she have children?*

T 7.2 Play the recording through once and get students to check the predictions above (*She's a movie star. She's from the United States. She's in her house in London now. Yes, she is. Yes, she does.*).

Play the recording again and get students to complete the conversation.

Get students to check their answers in pairs before checking them with the whole class.

Answers and tapescript
G = Gary   C = Celine
G This is a very beautiful house.
C Thank you. I like it very much, too.
G Celine, you're American. Why do you live here in London?
C Because I just love **it** here! The people are fantastic! I love them! And of course, my husband, Charles, is English, and I love him, too!
G That's a very nice photo. Who are they?
C My sons. That's Matt and that's Jack. They go to school here. My daughter's at school in the US. Her name's Lisa-Marie.
G **Why** does Lisa-Marie go to school in the US?
C **Because** she lives with her father. My first husband, you know—the actor Dan Brat. I hate **him** and all his movies. I never watch **them**.
G I see. So does Lisa-Marie visit you?
C Oh, yes. She visits me every vacation. She's here with **me** now.
G And is this a photo of **you** and Charles?
C Oh, yes. It's us in Hawaii. It's our wedding. We're so happy together!

2 Get students to practice the conversation in closed pairs while you monitor. If students have problems with pronunciation and intonation, drill key sentences and then get students to continue practicing the conversation in closed pairs.

3 This exercise reviews Present Simple questions and answers, and also practices object pronouns plus *why* and *because*. Focus on the example and remind students of the use of *does* in the third person question. Students complete the sentences, working individually.

Get students to check their answers in pairs before checking them with the whole class.

Answers
1. Why **does** Celine live in London?
   Because she **loves** it in England.
2. Does she like English people?
   Yes, she loves **them**.
3. How **many** children does she have?
   Three.
4. Where **do** her sons go to school?
   In England.
5. **Why** does Lisa-Marie go to school in the US?
   Because she lives with her father.

GRAMMAR SPOT (SB p. 44)

1 Focus attention on the examples *What* and *How old* from sentences 1 and 2 in *Starter* Exercise 1. Elicit the question words in sentences 3 and 4 (*What time* and *Where*). Students continue underlining the question word(s) in *Starter* Exercises 1 and 2. Check the answers with the whole class.

2 Check comprehension of the terms *subject* and *object pronouns* by writing this simple chart on the board.

Subject	Verb	Object
I	like	you.
You	like	it.
She	likes	them.
We	like	him.

Focus attention on the chart in the Student Book and on the examples. Get students to complete the object pronouns, working in pairs. Check the answers with the whole class.

Answers

Subject pronoun	I	you	he	she	it	we	they
Object pronoun	**me**	**you**	**him**	her	**it**	us	**them**

Ask students to underline the object pronouns in the conversation in Exercise 1.

3 Elicit the first examples of *this* and *that* in the conversation in Exercise 1 (*This is a very beautiful house. That's a very nice photo.*). Students continue to find examples of *this* and *that*.

Read Grammar Reference 7.1–7.3 on p. 127 together in class, and/or ask students to read it at home. Encourage them to ask you questions about it.

PRACTICE (SB p. 46)

What's that?

1 Pre-teach/check the use of *What's this?* by holding an object or picture of an object close to you and eliciting the answer *It's a (book)*. Repeat the procedure for *What's that?* by pointing to an object or picture of an object at a distance from you. Drill the questions and answer *It's a/an ...* chorally and individually. Make sure you include an object/picture of an object beginning with a vowel so that students review *It's an (orange)*.

Focus attention on the picture. Review the names of all the objects, without asking *What's this/that?* at this stage, and check the pronunciation. Focus attention on the examples in the speech bubbles. Drill the examples in open pairs and then get students to ask and answer about the objects in the pictures in closed pairs. Monitor and check for correct use of *What's this/that?* Check the answers by getting students to ask and answer across the class.

Answers
What's that? It's a dog/camera/bag/photograph/glass/computer.
What's this? It's a/an phone/television/orange/sandwich/dictionary/cat.

2 Focus attention on the examples in the speech bubbles. Drill the language around the class and then get students to continue asking about objects in the classroom in closed pairs. Encourage them to use the possessive *'s* where appropriate, e.g., *It's Jun's book*. Monitor and check for correct use of *What's this/that?* and the possessive *'s*.

ADDITIONAL MATERIAL

Workbook Unit 7
Exercises 4 and 5   provide more practice with *this* and *that*.

I like them!

3 This section practices object pronouns and allows students to personalize the language by talking about people and things. Pre-teach/check *hate* and *of course*. Focus attention on the example and make sure students understand what the answer *it* refers back to (*ice cream*). Students complete the other sentences, working individually.

T 7.3 Get students to check their answers in pairs before letting them check against the recording. Ask students what the pronoun refers back to each time (given in parentheses in the Answer Key below). Sentence 5 assumes the teacher is a woman. Check what pronoun would be used if the teacher were a man (*him*).

What do you like?

4 Check comprehension of the items in the list. Focus attention on the speech bubbles and check comprehension of *love*, *hate*, and *all right*. This can be done with simple board drawings of faces—a smiling face ☺ for *love*, a neutral face ☺ for *all right*, and a frowning face ☹ for *hate*.

Drill the language in the speech bubbles chorally and individually. Check for correct sentence stress in the answers:

●

Yes, I do. I love it.

●

No, I don't. I hate it.

●

It's all right.

Get students to give two or three more examples in open pairs across the class. Then get students to continue in closed pairs. Monitor and check for the correct use of object pronouns.

ADDITIONAL MATERIAL

Workbook Unit 7
Exercises 1–3 consolidate object pronouns.

Questions and answers

5 Pre-teach/check *marry*, *math*, *homework*, *present* (noun). Focus attention on the question in the example and review the formation of the third person Present Simple question. Focus attention on the answer and review the use of third person -*s* and the object pronoun *it*. Check that students know what the pronoun refers back to *(tea)*.

T 7.4 Give students time to write the questions and answers individually and then ask and answer in pairs. Monitor and check for grammatical accuracy. Play the recording and get students to check their answers.

If students had a lot of problems with the question formation or the object pronouns, go over the key grammar in each question and answer, and then get students to listen and repeat each exchange.

6 Pre-teach/check *learn*, *start* (verb), *a lot (of groups)*. Check comprehension of *How?* to refer to manner by focusing on the answer to question 1 *(By bus.)*. Then get students to continue matching the questions and answers, working individually.

T 7.5 Play the recording and get students to check their answers.

Get students to practice the questions and answers in closed pairs. Monitor and check for correct pronunciation and intonation. If students have problems, drill the questions and answers chorally.

Demonstrate the personalization phase by getting the students to ask you the questions. Students then continue in closed pairs, talking about themselves.

Check it

7 Focus attention on the first pair of sentences as an example. Students continue working individually to choose the correct sentence.

Get students to check their answers in pairs before checking them with the whole class.

Answers
1. What do you do on the weekend?
2. Who is your boyfriend?
3. How much money do you have?
4. I don't drink tea. I don't like it.
5. Our teacher gives us a lot of homework.
6. She loves me and I love her.

ADDITIONAL MATERIAL

Workbook Unit 7
Exercise 6   provides practice with *why* and *because*.
Exercises 7 and 8   provide further practice of question words.

VOCABULARY (SB p. 48)

Adjectives

1   This exercise introduces some key adjectives and their opposites and also reviews *it's* and *they're*. Focus attention on the pictures and the example. Get students to tell you any other of the adjectives they recognize or let them guess. Pre-teach the remaining adjectives using mime. Elicit a plural example to remind students of the use of *They're*. Make sure students understand they only have to write *It's/They're* and the appropriate adjective, not the name of the objects.

T 7.6 Play the recording and get students to check their answers in pairs.

Answers and tapescript
1. It's great.
2. It's awful.
3. He's hot.
4. She's cold.
5. They're old.
6. They're new.
7. It's big.
8. It's small.
9. They're expensive.
10. They're cheap.

Drill the pronunciation of the sentences chorally and individually.

2   Focus attention on the adjectives and opposites. Elicit the opposite of *new* as an example *(old)*. Get students to write the other opposites in the chart and then to check their answers in pairs.

Answers

Adjective	Opposite
new	old
expensive	cheap
great	awful
small	big
cold	hot

SUGGESTION

You can practice adjective and noun combinations in the "pictionary"-type activity on TB p. 101.
Ask students to work in pairs. You will need one copy of the worksheet cut up into cards for each pair. Each student takes an adjective card and a noun card. If their noun card cannot be matched with their adjective card, they replace it at the bottom of the pile and take another until they find a combination which they are able to depict in a drawing. Each student then draws a picture of their combination. When they have finished drawing, they show their pictures to their partner, asking *What this?* Partners have to guess which adjective/ noun combinations have been depicted, and reply using *It's a/an ....* Continue until all the adjective cards have been used.

ADDITIONAL MATERIAL

Workbook Unit 7
Exercises 11–13   consolidate adjectives from the unit.

READING AND WRITING (SB p. 49)

A postcard from San Francisco

1   This section extends the focus on adjectives in the context of a description of a place. Focus attention on the photos and elicit information about the places shown, e.g., *Is it a hot place? Is it in Canada? Where do you think it is?* Tell students they are going to read and listen to the postcard. Encourage them to guess the meaning of new words.

T 7.7 Play the recording and get students to follow along in their books. Check comprehension of the following, using the context to help where possible: *on vacation, comfortable, friendly, delicious, building, weather, wet, see you soon.*

2   Elicit the answer to question 1 as an example *(It's from Diana and Davi.)*. Get students to answer the other questions, working individually. Check the answers with the whole class.

Answers
1. It's from Diana and Davi.
2. They're in San Francisco.
3. They're on vacation.
4. Yes, it is.
5. The weather.

3   Focus attention on the adjectives Diana and Davi use to describe their hotel. Get students to continue finding the appropriate adjectives. Point out that for San Francisco they will need to use a negative formed with *not*.

Get students to check their answers in pairs before checking them with the whole class.

Answers

	Adjectives
their hotel	nice, old, comfortable
people	friendly
the food	delicious, cheap
the cafes	wonderful
San Francisco	beautiful, big, new, not expensive
the weather	awful, wet, cold

4 Focus attention on the skeleton of the postcard. Check comprehension of *beach*. You can get students to write their postcard in full in class, providing vocabulary where relevant, or give it for homework. With a weaker class, you could draft the postcard as a class activity on the board, and then get students to write a different postcard for homework, based very closely on the draft.

ADDITIONAL MATERIAL

Workbook Unit 7
Exercise 15   provides further reading practice.

EVERYDAY ENGLISH (SB p. 50)

Can I ...?

1 This section focuses on requests in everyday situations. Students are introduced to *Can I ...?*, but do not give a detailed explanation of the grammar of *can* at this stage. Check comprehension of the vocabulary in the activities list by reading out each activity and getting students to point to the correct picture. Check comprehension of any other individual words, e.g., *tuna, round-trip ticket, traveler's check*. Repeat this procedure for the places vocabulary. Students then write the correct numbers and letters for each picture. Check the answers.

Answers (clockwise from top left)
5. a   2. c   1. d   4. e   3. b

2 **T 7.8** Explain that students are going to hear Keiko, a Japanese woman, in different places in town. Focus on the example and play the first conversation. Play the other four conversations, pausing after each one. Get students to complete their answers, choosing from the options in Exercise 1. Play the conversations through again if necessary. Check the answers with the whole class. Highlight the use of *at* with *train station*, rather than *in*.

Answers

Where is she?	What does she want?
1. In a cafe.	To have a tuna sandwich.
2. In a clothing store.	To try on a sweater.
3. In an Internet cafe.	To send an e-mail.
4. In a bank.	To change a traveler's check.
5. At a train station.	To buy a round-trip ticket.

3 Focus attention on the fill-in-the-blank conversations. Pre-teach/check *fitting room, pay, at the end, Can I help you?, change* (noun in money context). Elicit as many answers for conversation 1 as the students can remember. Play the recording and get students to check. Students continue to complete the other conversations, working in pairs.

Play the recording again and get students to check/complete their answers.

Answers and tapescript
K = Keiko
1. **A** Next, please!
    K Can I have a tuna sandwich, please?
    A OK.
    K How **much** is that?
    A That's **three** ninety-five, please.
    K Here you are.
    A Thanks **a lot**.
2. **K** Hi. Can **I try on** this sweater, please?
    B **Of course**. The fitting rooms are over there.
3. **K** **Can I send an** e-mail, please?
    C OK. Computer **number two**.
    K **How much** is it?
    C Forty-five cents a minute. You pay at the end.
4. **D** Good morning. Can I help you?
    K Yes, please. **Can I change** this traveler's check?
    D How much is it?
    K **Fifty** dollars.
    D OK.
5. **K** **Can I buy** a round-trip ticket to Milford, please?
    E Sure.
    K How much **is that**?
    E Eighteen **dollars**, please.
    K Thank you.
    E Twenty dollars. Here's **your ticket**, and $2.00 change.

Get students to practice the conversations in closed pairs. Monitor and check for correct pronunciation and intonation. If students have problems, drill key sections chorally and then get students to repeat the closed pair work.

4 Check comprehension of *jacket, T-shirt,* and *one-way ticket*. Put students into pairs and assign a role, A or B, to each student. Make sure they understand that they have to ask about the things in their list. Check that students know which item can go with which conversation:

Conversation 1   a coffee, an ice cream

Conversation 2   this jacket, this T-shirt

Conversation 5   a round-trip ticket to Dallas, a one-way ticket to Houston

Elicit likely prices for a coffee and an ice cream. Choose a pair of students to demonstrate the conversation with Student A asking for a coffee. Then choose another pair, with Student B asking for ice cream. Get students to continue practicing the conversations, working in closed pairs and taking turns to be the sales assistant and the customer. Monitor and check for correct pronunciation and intonation. If students have problems, drill key sections of the conversations and get them to practice again in pairs.

ADDITIONAL MATERIAL

Workbook Unit 7

Exercise 16   provides further practice in making requests with *Can I ...?*

Don't forget!

Workbook Unit 7

Exercises 9 and 10   provide further practice with questions and answers.

Exercise 14   In this exercise, students translate sentences containing the main grammar points presented in the unit.

Word List   Ask the students to turn to SB p. 133 and go through the words with them. Ask them to learn the words for homework, and test them on a few in the following lesson.

> **EXTRA IDEAS UNITS 1–7**
> On p. 102 of the Teacher's Book there is a song, "You're My Everything," and suggested activities to exploit it. You will find the song after Unit 7 on the Student Book Cassette/CD. If you have the time and feel that your students would benefit from this activity, photocopy the page and use it in class.
> The answers to the activities are on p. 129 of the Teacher's Book.

Rooms and furniture

There is/are • *any*

Prepositions • Directions

Where I live

Introduction to the unit

The title of this unit is "Where I live" and the theme is homes. *There is/are* and *any* are introduced in the context of talking and asking about rooms and furniture. Prepositions of place are reviewed and extended. There is a range of skills practice, including a reading and speaking section on the city of Sydney, and a listening and writing section on the students' own hometown.

The lexical set of rooms and furniture is introduced. The language of asking about local amenities and giving directions is introduced and practiced in the *Everyday English* section.

Language aims

There is/are *There is/are* are introduced in the affirmative, question, and negative forms.

any *Any* is introduced for negatives and plural questions with the structure *there is/are*. It is not used with any other structures at this stage so that students have the opportunity to get used to using it. *Some* is included for recognition, but is not given a full presentation or contrasted with *any*, as this is covered in *American Headway 1*.

> **POSSIBLE PROBLEMS**
>
> - *There is/are*
>   Students will be familiar with the forms *is/are* from their knowledge of the verb *to be*. However, students may find it confusing to have a singular and plural form to talk about what exists, especially if the equivalent structure has a single form in their own language. Students can also confuse *there* and *their*, so they may need help in this area in written work. In terms of pronunciation, students need practice with the /ð/ sound in *there* and also need help with linking *There's a* and *There are*. The intonation of the question form may need to be drilled carefully. Students should be encouraged to use a broad voice range, starting high with a fall in the voice and then ending the question with a rise.
>
> - *any*
>   Students often ask what *any* means as there is usually no direct equivalent in their own language. There is of course no real answer to this, so simply tell students that they need to use *any* in negatives and plural questions with *There is/are*. Students also sometimes have a tendency to use *any* in the affirmative, so be prepared to monitor and check for this.

Prepositions of place *In, on, under,* and *next to* are introduced and practiced in the context of talking about furniture in rooms.

Vocabulary The lexical set is of rooms and furniture. Students are given the opportunity to personalize the language by talking about their own home.

Everyday English This covers the language of asking about local amenities and giving simple directions.

Workbook The lexical set of rooms and furniture is consolidated.

There is/are and *any* are practiced in a range of exercises.

There is a word-stress exercise, reviewing key language from this and earlier units.

The prepositions of place from the unit are practiced.

There is further practice in reading and writing.

The language of local amenities and directions from *Everyday English* is consolidated in a range of exercises.

Notes on the unit

STARTER (SB p. 52)

1 Focus attention on the questions in Exercise 1. Pre-teach/check *yard* and the difference between *house* and *apartment*. You can draw these on the board to highlight the difference. Demonstrate the activity by talking briefly about your own home. Only include language that students have already met, e.g., adjectives *big, small*, etc. As a class, students talk briefly about where they live.

2 **T 8.1** Focus attention on the picture of the house. Play the recording and get students to point to the correct room and repeat the words chorally and individually. Check for accurate pronunciation of:

kitchen   /ˈkɪtʃn/

> **Tapescript**
> living room
> dining room
> kitchen
> bedroom
> bathroom

3 Focus attention on the example. Then get students to find the rest of the things in the house and write the correct number, working in pairs. Check the answers with the class.

> **Answers**
> 12 a picture   8 a CD player
> 7 a sofa   9 an armchair
> 5 a TV   4 a lamp
> 2 a shower   13 a stove
> 11 a table   10 a magazine
> 1 a toilet   6 a VCR

T 8.2 Students listen and repeat the words chorally and individually. Check for accurate pronunciation and word stress on:

shower   /ˈʃaʊər/
picture   /ˈpɪktʃər/
sofa   /ˈsoʊfə/
magazine   /mægəˈzin/
toilet   /ˈtɔɪlət/

JANET'S LIVING ROOM (SB p. 53)

There is/are, any

1 Focus attention on the photograph and the instructions for Exercise 1. Ask *What's her name? (Janet)* and *Where is she? (In her living room.)*

T 8.3 Play the recording through once and get students to read and listen to the text, but not write anything at this stage. Write the sentence *There's a sofa, and there are a lot of books* on the board. Underline *There's* and *there are*. Focus attention on the first blank and review the answer *(There)*. Play the recording again and get students to complete the text. Check the answers with the whole class.

> **Answers and tapescript**
> My living room isn't very big, but I love it. There's a sofa, and there are two armchairs. **There's** a small table with a TV on it, and there **are** a lot of books. **There's** a CD player, and **there are** some CDs. **There are** pictures on the wall, and **there are** two lamps. It's a very comfortable room.

If students query the use of *some*, ask *How many CDs?* and elicit *We don't know* to convey the idea of indefinite quantity.

2 Focus attention on the speech bubbles. Write the sentences on the board and ask *Singular or plural? (There's a sofa—singular and There are two armchairs—plural)*. If you know the students' mother tongue, you can translate *There is/are*. If you don't, they should be able to pick up the meaning from the context.

Drill the language in the speech bubbles chorally and individually. Check students can accurately reproduce the linking in both forms:

There's a sofa.

There are two armchairs.

Elicit more singular and plural examples from the class, using the other nouns in the exercise. Students then repeat the sentences working in closed pairs. Monitor and check for correct use of *there is* and *there are*.

Get students to practice *there is* and *there are* with the objects in the classroom. Write lists on the board of the things you have in your classroom, e.g.:

Singular   *a picture, a table, a TV, a photo*
Plural   *lots of books, chairs, desks, bags*

Students work in pairs and take turns making sentences about objects in the classroom. Monitor and check for correct use of *there is* and *there are*.

3 **T 8.4** In this exercise, students practice the question form and short answers. Focus attention on the questions and answers. Play the recording and get students to listen to the questions and repeat chorally and individually. Check students can accurately

reproduce the intonation in the question, and the linking in the short answers:

Are there any photographs?

Yes, there is.

No, there isn't.

Yes, there are.

No, there aren't.

Highlight the singular and plural forms and point out that we use *any* in questions in the plural. Get students to practice the questions and answers in closed pairs. Monitor and check for correct formation of the questions and short answers, and the correct use of *any*.

GRAMMAR SPOT (SB p. 53)

Focus attention on the completed examples. Check that students know *there's* is singular and the contracted form of *there is*, and that *Are there* is plural.

Focus attention on the fill-in-the-blank sentences. Check that students notice that the first and third blanks require plural forms and that the second blank requires singular by focusing on the nouns. Students then complete the sentences.

Give students the opportunity to practice the negative statements by referring to the classroom, e.g., *There isn't a CD player. There aren't any magazines.* Write a list of nouns on the board and get students to make negative sentences.

Read Grammar Reference 8.1 and 8.2 on p. 128 together in class, and/or ask students to read it at home. Encourage them to ask you questions about it.

4 Tell students they are going to talk about Janet's living room. Check comprehension of the items in the list. Focus attention on the speech bubbles and get students to ask and answer the questions in open pairs. Elicit one or two more exchanges using different nouns and then get students to continue in closed pairs. Monitor and check for correct formation of the questions and short answers, and the correct use of *any*.

Check the answers with the whole class by getting students to ask and answer across the class.

Answers

Is there a TV?	Yes, there is.
Are there any photographs?	No, there aren't.
Is there a radio?	No, there isn't.
Is there a CD player?	Yes, there is.
Is there a telephone?	No, there isn't.
Is there a VCR?	Yes, there is.
Are there any lamps?	Yes, there are.
Are there any pictures?	Yes, there are.

5 Demonstrate the activity by describing your own living room. Include affirmative and negative sentences. Get students to work in closed pairs. Encourage students to ask questions if their partner runs out of things to say. Monitor and check for correct use of *There is/are* in all forms, *any*, and pronunciation and intonation. Provide feedback on common errors with the whole class.

ADDITIONAL MATERIAL

Workbook Unit 8

Exercises 1–3 provide further practice of rooms and furniture vocabulary.

Exercises 4–8 provide further practice of *There is/are* in a range of exercises.

JANET'S BEDROOM (SB p. 54)

Prepositions

1 Focus attention on the prepositions. Check that students understand the difference between *in* and *on* by putting something in your book and then on your book and eliciting the correct preposition.

2 Focus attention on the photograph. Ask *What room is this?* (*It's Janet's bedroom.*). Briefly review the vocabulary in the picture by pointing to the objects/furniture and eliciting the correct word. Pre-teach/check the new vocabulary in the sentences: *car keys*, *drawer*, and *floor*.

Focus attention on the example. Students then complete the sentences, working individually.

T 8.5 Get students to check their answers in pairs before checking them with the whole class.

Answers and tapescript
1. Janet's cell phone is **on** the bed.
2. The magazine is **next to** the phone.
3. Her CD player is **on** the floor **next to** the desk.
4. Her car keys are **in** the drawer.
5. Her bag is **on** the floor **under** the chair.
6. The books are **under** her bed.

Students practice the sentences. Monitor and check for accurate pronunciation. If students have problems, drill the sentences and get students to practice them again.

3 This exercise practices questions with *Where?* and the prepositions. Focus attention on the speech bubbles. Remind students of the singular form *is* and the plural form *are*. Highlight the use of *It's* in the singular answer and *They're* in the plural. Drill the questions and answers chorally and individually. Make sure students can reproduce the falling intonation on the questions. Check comprehension of the items in the lists. Elicit two or three more exchanges using the nouns in the list. Students then continue in closed pairs. Monitor and check for correct use of *is/are*, *It's/They're*, and the prepositions.

Check the answers with the whole class by getting students to ask and answer across the class.

Answers
1. Where's her CD player? It's on the floor next to the desk.
2. Where are her CDs? They're on the desk.
3. Where's her lamp? It's on the desk.
4. Where's her computer? It's on the desk.
5. Where are her pens? They're in her bag.
6. Where are her shoes? They're under the bed.
7. Where are her car keys? They're in the drawer.
8. Where are her clothes? They're on the chair.
9. Where are her credit cards? They're in the drawer under the keys.

4 Give students time to write about six questions each. Demonstrate the activity by closing your eyes and getting students to ask you one or two questions. Then get them to continue in closed pairs. Monitor and check for correct use of *is/are*, *It's/They're*, and the prepositions.

SUGGESTION
You can use the picture of Janet's bedroom on p. 54 to review *There is/are* in the affirmative, negative, and in questions. This can be done as a warm-up activity at the beginning of class or as a filler. For further practice, bring in pictures of rooms from magazines. These can be used for vocabulary consolidation, question and answer practice, and describe and draw activities.

ADDITIONAL MATERIAL

Workbook Unit 8
Exercises 10–12   provide further practice of the prepositions of place from the unit.

PRACTICE (SB p. 55)

Questions and answers

1 Focus attention on the example. Then get students to write the words in the correct order to form questions.
T 8.6 Play the recording and get students to check their answers.

Answers and tapescript
1. Do you live in a house or an apartment?
2. How many bedrooms are there?
3. Is there a telephone in the kitchen?
4. Is there a television in the living room?
5. Is there a VCR under the television?
6. Are there a lot of books in your bedroom?
7. Are there any pictures on the wall?

2 Demonstrate the activity by asking a few students the questions in Exercise 1. Students continue asking and answering in closed pairs. Encourage them to ask different questions from those in Exercise 1. Monitor and check.

Different rooms

3 This is an information gap using different pictures. Tell students that they are going to work with a partner and ask questions to find the difference between two similar pictures of a room. Pre-teach/check *window*. Divide the class into pairs. Refer the A students to p. 55 and B students to p. 111. Tell them they shouldn't look at each other's picture. Focus attention on the examples in the speech bubbles and drill the language. Tell students to circle the differences they find in their pictures. Students work in pairs to find all six differences. Monitor and check.

Students compare their pictures to check they have found the differences.

4 **T 8.7** Tell students they are going to hear a description of one of the rooms and that they have to decide which one it is. Play the recording through once and get them to vote for either picture A or B. If there is disagreement, play the recording again. Check the answer with the whole class.

Answer and tapescript
Student A's picture, p. 55

T 8.7
The living room
There's a cat on the sofa, and there's a telephone on a small table next to the sofa. There's a CD player with some CDs under it. Not a lot of CDs. There isn't a TV, and there aren't any pictures or photographs on the walls. There's one lamp; it's next to the table with the telephone. There are two tables and two armchairs. There are some books under one of the tables.

Check it

5 Focus attention on the first pair of sentences as an example. Students continue working individually to choose the correct sentence.

Get students to check their answers in pairs before checking them with the whole class.

Answers
1. Is there a sofa in the living room?
2. There's a CD player.
3. Are there any lamps?
4. Your keys are in the drawer.
5. The lamp is next to the bed.

Sydney

1 Ask students *What do you know about Australia?* and let them give any information they know. Focus attention on the photos. Ask students to find the Opera House as an example and then get them to find the other things in the list, working in pairs. Monitor and help as necessary.

2 This text is slightly longer than in previous units and there are some new words. Tell students not to worry if they don't understand every word and just to focus on the matching task. Check comprehension of the headings. Get students to read the text as far as *it is very hot.* Elicit which heading goes in the first space *(When to go).* Students continue reading and putting in the headings.

T 8.8 Play the recording and get students to check their answers.

Answers and tapescript
How to have a good time in ...

Sydney
Sydney has everything you want in a city. It's beautiful, it has old and new buildings, there are fantastic beaches, and the food is delicious.

When to go
The best times to visit are the spring and fall. In the summer it is very hot.

Where to stay
There are cheap hotels in King's Cross. A room is about $50 a night. There are international hotels in the center. Here a room is about $150 a night.

What to do
Sydney has theaters and movie theaters, and of course, the Opera House. The best stores are on Pitt Street.
Go to the harbor. There are beaches, walks, parks, cafes, and, of course, the wonderful bridge.
Sydney has the famous Bondi Beach. People go swimming, surfing, windsurfing, and sailing.
For nightlife, there are a lot of clubs on Oxford Street.

What to eat
There are restaurants from every country—Italian, Turkish, Lebanese, Japanese, Thai, Chinese, and Vietnamese. Australians eat a lot of seafood—it's very fresh!

How to travel
There are fast trains and slow buses. The best way to see Sydney is by ferry.

Check comprehension of the following vocabulary: *everything, spring, fall, summer, theater, walk* (noun), *park, surfing, nightlife, club, Turkish, Lebanese, Thai, Vietnamese, seafood, fresh, fast, train, slow.*

3 Focus attention on the examples in the chart. Students continue finding the nouns and adjectives, working in pairs. Check the answers with the whole class.

Answers
Adjective	Noun
old/new	buildings
fantastic	beaches
delicious	**food**
cheap	hotels in King's Cross
international	hotels in the center
best	stores
famous	Bondi Beach
fresh	**seafood**
fast	**trains**
slow	buses

4 Elicit the answer to the first question as an example *(The best times to go are the spring and fall.).* Students ask and answer in closed pairs. Monitor and help where necessary. Check the answers.

Answers
1. The best times to go are the spring and fall.
2. No. There are cheap hotels in King's Cross.
3. People go shopping on Pitt Street.
   They go to the beaches, walks, parks, and cafes at the harbor.
   They go swimming, surfing, windsurfing, and sailing at the beach.
   They go to clubs on Oxford Street.
4. There are Italian, Turkish, Lebanese, Japanese, Thai, Chinese, and Vietnamese restaurants in Sydney.
5. The best way to see Sydney is by ferry.

My hometown

1 **T 8.9** Focus attention on the photograph. Ask *What's his name? (Darren)* and *Where does he live? (Bondi, Sydney).* Focus attention on the example. Play the recording as far as *We live in Bondi and we all love surfing.* Tell students they are going to listen to the rest of the recording. Tell them to focus just on the list of things at this stage and not to worry about the details of what Darren says. Make sure students understand they have to write a check mark (✔) for the things Darren talks about and an ✗ for the things he doesn't. Play the recording through once and get students to complete the task. Let them check their answers in pairs and play the recording through again if necessary. Check the answers with the whole class.

Focus attention on the information Darren gives about his brother. Tell students to listen to the recording again and to focus on the details of what Darren says about each thing. Play the recording through again if necessary. Check the answers with the whole class. (If students question the use of *clothes shop*, explain to them that Darren is from Australia, where some of the vocabulary is different from that used in the United States and in *American Headway*.)

Answers and tapescript
Darren says:
his brother: Darren lives in a house with his brother and a friend.
surfing: They (Darren, his brother, and a friend) all love surfing. They often go surfing in the morning before work.
train: He goes to work by train.
the Harbor: His office is on Macarthur Street, very near the Harbor.
the Opera House: They go running near the Opera House.
his girlfriend: His girlfriend likes to go shopping on Saturday.
Oxford Street: There are some great clothes shops on Oxford Street.
Manly Beach: They go to Manly Beach on Sunday if the weather is good.
ferry: They go to the beach by ferry.

T 8.9

G'day! My name is Darren, and I live in a house with my brother and a friend. We live in Bondi and we all love surfing. We often go surfing in the morning before work.
I'm an engineer. I work in the center of Sydney for a big international company. I go to work by train. My office is on Macarthur Street, very near the Harbor. On Monday, Wednesday, and Friday I go running at lunchtime. It's very hot in the summer, but it's beautiful. I sometimes go with friends from work. We run near the Opera House.
My girlfriend likes to go shopping on Saturday. There is a great market in Paddington, and there are some great clothes shops on Oxford Street. On Saturday night, we often go to Chinatown. The food is fantastic and really cheap. Or we stay in Bondi because there are a lot of really good little Thai and Italian restaurants here.
I usually relax on Sunday. When the weather is good, we go to the beach—Manly Beach. We go by ferry. When it's wet, we go to the movies.

2   Get students to ask you the questions in the Student Book and give true answers. Write relevant vocabulary on the board in the categories given below and get students to add to each list, e.g.:

Where/live? *house with a yard, apartment, in the center, near the beach*
Where/work/go to school? *in a hospital/office/school/store/restaurant/cafe, in the center of town, near my house*
What do/with your friends? *go to restaurants/the movies/theater/Internet cafe, watch TV/videos, play soccer/tennis, go shopping/swimming/sailing/surfing/windsurfing*
Where/go shopping? *in the town center, at the supermarket/department store/clothing store/market*
What do/when go out? *see friends, go to clubs* (also see above examples of pastimes with friends)

Put the students into groups and get them to talk about their hometown or a town they like. Get them to refer to the ideas on the board to help them, but also encourage them to say as much as they can for themselves. Monitor and check, but only help if asked. It's important for students to have the opportunity for free practice and to rely on each other for help. Provide feedback on any common errors but only focus on things which are potential blocks to communication. Correcting every small mistake will only discourage the class.

3   This writing task can be done in class or for homework. Tell students they are going to write about a town they know. Focus attention on the paragraph headings and the ideas. If you have time, you might want to build up a full writing model on the board, based on the town where students are studying. If the writing is done in class, get students to exchange their descriptions with a partner for checking/editing. If you check the writing, provide feedback on any general errors, but again do not pick up on every small mistake.

ADDITIONAL MATERIAL

Workbook Unit 8
Exercises 13 and 14   provide further reading and writing practice.

EVERYDAY ENGLISH (SB p. 59)

Directions

1   Pre-teach/check the items in the box. Drill the pronunciation chorally. Demonstrate the activity by getting students to find and point to the bank and the drugstore. Students then continue locating the places on the map.

2   Focus attention on the signs. Copy them onto the board and drill the pronunciation of *turn left, turn right,* and *go straight ahead.*

Answers
a. turn left
b. turn right
c. go straight ahead

3 **T 8.10** Tell students they are going to listen to some directions which they have to follow on the map. Tell students to find the start point YOU ARE HERE on the map. Play the first conversation as an example and get students to follow on the map.

Play the rest of the conversations, pausing after each one and getting students to write in their final location. Get students to check their answers in pairs. Play the recording again and get students to check/complete their answers.

Check the answers with the whole class. If students had problems, go over the exercise again, holding up your book and following the route as you read the tapescript aloud.

Answers and tapescript
1. At the drugstore.
2. At the park.
3. At the school
4. At the Chinese restaurant.
5. At the Internet cafe.

T 8.10
1. Go down Main Street. Turn right at the Grand Hotel onto Charles Street. It's next to the movie theater.
2. Go straight ahead, past Charles Street and turn left onto Cherry Lane. It's on the right, next to the Italian restaurant.
3. Go down Main Street. Turn right at the bookstore. Go down River Road. It's a big building on the right.
4. Go down Main Street. Turn left at the bank onto Charles Street. It's on the right, next to the theater.
5. Go straight ahead. It's on Main Street, on the left, past the theater.

Refer students to the tapescript on p. 120. Get students to practice in pairs. Monitor and check. If they have problems with pronunciation, drill key phrases and then get them to repeat the pair work.

4 Focus attention on the language in the speech bubbles. Drill the language chorally and individually. Check students can reproduce the falling intonation on *Excuse me!* and the rise on *Is there a ... near here?*

Excuse me!   *Is there a ... near here?*

Elicit the directions to the movie theater and the post office as examples. Students continue in closed pairs. Monitor and check.

5 Focus attention on the speech bubbles. Check comprehension of *get to, post office, go out,* and *far.* Drill the language chorally and individually. Briefly review the numbers 1–50 by getting students to count around the class in fives. This will help students with the numbers of minutes. Get one pair of students to practice the conversation in front of the class. Students then continue in closed pairs. Monitor and check.

ADDITIONAL MATERIAL

Workbook Unit 8
Exercises 16–18   provide further practice of giving directions.

Don't forget!

Workbook Unit 8
Exercise 9   is a word-stress exercise.
Exercise 15   In this exercise, students translate sentences containing the main grammar points presented in the unit.
Word List   Ask the students to turn to SB p. 134 and go through the words with them. Ask them to learn the words for homework, and test them on a few in the following class.

EXTRA IDEAS UNITS 5–8
On TB p. 103 there are additional photocopiable activities to review the language from Units 5–8. There is a reading text with tasks, a question formation exercise, and a matching activity on everyday English. You will need to pre-teach/check *refrigerator, message,* and *light* (adjective) for the reading text.

Saying years • *was/were born*

Past Simple—irregular verbs

When's your birthday?

Introduction to the unit

The title of this unit is "Happy birthday!" and it focuses on the birth dates and lives of famous people. This is the vehicle for the presentation of *was/were born,* which is extended to general uses of the past of *to be.* The affirmative forms of Past Simple irregular verbs are also presented in a story context. Students learn how to say dates in English with focuses on months, ordinal numbers, and years. Skills practice is provided in the *Vocabulary and reading* section.

Language aims

Saying years   The *Starter* section teaches students how to read dates in English. This highlights dates before 2000, e.g., *1961—nineteen sixty-one,* and the use of *two thousand* in dates after 1999, e.g., *2008—two thousand eight.* (Note: In British English, it is common to use *and* in dates after 2000, e.g., *2008—two thousand and eight.*)

> **POSSIBLE PROBLEMS**
>
> How students say dates in their own language can often create problems with dates in English. Some languages divide the year differently, e.g., *1999—*one thousand nine hundred and ninety-nine,* so students need help with dividing the century and years correctly.

was/were   The past of *to be* is introduced in all forms. Students' first contact with the past forms is with *was/were born,* and then students move on to general uses of *was/were.*

> **POSSIBLE PROBLEMS**
>
> Students usually make the switch from the present tense of *be* to the past tense relatively smoothly, although they need a lot of practice with which subjects take *was* and which take *were.* Pronunciation can present a problem in that the vowels in *was* and *were* have weak and strong forms: *was* /ə/ and /ʌ/; and *were* /ə/. The weak form /ə/ is in the affirmative and question forms, and strong form /ʌ/ is in negatives and short answers:
>
> | | |
> |---|---|
> | *She was at school.* | /ʃi wəz ət skul/ |
> | *She wasn't at school.* | /ʃi wʌznt ət skul/ |
> | *Was she at school?* | /wəz ʃi ət skul/ |
> | *Yes, she was./No, she wasn't.* | /yɛs ʃi wʌz/ /noʊ ʃi wʌznt/ |
> | *They were at school.* | /ðeɪ wər ət skul/ |
> | *They weren't at school.* | /ðeɪ wərnt ət skul/ |
> | *Were they at school?* | /wər ðeɪ (y)ət skul/ |
> | *Yes, they were./No, they weren't.* | /yɛs ðeɪ wər/ /noʊ ðeɪ wərnt/ |
>
> The pronunciation of the negative forms is highlighted and practiced in the *Negatives and pronunciation* section on p. 63.

was/were born   The equivalent structure in the students' own language is often different, leading students to say **I am born* or **I born.* The unit provides a whole section on this structure to help students become familiar with the correct forms.

Past Simple—irregular verbs The unit introduces the Past Simple in the affirmative. The focus is on a limited number of irregular verbs which are presented as a lexical set in a story context. This allows students to get initial familiarization with some of the highest frequency irregular past forms before they move on to the use of *did* in negatives and questions in Unit 10.

POSSIBLE PROBLEMS

There are a lot of irregular verbs for students to learn in the course of their studies. The initial presentation is limited to a small number of verbs and students access them by matching to their present forms. Students are referred to the irregular verb list on p. 137 to help them do this and they should be encouraged to refer to the list as they work through the remaining units in the book.

Vocabulary This is the small number of irregular past forms that students use to complete a story.

Everyday English This covers months of the year, ordinal numbers in dates, and personalizes the language by talking about students' birthdays.

Workbook Saying years is consolidated in writing and listening exercises.

A reading exercise reviews family vocabulary and further consolidates years.

was/were born is further practiced.

was/were is consolidated through a variety of exercises, including guided writing, question formation tasks, cued sentences, and fill-in-the-blank exercises. Some of these exercises are based on profiles of famous people from the past.

Irregular past tenses are practiced.

Vocabulary from earlier units is reviewed and consolidated in a categorizing activity.

The *Everyday English* section focuses on months, ordinal numbers, and dates.

Notes on the unit

STARTER (SB p. 60)

1 **T 9.1** Briefly review the numbers 1–20 around the class. Write numbers in the 30s, 40s, 50s, etc., on the board to review numbers up to 100. Pre-teach/check *a thousand*. Play the recording for the first date and focus attention on the answer. Play the rest of the recording and get students to underline the correct date.

Get students to check their answers in pairs. Then check the answers with the whole class.

Answers and tapescript
1. fourteen twenty-six
2. seventeen ninety-nine
3. eighteen eighty
4. nineteen thirty-nine
5. nineteen sixty-one
6. two thousand seven

 Focus attention on the Caution Box. Read the first two dates aloud and write them on the board. Highlight that we divide the dates like this in English:
18–41   19–16
T 9.2 Focus attention on the last three dates. Read them aloud. Play the recording and get students to repeat chorally and individually. Elicit how we read each of the dates in Exercise 1. Then get students to practice saying the dates in closed pairs. Monitor and check.

2 Elicit the answers to the questions. The second question includes *was* for recognition. If students query it, tell them it's the past of *be*, but do not go into a full presentation of *was/were* at this point.

WHEN WERE THEY BORN? (SB p. 60)

was/were born

1 **T 9.3** Focus attention on the photos. Ask *Who was he/she?* about each of them to check the names. Check comprehension of *When were they born?* Focus attention on the information about the people. Check comprehension of *painter, scientist,* and *Poland.* Tell students that they will hear a short description of each person and that they have to write the year they were born. Play the recording and get students to write the years. Check the answers with the class.

Answers and tapescript
Leonardo da Vinci was a painter and scientist. He was born in **1452** in Tuscany, Italy.
Marie Curie was a scientist. She was born in **1867** in Warsaw, Poland.

---

2 **T 9.4** Focus attention on the sentences. They present the *I/he/she* forms with *was.* Play the recording and get students to repeat chorally and individually. Encourage students to reproduce the weak form /ə/ in *was.*

3 Focus attention on the speech bubbles. Get students to ask you the questions and give the answers. Drill the language chorally and elicit a few exchanges in open pairs. Students continue in closed pairs. Monitor and check for correct use of *am* and *was* and correct pronunciation.

4 **T 9.5** This exercise presents the *you* and *they* forms with *were*, the *Wh-* question form, and also reviews dates. Play the recording and have students just listen. Play the recording again and get students to repeat chorally and individually. Encourage students to reproduce the weak form /ə/ in *was* and *were*, and the correct intonation and sentence stress:

When were you born? I was born in 1986.

Get students to practice the questions and answers in open pairs and then in closed pairs. Monitor and check for correct reading of dates, pronunciation, and intonation.

GRAMMAR SPOT (SB p. 61)

Focus attention on the chart. Read out the present forms of *to be* and focus on the past examples *was* and *were*. Elicit the *you* form in the past *(were)*. Then get students to complete the rest of the chart.

Answers

	Present	Past
I	am	was
You	are	**were**
He/She/It	is	**was**
We	are	were
They	are	**were**

Read Grammar Reference 9.1 on p. 128 together in class, and/or ask students to read it at home. Encourage them to ask you questions about it.

---

5 **T 9.6** Focus attention on the photo. Ask *What's her name? (Calico Jones.) How old is she, do you think?* (Encourage students to guess her age—about 15.) Draw a family tree on the board and review the following vocabulary: *brother, sister, mom, dad, grandmother.* Focus attention on the names of Calico's family. Read the names aloud so that students will become familiar with the pronunciation. Tell the students they are going to hear Calico describing her family. Ask *When was Calico born?* Play the recording as far as *I was born in 1988,* then elicit the answer. Play the next part of the recording as far as *one year later in 1993.* Elicit the answers about Henry and William *(Henry—1992, William—1993).* Play the rest of the recording and get students to complete their answers.

Get students to check their answers in pairs. Play the recording again if necessary to allow students to check/complete their answers. Check the answers with the whole class.

Answers and tapescript
Calico Jones

Henry and William	1992, 1993
Cleo	1999
Linda and Adam	1961
Violet	1937

T 9.6

My name is Calico. I know, it's a funny name! I was born in 1988. My two brothers are Henry and William, they were born ... umm ... Henry in 1992, and William just one year later in 1993. Ugh! They're awful! My little sister is Cleo, she's OK. She was born in 1999. Mom and Dad are Linda and Adam. My mom was born in 1961 and my dad ... umm ... I think he was born in 1961, too. And my grandmother ... oh, she was born ... uhh ... in 1930 something, I think. ... Yeah, in 1937. Her name's Violet. I think it's a beautiful name.

Focus attention on the speech bubbles. Highlight the uses of the present and past forms. Ask the questions and get students to give complete answers *(She was born in 1999. They're her parents. Linda was born in 1961. Adam was born in 1961, too.).*

Drill the questions and answers chorally. Elicit some questions and answers about the other people in Calico's family with students working in open pairs. Students continue in closed pairs. Monitor and check for correct use of *is/are, was/were born,* dates, pronunciation, and intonation.

6 Demonstrate the activity by writing the names of some of your family on the board. Focus attention on the speech bubbles. Elicit similar questions about your family from the class. Briefly review *he/she* if students have problems with this and make sure they use *is* and *was* correctly. Students work in closed pairs and ask and answer about their respective families. Encourage them to make brief notes of the dates when people were born in preparation for the next exercise. Monitor and check for correct use of *is/are, was/were born,* dates, pronunciation, and intonation.

7 This is a transfer activity to consolidate the third person singular form. Elicit information from several students about their partner's family.

ADDITIONAL MATERIAL

Workbook Unit 9
Exercise 1 provides further practice of writing and saying years.
Exercise 2 is an exercise to review family vocabulary and years.
Exercises 3 and 4 provide further practice of *was/were born* in affirmative and question forms.

PRACTICE (SB p. 62)

Who were they?

1 Pre-teach/check the words in the box, and *India*. Drill the pronunciation chorally and individually. Focus attention on the example. Get students to continue matching the people to the jobs in the box.

Answers
1. writer
8. politician
4. musician
2. painter
7. race-car driver
3. actor
6. princess

2 **T 9.7** Tell students they are going to hear when each of the people in Exercise 1 was born. Play the first sentence and review the answer *(1564)*. Play the rest of the recording and get students to write the other years.

Get students to check their answers in pairs. Play the recording again if necessary to allow students to check/complete their answers. Check the answers with the whole class.

Answers and tapescript
1. Shakespeare was born in England in **1564**.
2. Frida Kahlo was born in Mexico in **1907**.
3. Marilyn Monroe was born in the US in **1926**.
4. Beethoven was born in Germany in **1770**.
5. Elvis Presley was born in the US in **1935**.
6. Diana Spencer was born in England in **1961**.
7. Ayrton Senna was born in Brazil in **1960**.
8. Indira Gandhi was born in India in **1917**.

3 **T 9.8** This exercise extends *Wh-* question forms with *was*. Play the recording and get students just to listen. Play the recording and get students to repeat chorally and individually. Encourage students to reproduce the weak form /ə/ in *was* and the correct intonation and sentence stress.

Get students to practice the questions and answers in open pairs and then in closed pairs. Monitor and check for correct pronunciation and intonation.

Focus attention on the speech bubbles. Ask the question about Frida Kahlo and elicit the answer *(She was a painter.)*. Elicit the other questions with *Where* and *When* and get students to practice in open pairs. Students continue asking and answering in closed pairs. Monitor and check for correct question formation and intonation, and for correct reading of the dates.

SUGGESTION

You can give students additional practice with *was born* and dates with the photocopiable information-gap activity on TB p. 104. Student A and Student B have six pictures of famous people from the past, but only information for three of those people. They have to ask questions to complete the information. Photocopy enough pages for your class. Pre-teach *president*, *dancer*, and *Jamaica*. Divide the class into pairs and hand out the copies, one for Student A and one for Student B. Elicit the questions students will need to ask: *Who was number (1)? What did he/she do? When was he/she born? Where was he/she born?* Remind students to ask *How do you spell that?* when they don't know the spelling of the proper nouns. Demonstrate the activity by getting one pair of students to ask about picture 1 *(Einstein)*. Students then complete the task, working in closed pairs. Monitor and check for correct use of *was*, reading of the dates, and use of the alphabet. Get students to compare their sheets to check they have exchanged the information correctly.

Negatives and pronunciation

4 This exercise introduces the negative forms and highlights the change in pronunciation of the vowel from affirmative to negative. It also highlights the need for contrastive stress when students correct information.

T 9.9 Focus attention on the examples. Remind students that the circles indicate the main stress of each sentence. Play the recording and get students to repeat chorally and individually. Encourage them to reproduce the correct sentence stress and strong vowel form in *wasn't*.

 Focus attention on the Caution Box.
1 Make sure students understand that *wasn't* and *weren't* are contracted forms and what the corresponding full forms are.
2 Focus attention on the examples and read the full sentences aloud. Then read the affirmative and negative verb forms in isolation, emphasizing the change from the weak form /ə/ in *was* and *were* to the strong form /ʌ/ in *wasn't*. Drill the sentences and individual verb forms chorally and individually.

5 Elicit the answer to number 1 as an example *(No, he wasn't. He was a race-car driver.)*. Remind students they will need a plural verb form in numbers 3 and 5. Students continue correcting the information working individually.

T 9.10 Play the recording and get students to check their answers.

Answers and tapescript

1. Ayrton Senna was an actor.
   No, he wasn't. He was a race-car driver.
2. Marie Curie was a princess.
   No, she wasn't. She was a scientist.
3. Marilyn Monroe and Elvis Presley were Mexican.
   No, they weren't. They were American.
4. Beethoven was a scientist.
   No, he wasn't. He was a musician.
5. Leonardo da Vinci and Frida Kahlo were musicians.
   No, they weren't. They were painters.
6. Indira Gandhi was a singer.
   No, she wasn't. She was a politician.

Play the recording again and get students to repeat. If students have problems, highlight the weak and strong verb forms in the *Caution Box* again and elicit where the main stress goes in each sentence. Then get students to repeat again. Get students to practice the sentences in pairs, Student A reading the first sentence and Student B the correction. Monitor and check for correct sentence stress and correct pronunciation of the past verb forms.

ADDITIONAL MATERIAL

Workbook Unit 9

Exercises 5 and 6   provide a fill-in-the-blank and guided writing task to consolidate *was/were* and *was/were* born.

Exercise 7   provides further practice of *was/were* in questions, short answers, and affirmative forms.

Exercise 8   provides further practice of *was/were* in affirmative and negative forms.

Exercise 9   consolidates *was/were* in all forms.

Today and yesterday

6   Pre-teach/check *yesterday* and briefly review the days of the week around the class. Briefly elicit other items that can fit in the sentences, e.g.:

Today/Yesterday ...

I'm/I was *in town/at the store/at the movies/in the country/in the park*

the weather is/was *good/all right/bad*

my parents are/were (see above examples)

Demonstrate the activity by saying where you and your parents are today and were yesterday. Elicit an example of the days of the week and the weather and then get students to continue in closed pairs. This exercise can be extended also to practice the negative. Monitor and check for correct present and past verbs forms, and for correct pronunciation.

Check it

7   Elicit the answer to number 1 as an example *(was)*. Students complete the other sentences, working individually.

Get students to check their answers in pairs before checking them with the whole class. Have them read the complete sentences aloud for more pronunciation practice.

Answers

1. Where **was** your mother born?
2. When **were** your parents born?
3. No, my parents **weren't** both born in 1951. My *father* **was** born in 1951, and my *mother* in 1953.
4. Yes, I **was** in New York in 1999.
5. **Was** he at home yesterday? No, he **wasn't**.
6. **Were** you at work yesterday? Yes, we **were**.
7. **Were** they at school yesterday morning? No, they **weren't**.

VOCABULARY AND READING (SB p. 64)

Past Simple—irregular verbs

1   This section introduces a small set of irregular past forms in a story context. Students access the verbs through their knowledge of the verbs in the Present Simple and the main focus is a lexical rather than grammatical one. It is therefore not advisable to go into a detailed presentation of the Past Simple at this stage. This is covered in Unit 10.

Check the meaning of *present* and *past* and review the meaning of the verbs in their present form. Demonstrate the activity by eliciting the past of *is* and *are (was* and *were)*. Refer students to the irregular verbs list on p. 137. Get students to match the verb forms, working in pairs.

T 9.11   Play the recording through once and get students to check their answers.

Answers and tapescript

are	were
is	was
buy	bought
go	went
say	said
see	saw
take	took

Play the recording and get students to repeat chorally and individually. Make sure students aren't confused by the spelling of *bought* /bɔt/. Say the present forms and get students to say the past equivalent around the class.

Refer students to Grammar Reference 9.2 on p. 128.

2 Pre-teach the new vocabulary in the sentences: *market, painting, expert* (noun), *be worth, million, franc, upset, dirty, for sale*, using the pictures where appropriate. (Note: As of January 2002, the common European currency is the Euro, but because the story is set in 1999, the currency quoted is the French franc.)

Focus on the example to demonstrate the activity. Students continue matching the pictures and sentences, working in pairs. Check the answers with the whole class.

> **Answers**
> 1. d 2. f 3. a 4. c 5. e 6. b

3 Tell students they are going to read a report of the story about the painting. Focus attention on the example to demonstrate the activity. Tell students to complete the rest of the story, working individually. Encourage them not to worry if they come across new words and to try to understand them from the context.

T 9.12 Get students to check their answers in pairs before checking them with the whole class.

> **Answers and tapescript**
> In August 1999 three friends, Charles Proust, Robert Fadat, and Georges Leclerc, **were** on vacation in the town of Laraque in France. On Sunday they **went** shopping at the market and they **saw** a dirty, old painting. They **bought** it for 1,400 francs and they **took** it to Paris. In Paris, an expert said that the painting was by Leonardo da Vinci and it **was** worth 500,000,000 francs. The man at the Laraque market said, "I was happy to sell the painting, but now I'm very upset. I don't want to think about it!"

Check any vocabulary students had problems with. Students then read the story to a partner. Monitor and check for pronunciation. If students have problems, drill key sections and get students to repeat the task.

4 Get students to cover the text in Exercise 3. Focus attention back on the pictures. You can either retell the story as a class activity first and then get students to repeat in pairs; or set up the pair work first and then retell as a class in a review phase. Either way, when you monitor, don't expect students to reproduce the story with complete accuracy. Do not over-correct in the feedback stage—just pick up on common errors in the irregular past forms.

ADDITIONAL MATERIAL

Workbook Unit 9
Exercises 10 and 11   provide further practice of irregular Past Simple forms.

When's your birthday?

1 Focus attention on the months. Pre-teach *calendar* and elicit the second month of the year (*February*). Get students to continue writing the months in order on the calendar.

T 9.13 Play the recording and get students to check their answers.

> **Answers and tapescript**
> January, February, March, April, May, June, July, August, September, October, November, December

Focus attention on the stress marks over each word. Play the recording again and get students to repeat chorally and individually. Get students to say the months in order around the class. Check for accurate pronunciation and drill the months again if necessary.

2 Focus attention on the speech bubbles. Check comprehension of *So is **my** birthday!* Drill the language chorally and then get students to stand up and practice the language in a mingle activity. Get them to note down the months of other students' birthdays as they ask. Elicit the answers to the follow-up questions and establish which is the most common month for birthdays in your class.

3 This exercise presents ordinal numbers. Check that students understand the difference between cardinal numbers and ordinal numbers with the following examples: *There are seven days in a week and there are twelve months in a year. The first day is Monday and the seventh day is Sunday. The first month is January and the twelfth month is December.* Get students to tell you the ordinal numbers (*first, seventh*, and *twelfth*).

T 9.14 Focus attention on the numbers and on how we form the abbreviations with the numeral and the last two letters of the ordinal number. Play the recording and get students to repeat chorally and individually. Write the abbreviated numbers on the board in random order and elicit the ordinal from individual students.

4 Elicit the first ordinal as an example (*sixteenth*). Get students to say the other ordinal numbers, working in pairs. Monitor and check and note any common errors.

T 9.15 Play the recording and let students check their answers. If necessary, drill any ordinals students had problems with.

5 **T 9.16** This exercise presents how we read dates in English. Tell students they are going to hear eight dates and that they should write down the correct ordinal. Play the first date and focus on the example answer (*January first*). Play the rest of the dates and get students to complete the task.

Get students to check their answers in pairs before checking them with the whole class.

 Focus attention on the *Caution Box* and highlight the use of the ordinal in spoken dates and the use of the abbreviation, but note that the ordinal is not used in writing.

Elicit the dates in Exercise 5 orally and then get students to continue practicing in closed pairs. Monitor and check for correct use of ordinals and pronunciation of the months.

6 Focus attention on the speech bubbles. Get students to ask you the questions and give answers. Drill the language chorally and then get students to practice in open pairs. Students continue in groups. Monitor and check for correct falling intonation in the questions and for the correct use of prepositions—*on* + date and *at* + time. Tell the class the date and time of your birth, following the example in the last speech bubble. Elicit more examples from the class.

SUGGESTION
You can give students regular practice in dates by asking *What's today's date?* at the beginning of every class. Encourage students to write the dates in full at the top of any written work, i.e., *January 3, 2003*, rather than *1/3/03*.

ADDITIONAL MATERIAL

Workbook Unit 9
Exercises 14 and 15 consolidate the months of the year.
Exercise 16 consolidates ordinal numbers.
Exercises 17 and 18 provide consolidation of dates.

Don't forget!

Workbook Unit 9
Exercise 12 In this exercise, students translate sentences containing the main grammar points presented in the unit.

Exercise 13 A review of the key lexical sets from previous units.
Word List Ask the students to turn to SB p. 134 and go through the words with them. Ask them to learn the words for homework, and test them on a few in the following class.

Past Simple—regular and irregular

Questions and negatives

Sports and leisure • Filling in forms

We had a good time!

Introduction to the unit

The title of this unit is "We had a good time!" and the overall theme is leisure and vacations. The unit follows up on Unit 9 with the introduction of all forms of the Past Simple for both regular and irregular verbs. Skills practice is provided with speaking, listening, and writing tasks.

The vocabulary of sports and leisure is reviewed and extended. The *Everyday English* section focuses on filling in an application form.

Language aims

Grammar—Past Simple regular and irregular; questions and negatives

The irregular past-tense verbs from Unit 9 are extended and the regular verbs are also introduced. The unit covers affirmative, negative, and question forms. Students' knowledge of the Present Simple usually helps them with the Past Simple, in that students are already familiar with the uses of the auxiliary *do*, and so will grasp how *did* functions. The past auxiliary is easier in that it is the same in all persons. It is important for students to see the contrast in the use of Present Simple and Past Simple and practice using the two tenses in parallel is provided in the unit.

> **POSSIBLE PROBLEMS**
> - Although knowledge of the Present Simple helps students to access the Past Simple, students often make mistakes in the new tense. Common errors are:
>   * *Did they watched TV?*
>   * *They no played tennis.*
>   * *When you lived in the US?*
> - Irregular verbs need to be used and reviewed constantly. Students often try to apply the regular *-ed* ending to irregular verbs, e.g.:
>   * *I goed to the movie theater.*
>   Encourage students to refer to the irregular verbs list on p. 137 of the Student Book, and have them review the verbs regularly for homework.
> - There are different ways of pronouncing the *-ed* regular ending and students need help with this. There is a pronunciation focus on p. 68 highlighting the /t/ and /d/ *-ed* endings, e.g.:
>   *worked* /wərkt/
>   *played* /pleɪd/
>   Students often try to divide out the *-ed* ending in the pronunciation incorrectly, e.g.:
>   *watched* */wɑtʃɛd/ rather than /wɑtʃt/
>   Monitor and check for this mistake. Also help students to perceive the different *-ed* endings, but do not insist that they produce the endings each time.

Vocabulary   The lexical set of sports and leisure activities is reviewed and extended. Students focus on sports and activities collocations with *go* and *play*, e.g., *go swimming, play hockey*, etc.

Everyday English   This section focuses on filling in an application form. The theme of leisure and sports is maintained with a form to join a sports center.

Workbook   Regular and irregular Past Simple verbs in the affirmative are reviewed and consolidated in a variety of exercises.

There is a Reading and matching section focusing on a day in the life of a character.

A Writing section lets students talk about what they did last Saturday.

Past Simple questions and negatives are reviewed in a number of exercises.

There is more practice with the vocabulary of sports and leisure.

A short Reading section consolidates negative and affirmative Past Simple forms.

There is additional practice filling in forms in the *Everyday English* section.

Notes on the unit

STARTER (SB p. 68)

1 This section reviews days and dates, Present and Past Simple forms, and key time expressions. Focus attention on the questions and elicit the answers. Make sure students use *is/was* correctly, pronounce the days correctly, and use ordinal numbers in the dates.

2 **T 10.1** Focus attention on the sentences. Go through and ask *Past or present?* about each one, and then elicit which verb is used in each sentence. Demonstrate the activity by eliciting the time expression for line 1 *(now)*. Elicit from students the fact that the other time expressions are not possible and establish that this is because they refer to the past. Students then match the remaining lines and time expressions. Play the recording and have students check their answers.

> **Answers and tapescript**
> 1. We're at school now.
> 2. You were at home yesterday.
> 3. I went to Australia in 1997.
> 4. She lives in Chicago now.
> 5. They bought their house in 1997.
> 6. It was cold and wet yesterday.

Play the recording again and get students to repeat chorally and individually.

YESTERDAY (SB p. 68)

Past Simple—regular and irregular

1 This section reviews and extends the irregular verbs students met in Unit 9 and also presents regular *-ed* forms. Focus attention on the photo and ask *What's her name? (Becky.) Where is she? (At home.)* Tell students they are going to hear Becky talking about what she did yesterday. Pre-teach/check *newspaper* and *dinner*. Focus attention on the list of verbs and ask *Past or present?* Check comprehension of each verb and get students to

tell you the infinitive of the irregular past forms. (If students query the regular *-ed* endings, tell them this is the ending for most verbs in the Past Simple, but do not go into a long explanation at this stage.)

T 10.2 Play the first line of the recording as far as *eleven thirty* and focus attention on the example. Play the recording through to the end and get students to write a check mark next to the remaining verbs. Have students check their answers in pairs before checking with the whole class.

> **Answers and tapescript**
> ✔ had a big breakfast
> ✔ went shopping
> ✔ stayed home
> ✔ bought a newspaper
> ✔ listened to music
> ✔ watched TV
> ✔ cooked dinner
> ✔ went to bed early

> **T 10.2**
> Yesterday was Sunday, so I got up late—eleven thirty. I had a big breakfast: orange juice, toast, eggs, and coffee. Then I went shopping, to the supermarket, and I bought some chocolate and a newspaper, the *Sunday News*. In the afternoon I listened to music a little and then I watched a movie on TV. In the evening I cooked dinner just for me—not a big meal, just soup and a salad. I went to bed early. It was a wonderful, lazy day.

2 Focus attention on the speech bubble and highlight the use of *then* to link a series of actions. Elicit from the class what Becky did yesterday. Students then take turns saying what Becky did, working in closed pairs. Monitor and check for pronunciation of the *-ed* regular endings but do not over-correct if they have problems during this initial production stage.

GRAMMAR SPOT (SB p. 68)

1 Focus attention on the list of verbs and on the examples *worked* and *played*. Ask students to write the other past forms. Check the answers with the whole class.

> **Answers and tapescript**
>
> | /t/ | work | watch | cook |
> | --- | --- | --- | --- |
> | | worked | **watched** | **cooked** |
> | /d/ | play | stay | listen |
> | | played | **stayed** | **listened** |

Explain that these are regular verbs, so they are different from those students used in Unit 9. Elicit the last two letters in each of the verb forms: *-ed*. Establish that adding *-ed* is the rule for the formation of the Past Simple in the majority of verbs.

T 10.3 Pronounce the sounds /t/ and /d/ and then play the recording. Get students to repeat chorally and individually. Make sure students don't separate the -ed ending into a syllable of its own, e.g., */kʊkɛd/. Encourage them to reproduce the /t/ and /d/ endings accurately, but do not overdo this if students find it difficult. It is enough at this stage for them to perceive the difference.

2 Ask students to write the past tense of the verbs ending in /ɪd/. Check the answers.

T 10.4 Pronounce the sound /ɪd/ and then play the recording. Get students to repeat chorally and individually. Elicit the difference between these verbs and the ones in Exercise 1: the -ed ending is pronounced /ɪd/.

> **Answers and tapescript**
>
> | /ɪd/ | visit | want | hate |
> |------|-------|------|------|
> | | **visited** | **wanted** | **hated** |

3 Read the sentence aloud. Check students understand that there is no difference in the verb forms for different persons in the Past Simple. Contrast this with the third person -s in the Present Simple. Read Grammar Reference 10.1 on p. 128 together in class, and/or ask students to read it at home. Encourage them to ask you questions about it.

3 Refer students back to the list in Exercise 1. Get students to underline the things that they did yesterday. Demonstrate the activity by telling the class things that you did yesterday. If appropriate, write the sentences on the board and underline the verbs, e.g., *I had a big breakfast*. Elicit a few more short examples from the class and then get students to continue in closed pairs. Monitor and check for correct use of regular and irregular past forms.

ADDITIONAL MATERIAL

Workbook Unit 10
Exercises 1–3   provide practice of Past Simple regular verbs.
Exercises 4 and 5   provide practice of Past Simple irregular verbs.
Exercise 6   is a reading and ordering exercise to practice and review the Past Simple.
Exercise 7   provides personalized writing practice.

Questions and negatives

4 **T 10.5** This section presents the Past Simple question and negative forms. Focus attention on the photo. Ask *What's her name? (Becky.)* and *What's his name? (Dan.)*. Tell students they are going to hear Becky and Dan talking about their weekend. Play the recording as far as *tennis with some friends* and elicit the verb for the first blank *(played)*. Play the recording to the end and get

students to complete the conversation. Have students check their answers in pairs. Play the recording again if necessary. Check the answers with the whole class.

> **Answers and tapescript**
>
> **B = Becky   D = Dan**
> **B** Hi, Dan. Did you have a good weekend?
> **D** Yes, I did, thanks.
> **B** What did you do yesterday?
> **D** Well, yesterday morning I got up early and I **played** tennis with some friends.
> **B** You **got up** early on Sunday!
> **D** I know, I know. I don't usually get up early on Sunday.
> **B** Did you go out yesterday afternoon?
> **D** No, I didn't. I just **stayed** home and watched basketball on TV.
> **B** Ugh, basketball! What did you do yesterday evening?
> **D** Oh, I didn't do much. I **worked** a little on my computer. I didn't go to bed late, about 11:00.

5 **T 10.6** Focus attention on the first question in the conversation and the example *(Did you have a good weekend?)*. Ask students to complete the rest of the conversation. Play the recording and get them to check their answers. Play the recording again and get students to repeat chorally and individually. Encourage use of a falling intonation on the *Wh-* questions.

> **Answers and tapescript**
>
> 1. **B Did** you **have** a good weekend?
>   **D** Yes, I did.
> 2. **B** What **did** you **do** yesterday?
>   **D** I played tennis.
> 3. **B Did** you **go** out yesterday afternoon?
>   **D** No, I didn't.
> 4. **B** What **did** you **do** yesterday evening?
>   **D** I didn't do much. I **didn't** go to bed late.

> **GRAMMAR SPOT** (SB p. 69)
>
> 1 Read the notes on the formation of questions and negatives. Highlight the use of *did* and *didn't* and make sure students understand that *didn't* is the contracted form of *did not*.
>
> **T 10.7** Play the recording. Get students to repeat the sentences chorally and individually.
>
> 2 Read the notes on the difference between Present Simple and Past Simple. Highlight the use of *do/did* in the questions. Remind students that *did* is used for all persons in Past Simple questions. Highlight the use of *doesn't/didn't* in the negatives and remind students that the other present forms require *don't*. Ask students to underline the time expressions that are used with the different tenses (Present Simple: *every morning, every Sunday*; Past Simple: *yesterday*

morning, last Sunday). Elicit other time expressions that can be used with the tenses, e.g.:
Present Simple: *every day/week/month, on Sunday, on the weekend, on Saturday afternoon*
Past Simple: *last week/month/year/weekend, yesterday*
Refer students to Grammar Reference 10.2 on p. 128.

6 Focus attention on the speech bubbles. Drill the questions and answers chorally and individually. Elicit other questions and answers in open pairs.

7 Focus attention on the examples, and then get students to continue in closed pairs. Encourage accurate pronunciation of *didn't*. Monitor and check for correct formation of the negatives. A common error is the repetition of the affirmative past form after the auxiliary *didn't*: *He didn't cooked a meal.* If students have this problem, highlight the errors in a general feedback session, then refer students to the Grammar Spot.

ADDITIONAL MATERIAL

Workbook Unit 10
Exercise 8 provides practice of Past Simple Yes/No questions and short answers.
Exercises 9 and 10 provide practice of Past Simple *Wh-* questions and answers.
Exercise 11 provides practice of Past Simple negatives.

PRACTICE (SB p. 70)

Did you have a good weekend?

1 Exercises 1, 2, and 3 focus on Yes/No questions in the Past Simple. Tell students they are going to talk about what they did last weekend. Focus attention on the list of activities in the chart and check comprehension of each one. Check comprehension of the difference between *do homework* and *do housework*. Students then continue to form the questions, working individually. Explain that there are three columns in the chart—one each for the student, the teacher, and the student's partner. Tell students to check the activities they did last weekend in the *You* column.

2 Focus attention on the speech bubbles. Drill the question chorally and individually and then give your answer. Get students to ask you the rest of the questions and record the answers in the *Teacher* column.

3 Demonstrate the activity in open pairs and then get students to continue in closed pairs. Monitor and check for correct question formation and short answers.

Focus attention on the example and have students tell the class about what they and their partner did last weekend.

4 This is an information-gap activity that practices Past Simple *Wh-* and Yes/No questions and can be conducted

as a memory game. There are pictures of two apartments, one for Student A and one for Student B, which show what the occupants did yesterday.

Pre-teach/check *write a letter* and its irregular past *wrote, read a book/newspaper* and its irregular past *read* /rɛd/, *take a bath, take a shower,* and *play the guitar* /gɪ'tɑr/.

Divide the class into pairs and make sure students know if they are Student A or Student B. Students A should look at page 112, and Students B should look at page 114. Demonstrate the activity with two confident students. Get Student B to look carefully at the picture of Paul's apartment for 30 seconds and then put it out of sight. Student A then uses the question cues to ask about what Paul did yesterday. Pre-teach *I can't remember.* Get students to complete the task in closed pairs for Student B's picture. Students then change roles with Student A looking at Jane's apartment for 30 seconds and Student B using the question cues to ask about what Jane did yesterday.

Monitor and check for correct question formation and use of regular and irregular pasts. (With a weaker class, you could separate the A and B students into groups to give them time to write out the cues as full questions. Then divide the class into A and B pairs and continue as above.)

5 This exercise focuses on *Wh-* questions in the Past Simple. Briefly review the question words *what, who, where, what time,* and *how much.* Focus attention on the example.

T 10.8 Tell students they are going to hear the questions, each preceded by a statement. Play the recording through once and get students to listen to the statements and check that they have formed the questions correctly. Play the recording again and elicit what the man says before each question.

Answers and tapescript
1. **A** I went to the movies.
    B What did you see?
2. **A** I went shopping.
    B What did you buy?
3. **A** I had dinner in a restaurant.
    B What did you have?
4. **A** I saw my friends.
    B Who did you see?
5. **A** I played soccer.
    B Where did you play?
6. **A** I went to a party.
    B What time did you leave?
7. **A** I did my homework.
    B How much homework did you do?
8. **A** I did the housework.
    B How much housework did you do?

6 **T 10.9** Pre-teach/check *steak* and *fries*. Play the recording and get students to listen. Get them to practice the conversations in closed pairs. Monitor and check for pronunciation. If students have problems, drill key sections, and get them to practice again in closed pairs.

Refer students back to Exercises 1 and 5. Explain that they are going to ask each other about the activities in question 1 again. If their partner answers "Yes" about an activity, they should ask the appropriate follow-up question from Exercise 5. If you think they need it, demonstrate by building a model conversation on the board.

Model conversation
A Did you go shopping last weekend?
B Yes, I did.
A What did you buy?
B A new sweater.
A Was it expensive?
B Yes, it was.

Get students to continue working in closed pairs. Monitor and check for the correct form of Past Simple questions, short answers, and affirmative forms, and for the use of *was/were*.

7 This exercise reviews short answers in the Present and Past Simple. Pre-teach/check *party*. Focus attention on the examples and then get students to complete the answers, working individually.

T 10.10 Get students to check their answers in pairs before checking them with the whole class.

Answers and tapescript
1. Do you work in New York?	No, I **don't.**
2. Did she like the movie?	Yes, she **did.**
3. Does he watch TV every night?	Yes, he **does.**
4. Did you go out last night?	No, we **didn't.**
5. Did he go to the party?	Yes, he **did.**
6. Do you buy a newspaper every morning?	Yes, I **do.**
7. Does she usually go to bed late?	No, she **doesn't.**
8. Did they have a good time?	No, they **didn't.**

Get students to practice the questions and answers in open and then in closed pairs. Monitor and check for pronunciation. If students have problems, drill key sentences and then get students to practice again in closed pairs.

Check it

8 Focus attention on the first pair of sentences as an example. Students continue working individually to choose the correct sentence.

Get students to check their answers in pairs. Then check the answers with the whole class.

Answers
1. She bought an expensive car.
2. Did they go shopping yesterday?
3. Where did you go last weekend?
4. We didn't see our friends.
5. "Did you like the movie?" "Yes, I did."
6. I played tennis yesterday.

SUGGESTION
Take the opportunity to review the Past Simple by getting students to ask and answer about the weekend in the first class that you have each week. This provides a useful review and also highlights the value of what students are learning in a realistic situation.

VOCABULARY AND SPEAKING (SB p. 72)

Sports and leisure

1 Focus attention on the photographs. Elicit the activity that goes with photo 1 *(tennis)*. Students continue to match the photos and activities. Check the answers with the whole class.

Answers
2. skiing	8. swimming
3. windsurfing	9. ice skating
4. dancing	10. soccer
5. sailing	11. cards
6. walking	12. ice hockey
7. baseball	13. golf
7. tennis	

Check the pronunciation of the activities and drill if necessary.

2 This exercise focuses on collocations with *play* and *go + -ing*. Focus attention on the examples and then get students to complete the categorizing, working in pairs. Check the answers with the whole class. As a general rule, you could tell students that sports with a ball and games like cards, chess, etc., take *play*, and physical activities ending in *-ing* take *go*.

Answers
play	**go + -ing**
tennis	skiing
soccer	sailing
golf	windsurfing
baseball	ice skating
cards	dancing
ice hockey	walking
	swimming

3 This exercise practices Yes/No and *Wh-* questions with the collocations from Exercise 2. Focus attention on the speech bubbles. Highlight the use of the tenses—Present Simple to talk about general habits in the present and Past Simple to ask *When?* in the past. Drill the language chorally and individually. Elicit two or three more examples from students working in open pairs. Students continue in closed pairs. Monitor and check for correct use of tenses, correct use of *play* and *go*, and pronunciation.

4 This exercise practices the third person forms. Focus attention on the examples. Elicit more examples from students about their partner. Check for accurate use of the third person forms in the Present Simple. Highlight common errors and get students to correct them.

ADDITIONAL MATERIAL

Workbook Unit 10
Exercise 13 consolidates the vocabulary of sports and leisure.

LISTENING AND SPEAKING (SB p. 73)

Vacations

1 This section provides further practice of the Present Simple and Past Simple in the context of vacations. It also reviews the sports and leisure activities from the *Vocabulary and speaking* section. Review the months of the year by getting students to say them around the class. Check for accurate pronunciation. Check comprehension of *season*. Elicit the seasons students have already met—*spring, summer,* and *fall,* and pre-teach *winter.* Get students to say the months that correspond to each season in their country, e.g., *In the United States, spring is March, April, and May.*

Focus attention on the speech bubble and give an example about yourself. Elicit more examples from the class, and then get students to continue in pairs.

2 **T 10.11** Focus attention on the photos. Ask *Who are they? (Bill and Kelly).* Focus attention on the lists of information, A and B. Check students recognize that A is Present Simple and B is Past Simple. Focus attention on the examples. Tell students to listen and underline the correct information about Bill and Kelly's vacations. Make sure they understand that the information will come in slightly different order from the order on the page. Play the recording through once and get students to complete the task.

Get students to check their answers in pairs. Play the recording through again and get students to check their answers. Check the answers with the whole class.

Answers and tapescript

A	B
They usually ...	**Last year they ...**
go in the summer	went in the winter
go to California	went to Colorado
stay in a hotel	stayed in an apartment
eat in restaurants	cooked their own meals
go swimming	went skiing and ice skating
play golf	played cards
have a good time	had a good time

T 10.11
B = Bill   K = Kelly
B Well, usually we go on vacation in the summer.
K Yes, and usually we go to California ..., but last year we ...
B ... last year we went to Colorado, and we went in the winter.
K We stayed in an apartment and we cooked all our own meals there. It was wonderful.
B Yes, in California we usually stay in a hotel and eat in restaurants.
K It was good to do different things, too. Usually we just go swimming and sit in the sun ...
B And I sometimes play golf. I love that!
K Ah, yes, you do. But of course in Colorado we went skiing every day, and sometimes we went ice skating in the afternoons—it was a lot of fun.
B And in the evenings we cooked dinner and then played cards. We had a very good time.
K We love vacations—we always have a good time in California, too.

3 This exercise practices questions in the Present Simple and Past Simple. Focus attention on the speech bubbles. Drill the questions and answers, encouraging students to reproduce the correct sentence stress:

● ● ● ●
When do they usually go on vacation?

● ● ●
When did they go last year?

Elicit the questions and answers for the second prompt in open pairs. (*Where do they usually go on vacation? To California. Where did they go last year? They went to Colorado.*) Remind students that the questions for the last prompt are a different type (Yes/No question). Get students to ask and answer in closed pairs. Monitor and check for correct question formation in both tenses, for correct sentence stress, and for correct use of the prepositions *to* and *in.* Check the answers by getting students to ask and answer in open pairs across the class. Provide feedback on any common errors if necessary.

Answers

- Where do they usually go on vacation? To Florida.
  Where did they go last year? They went to Colorado.
- Where do they usually stay? In a hotel.
  Where did they stay last year? They stayed in an apartment.
- Where do they usually eat? In restaurants.
  Where did they eat last year? They cooked their own meals.
- What do they usually do? Go swimming and play golf.
  What did they do last year? They went skiing and ice skating.
- Do they usually have a good time? Yes, they do.
  Did they have a good time last year? Yes, they did.

WRITING (SB p. 74)

My last vacation

1 This section reviews Past Simple negative and affirmative forms. Establish that this exercise is about Bill and Kelly's vacation last year so students will need to use the Past Simple tense. Focus attention on the example and highlight the need for a negative form, then an affirmative form. (With a weaker group, you might want to elicit the verbs students will use before they start: 2—*go*, 3—*stay*, 4—*eat/cook*, 5—*go*.) Have students complete the sentences working individually.

T 10.12 Let students check their answers in pairs before checking them against the recording.

Answers and tapescript

1. Last year Bill and Kelly **didn't go** on vacation in the summer.
   They **went** in the winter.
2. They **didn't go** to California.
   They **went** to Colorado.
3. They **didn't stay** in a hotel.
   They **stayed** in an apartment.
4. They **didn't eat** in restaurants.
   They **cooked** their own meals.
5. They **didn't go** swimming.
   They **went** skiing.

2 This exercise allows students to personalize the language of vacations and the Past Simple in a guided writing task. Tell students they are going to write to a friend about their last vacation. Ask *Present or past?* and establish that they need to use the past tense. Focus attention on the model sentences and elicit what language can complete the skeleton. Highlight the use of *was* in *Was the weather good?* and check that students recognize this as the past of *be*.

Tell the class about your last vacation; then let students write their descriptions, using the skeleton in the Student Book. Circulate and help, correcting as necessary.

Get students to read their description to the class. If time is short, or if you have a very large class, get students to read their descriptions in groups of four.

EVERYDAY ENGLISH (SB p. 75)

Filling in forms

> **NOTE**
>
> Students may need an explanation of the titles used with last names in English: *Mr./Mrs./Ms.* Be prepared to give a brief explanation of the titles.
> Mr. /mɪstər/   used for men
> Mrs. /mɪsəz/   used for married women
> Ms. /mɪz/   used before a woman's last name when you do not know whether she is married or not, or when she prefers to use this title

1 This section focuses on the language of forms and continues the overall theme of leisure. Focus attention on the form and ask *What does Jennifer Cotter want to do? (Join a sports center.) What's the name of the Sports Center? (Monroe.)* Focus attention on the categories that applicants have to fill in. Check comprehension of the titles *Mr./Mrs./Ms., full name, zip code, date of birth, running, squash, fitness training, signature, type of card* (= card that applicant will be allocated), *data input date* (= date when applicant's details were processed).

2 Get students to complete the form with their own information. Circulate and help as necessary.

3 Focus attention on the speech bubbles. Highlight the use of *both* to say students share interests, and the way of contradicting information with *but I'm not*. Also highlight the preposition *in*. Drill the language chorally and individually, encouraging students to reproduce the sentence stress correctly:

●　　　●　　●　●　　　　　●

Gabriel and I are both interested in golf.

　　●　　　　　　●　　　　　●

Maria is interested in fitness training, but I'm not.

Divide the class into groups and give students time to compare their forms and decide who is interested in what. Elicit examples from the class of similarities and differences in interests.

ADDITIONAL MATERIAL

Workbook Unit 10
Exercise 15 provides further practice filling in forms.

Don't forget!

Workbook Unit 10
Exercise 12 In this exercise, students translate sentences containing the main grammar points presented in the unit.
Exercise 14 provides reading practice.

Word List   Ask the students to turn to SB p. 134 and go through the words with them. (Note: In the split edition, this word list appears on SB p. 135.) Ask them to learn the words for homework, and test them on a few in the following class.

Stop and Check 3   There is a Stop and Check quiz for Units 7–10 on p. 116 of the Teacher's Book.

Progress Test 2   There is a Progress Test for Units 6–10 on p. 124 of the Teacher's Book.

11

can/can't • Requests and offers

Verbs and nouns that go together

What's the problem?

We can do it!

Introduction to the unit

The title of this unit is "We can do it!" and it introduces *can* for ability. The affirmative, negative, and question forms are introduced and practiced. The focus on *can* is extended to cover requests and offers. There is a *Reading and vocabulary* section with a text on the Internet, and a focus on verb and noun collocations. The *Everyday English* section focuses on basic problems.

Language aims

Grammar–*can/can't*   *Can* for ability is introduced in all forms. It is presented and practiced with key verbs and the adverbs *well* and *fast*. There is also a pronunciation focus highlighting the different sounds in *can/can't*. Students are given both receptive and productive practice in the different forms.

> **POSSIBLE PROBLEMS**
> * After having practiced the Present Simple, students sometimes want to use the auxiliaries *do/does* and *don't/doesn't* to form negatives and questions with *can*:
> * We don't can run fast.
> * Do you can swim?
> * The pronunciation of *can/can't* needs careful presentation and practice. Students often have problems with the different vowel sounds (weak form /ə/ and strong form /æ/ in *can*, and /æ/ in *can't*). Students may also have problems distinguishing affirmative from negative forms, as the final *-t* in *can't* is often not fully pronounced.
>
> | | |
> |---|---|
> | *I can swim.* | /aɪ kən swɪm/ |
> | *Can you swim?* | /kən yu swɪm/ |
> | *Yes, I can.* | /yɛs aɪ kæn/ |
> | *I can't swim.* | /aɪ kænt swɪm/ |
>
> The pronunciation is highlighted as part of the *Grammar Spot* and students are given both receptive and productive practice.

Requests and offers   Requests and offers with *can* are presented and practiced.

Vocabulary   There is a focus on key noun-verb collocations as an introduction to a text about what you can do on the Internet.

Everyday English   The language associated with describing and solving basic problems is introduced and practiced.

Workbook   The vocabulary and collocations syllabus is extended with a focus on activities. Vocabulary from previous units is also reviewed in an "odd one out" exercise.

Can/can't is consolidated in a variety of exercises.

There is a pronunciation exercise on *can*.

Requests and offers with *can* are further practiced.

The *Everyday English* focus on problems is consolidated.

Notes on the unit

STARTER (SB p. 76)

> **NOTE**
>
> In *American Headway*, we have chosen to spell *e-mail* with a hyphen. Students may have seen the non-hyphenated form *email* and both are acceptable in current usage.

1 This *Starter* section focuses on possible uses of a computer and provides a useful introduction to the overall topic of computing and the Internet. Pre-teach/check the language in the list of questions. Drill the pronunciation as necessary.

2 Focus attention on the examples in the speech bubbles. Highlight the contrastive stress in the first speech bubble (*don't, home, use, work*). Check that students understand what *it* refers back to in the second sentence of the second speech bubble (*a computer*). Give an example of how you use a computer.

Elicit one or two more examples from the students and then let them continue in closed pairs. Monitor and check.

Elicit a few more examples in a short review session.

WHAT CAN THEY DO? (SB p. 76)

can/can't

1 This section presents different people and their skills to highlight the use of the affirmative form *can*. It also reviews the use of *a/an* with jobs/roles.

Focus attention on the photos and on the example. Students continue matching the words and photos, working in pairs. Check the answers with the whole class.

> **Answers**
> 1. a student
> 2. an athlete
> 3. an architect
> 4. an interpreter
> 5. a farmer
> 6. a grandmother

2 Pre-teach/check *run fast, draw well, drive a tractor,* and *make cakes,* using the information in the photos. Focus attention on the example, highlighting the use of *a*. Students complete the rest of the sentences with *a* or *an*.

T 11.1 Play the recording and let students check their answers.

> **Answers and tapescript**
> 1. Josh is **a student.** He can use a computer.
> 2. Tamika is **an athlete.** She can run fast.
> 3. Laura is **an architect.** She can draw well.

> 4. Ted is **an interpreter.** He can speak Chinese and Japanese.
> 5. John is **a farmer.** He can drive a tractor.
> 6. Helen is **a grandmother.** She can make cakes.

Play the recording again line by line and have students repeat. Encourage them to reproduce the weak form for the affirmative of *can* /kən/. If students find this difficult, get them to highlight the main stresses in each sentence and then practice the sentences again. Students practice in closed pairs. Monitor and check for correct pronunciation of *can*.

3 Focus attention on the language in the speech bubble. Drill the example chorally and individually. Give another example about yourself and elicit one or two more examples from the class. Students then continue in closed pairs. Monitor and check for correct use and pronunciation of *can*. Do not overdo the practice of the weak form /kən/, as students will have the opportunity to review this in contrast with the other forms at various points in the unit.

Questions and negatives

4 **T 11.2** This section presents the question and negative forms of *can*. Play the recording through once and get students to just listen. Play the recording again and get students to repeat the questions and answers. Encourage them to reproduce the weak form /kən/ in the question, the strong form /kæn/ in the affirmative short answer, and the negative form /kænt/. Get students to ask and answer in open pairs across the class. Students then continue in closed pairs. Monitor and check for correct pronunciation of the different forms of *can*. If students have severe problems with the pronunciation, drill the sentences again, but do not make students self-conscious about using the new language.

5 Focus attention on the examples in the speech bubbles. Highlight the use of *can* for both the *she* and the *I* forms. Drill the examples in open pairs. Elicit some more examples about the people in Exercise 1, and also some student-student examples. Students then continue in closed pairs. Monitor and check for correct use and pronunciation of *can* and *can't*.

GRAMMAR SPOT (SB p. 77)

1 Read the notes with the whole class. Highlight that *can/can't* is used with all persons, and that *can't* is the contraction of *can not*.

2 Read the notes with the whole class. Highlight the use of *can* in the affirmative and question forms.

3 **T 11.3** Tell students they are going to hear the two ways of pronouncing *can*. Play the recording and get students to just listen. Play the recording again and get students to repeat chorally and individually.

Read Grammar Reference 11.1 on p. 129 together in class, and/or ask students to read it at home. Encourage them to ask you questions about it.

6 **T 11.4** Focus attention on the photo. Ask *What's his name? (Josh.) Does he have a job? (No, he's a student.)* Ask *What's her name? (Teresa.)* Pre-teach/check *a little, planes, grow up, cook* (verb), and *grandmother*. Play the recording through once and get students to fill in the blanks. Ask them to check their answers in pairs. Play the recording again and get students to check/amend their answers. Check the answers with the whole class.

Answers and tapescript

T = Teresa   J = Josh

T Can you use a computer, Josh?

J Yes, of course I **can**. All my friends **can**. I use a computer at school and at **home**.

T That's very good. What other things can you do?

J Well, I can run fast—very fast—and I can draw a little. I can draw planes and **cars** really well but I can't drive a car, of course. When I grow up I want to be a farmer and **drive** a tractor.

T And I know you can speak French.

J Yes, I can. I **can** speak French very well because my dad's Canadian, from Quebec. We sometimes **speak** French at home.

T Can you speak any other languages?

J No, I can't. I **can't** speak Spanish or Portuguese, just French— and English of course! And I can cook! I can **make** cakes. My grandmother makes delicious cakes and I sometimes help her. Yesterday we made a big chocolate cake.

Get students to practice the conversation in closed pairs. Monitor and check. If students have problems with pronunciation, drill key sections of the conversation and get students to practice again in closed pairs.

7 Elicit the answer to question 1 as an example *(He can use a computer, run fast, draw planes and cars, speak French and English, cook, and make cakes.).* Students continue asking and answering in closed pairs.

Check the answers by getting students to read the questions and answers across the class.

Answers

1. He can use a computer, run fast, draw planes and cars, speak French and English, cook, and make cakes.
2. He can't drive, or speak Spanish or Portuguese.
3. Yes, he does.
4. He wants to be a farmer.
5. He can speak French well because his dad is Canadian.
6. He made a chocolate cake with his grandmother.

ADDITIONAL MATERIAL

Workbook Unit 11

Exercise 1   is a vocabulary exercise on activities including some noun-verb collocations.

Exercises 2 and 3   provide further practice of *can/can't*.

Exercises 4 and 5   provide practice of questions and answers with *can*.

PRACTICE (SB p. 78)

Pronunciation

1 **T 11.5** This is a discrimination exercise to practice recognizing and producing *can* and *can't*. Play sentence 1 as an example and confirm the answer *(can)*. Play the rest of the sentences, pausing at the end of each one and get students to underline the correct word.

Get students to check their answers in pairs before checking them with the whole class.

Answers and tapescript

1. I **can** use a computer.
2. She **can't** speak Thai.
3. He **can** speak English very well.
4. Why **can't** you come to my party?
5. We **can't** understand our teacher.
6. They **can** read music.
7. **Can** we have an ice cream?
8. **Can't** cats swim?

Play the recording again line by line and get students to repeat chorally and individually. Students then practice the sentences in closed pairs. Monitor and check for correct pronunciation of *can/can't*, but don't insist on perfect pronunciation from all students.

Can you or can't you?

2 Focus attention on the chart. Check comprehension of the verbs in the list, and pre-teach/check *horse*. Tell students that they will get the answers for Tito from the recording, they will complete the *You* column, the teacher will give answers for the *T* column, and another student for the *S* column.

T 11.6 Focus attention on the photo. Ask *What's his name? (Tito.)* Tell students they are going to hear Tito on the recording and that they should check the things he can do in his column of the chart. Play the recording as far as *Portuguese, Japanese, and English*. Focus attention on the example, and elicit the next verb that requires a check (*speak Japanese*). Play the rest of the recording and get students to complete their answers.

Play the recording again and get students to check their answers before reviewing them with the whole class.

Answers and tapescript
speak Japanese
speak English very well
drive a car
ride a horse
ski
play the guitar

T 11.6
I come from Argentina, but now I live and work in the United States, in Los Angeles. I can speak four languages—Spanish, of course, Portuguese, Japanese, and English. I can speak English very well now, but in the beginning it was very difficult for me. I can drive a car and I can ride a horse. Back home in Argentina, I didn't drive a lot, but in Los Angeles I drive every day! I can ski, but I can't cook very well and I can't play the piano—but I can play the guitar.

3 Students complete the *You* column in the chart. Drill the pronunciation of the verbs in the list if necessary and then elicit the questions from the class. Give true answers for yourself and get students to complete the *T* column.

Then focus attention on the language in the speech bubbles. Drill the language chorally and individually. Elicit two or three more examples in open pairs. Then get students to continue asking and answering in closed pairs, noting their partner's answer to each question in the *S* column.

4 Focus attention on the example in the speech bubble. Drill the language and highlight the different pronunciation of *can* and *can't* and the contrastive stress in the second sentence:

/ə/
Isabel and I can speak Spanish.

● /ə/　　　　●　　　　●/æ/
She can speak French too, but I can't.

Elicit two or three more examples from the class and then get students to continue in closed pairs. Monitor and check for the correct use and pronunciation of *can/can't*. Provide feedback on any major common errors, but do not expect students to produce perfect pronunciation of *can/can't* as this may be demoralizing.

ADDITIONAL MATERIAL

Workbook Unit 11
Exercise 6 is an exercise to consolidate the pronunciation of *can/can't*.

Requests and offers

5 Focus attention on the example. Then get students to write the other questions, working individually. Get students to check their answers in pairs but don't check them with the whole class until after Exercise 6.

Answers
See **T 11.7** below

6 Elicit the answer to question 1 (*c. It's about three thirty.*). Students continue matching, working individually.

T 11.7 Play the recording and let students check their answers to the question formation and the matching phase.

Answers and tapescript
1. c　2. e　3. d　4. b　5. a

T 11.7
1. Can you tell me the time, please?
   It's about three thirty.
2. Can you come to my party?
   I'm sorry. I can't. It's my grandmother's birthday.
3. Can you speak more slowly, please?
   I'm sorry. Can you understand now?
4. Can I help you?
   Yes, please. I want to buy this postcard.
5. Can I have a cold drink, please?
   Yes, of course. Do you want soda or orange juice?

Focus attention on the examples in the speech bubbles. Highlight how the conversation can be continued. Get students to practice the conversation in open pairs. Have them continue with the other conversations in closed pairs. Remind students to continue the conversations in an appropriate way. With a weaker class, you could get them to repeat after the recording, and elicit ways of continuing the conversations before they start the pair work. Possible ways of continuing the conversations:

2. *That's 90¢, please.*
   Here you are.
   Thank you.
3. *Say "Happy Birthday" from me.*
   OK. Thanks.
4. *Orange juice, please.*
   Here you are.
   Thanks.
5. *Yes, I can. Thanks.*

Check it

7 Focus attention on the first pair of sentences as an example. Students continue working individually to choose the correct sentence.

Get students to check their answers in pairs before checking them with the whole class.

Answers
1. I can't understand.
2. He can speak three languages.
3. What can you see?
4. Can you swim fast?
5. "Can they come to the party?" "No, they can't."
6. Can she play tennis?

ADDITIONAL MATERIAL

Workbook Unit 11
Exercises 7 and 8   provide further practice of requests and offers.

READING AND LISTENING (SB p. 80)

The things you can do on the Internet!

> **NOTE**
> The reading text in this section contains a number of new vocabulary items and some topic-specific words, e.g., *computer network, the Net, go worldwide*. In order to save time in class, you might want to ask students to check the following words in their dictionary for homework before the reading lesson: *history, start* (verb), *Department of Defense, computer network, military* (noun), *telephone company, communicate, the Net, go worldwide, north, south, partner* (in a game), *list, endless*.

1   This section gives practice in vocabulary, reading, and listening based on a subject of interest to many students—the Internet. The first exercise reviews and extends useful verb-noun collocations and also pre-teaches some of the vocabulary used in the reading text.

   Pre-teach/check *chat with, reservation, plan* (verb), and *chess*. Focus attention on the example. Students continue matching, working individually. Get students to check their answer in pairs before checking them with the whole class.

> **Answers**
> | | |
> |---|---|
> | listen to a CD | read a magazine |
> | watch a video | chat with a friend |
> | play chess | make a reservation |

2   Focus attention on the web site addresses and elicit where you can find them *(on the Internet)*. Elicit what *www* means *(worldwide web)*.

3   Read through the questions as a class and elicit possible answers. Focus attention on the example in the speech bubble. Divide the class into pairs or groups of three and get students to discuss the questions. Allow them to use whatever language they can to express their ideas, but be prepared to supply vocabulary if students request it. Do

not give feedback on the questions at this stage as students will find answers to the questions in the reading text.

4   **T 11.8** If you did not assign the vocabulary for homework, pre-teach/check the items listed in the *Note* above. Ask students to read and listen to the text and to find the answers to the questions in Exercise 3. Get students to compare their predictions in Exercise 3 with the information in the text. Check the answers with the whole class.

> **Answers**
> 1. The Internet started in the 1960s.
> 2. It started because the US Department of Defense wanted a computer network to help the American military.
> 3. You can shop for a car or house; you can plan a vacation; you can watch a video; you can read an Australian newspaper or a Japanese magazine; you can buy books and CDs from North and South America; you can play chess with a partner in Moscow; you can chat with people from all over the world.

Elicit any other uses of the Internet that the students thought of in Exercise 3 but that don't appear in the text.

5   Get students to read the text again, and find and correct the false sentences. Ask students to check their answers in pairs before checking them with the whole class.

> **Answers**
> 1. The Internet started in the 1960s.
> 2. The US Department of Defense started it.
> 3. ✔
> 4. ✔

6   Give the names of a few good web sites that you know and describe what you can do at these sites. Provide useful language for talking about web sites:

   (Name of site) is good for (shopping).

   I visit (name of site) for (information on travel).

   You can (read the news) at (name of site).

   A good site for (games) is (name of site).

   Divide the class into groups and get them to talk about good web sites that they know. Monitor and check. Get students to tell the whole class of any interesting sites in a brief review session. Highlight any common errors to the class, but do not over-correct as this may be demoralizing.

7   **T 11.9** Tell students they are going to hear different people talking about when and why they use the Internet. Play the first extract and focus attention on the example. Play the rest of the recording and get students to note their answers in the chart.

   Get students to check their answers in pairs. Play the recording again and get students to check/amend their answers. Check the answers with the whole class.

T 11.9

Carmen

I use the Internet a lot. Every day, I think. It helps me with my homework. It helps me with everything. Yesterday I did an English test. It was quite difficult.

Anela

My brother's in Taiwan. I can't call Taiwan, it's very expensive—so Paul (that's my brother) and I—we "talk" in chat rooms on the Internet. We talk late, at about 11 o'clock in the evening—well, it's evening here, but it's 8 o'clock in the morning in Taiwan.

Tito

I play the guitar and I can find lots of songs on the Internet. Last week I got the words and music for "Can't Buy Me Love," you know, by the Beatles. I can play it now. I use the Internet on weekends because it's cheap then.

Liam

Well, my family's name is Connelly and I want to write about my family, so every day I chat with people from all over the world, Canada, South Africa, Australia—people who have the name Connelly. They send me information about their families. It's really interesting.

Tommy

I play games. And I go to chat rooms. And I visit web sites for my favorite groups and basketball players. I want to be on the web all the time, but my mom says I can't. She says I can only use it after school for an hour, and then I stop.

April

I go shopping on the Internet. Every Friday I go to my son's house and I use his computer. It's fantastic—the supermarket brings all my food to my home!

Getting information

8 This is an information-gap activity to review and extend the verb-noun collocations from the *Reading and listening* section. The exercise is a fill-in-the-blank conversation to practice the collocations.

Divide the class into pairs and make sure students know if they are Student A or Student B. Students A should look at page 112, and Students B should look at page 114. Pre-teach/check *show* (verb). Focus attention on the example and then get students to complete the conversation, working in pairs. Check the answers with the whole class.

Get students to practice the conversation in closed pairs.

EVERYDAY ENGLISH (SB p. 82)

What's the problem?

1 Focus attention on the problems and check that students understand them. Pre-teach/check the following words from the conversations as you elicit from the class which problem goes with which picture: *airport, push a button, borrow, What's the matter, maybe, it doesn't matter, flowers.*

2 Focus attention on the example in conversation 1 (*I can't find my passport.*). Students complete the other conversations, working individually. Get students to check their answers in pairs.

T 11.10 Play the recording and get students to check their answers.

5. **A** Oh, no!
   B What's the matter?
   A **The TV's broken.**
   B Good! Maybe we can talk this evening.
   A But I want to watch a movie.
   B Then go to the movie theater.
6. **A** I'm really sorry. **I forgot your birthday.**
   B It doesn't matter.
   A It was on the tenth, wasn't it?
   B Yes, it was.
   A Well, here are some flowers.
   B Oh, thank you. They're beautiful.

3 Get students to practice the conversations in closed pairs. Monitor and check for pronunciation. If students have problems, drill key sections from the recording and get students to repeat the pair work.

Have students choose two conversations to learn and act out for the rest of the class. Encourage them to stand up and role-play the situation, rather than just say the conversations face-to-face. This helps students with the acting out and with the overall delivery. Encourage the other students to listen carefully to the students who are acting and give feedback on pronunciation.

SUGGESTION

If class time is short, you could get students to learn their lines for homework and then give them a short time to rehearse in pairs. With a weaker group, you could put simple cues on the board to help if students forget their lines.

ADDITIONAL MATERIAL

Workbook Unit 11

Exercise 11   provides further practice talking about and solving problems.

Don't forget!

Workbook Unit 11

Exercise 9   In this exercise, students translate sentences containing the main grammar points presented in the unit.

Exercise 10   is an elimination exercise to review word groups from previous units.

Word List   Ask the students to turn to SB p. 135 and go through the words with them. Ask them to learn the words for homework, and test them on a few in the following class.

12

want and *would like*

Food and drink

In a restaurant • Going shopping

Thank you!

Introduction to the unit

The title of this unit is "Thank you!" and it focuses on the function of asking for things in a variety of contexts. The structures *want* and *would like* are practiced and the difference in register is highlighted. *Like* is also reviewed and contrasted with *would like*. The vocabulary of stores and amenities is reviewed and extended, and there is a *Vocabulary and speaking* section on food and drink, and ordering in a restaurant. The *Reading* section also focuses on food with a text on junk food. There is functional practice in the *Everyday English* section of the language used when going shopping.

Language aims

Grammar—*want* and *would like* Students have already met *want* as part of their practice of the Present Simple. In this unit, *want* + noun and *want* + *to*-infinitive are reviewed and practiced. *Would like* + noun and *would like* + *to*-infinitive are also introduced as more polite ways of asking for things, or saying that you want to do something. The question form *Would you like ...?* is also introduced for offering things.

POSSIBLE PROBLEMS

Students have already seen *like* as a main verb in the presentation of the Present Simple in Unit 5. This is the first time students have seen *would like* and it is easy for students to confuse the two.

Common mistakes:

* *Do you like a cup of coffee?*
* *I like to buy a dictionary.*
* *You like a tea?*

Students can usually understand the difference between liking in general (expressed with *like*) and a specific request (expressed with *would like*), but the similarity in form can lead to confusion. Students are given both receptive and productive practice of both forms, but be prepared to monitor and check for mistakes and to review as necessary. (There is no need to highlight that *would* is a modal verb at this stage. Students will meet *would* and its various uses in later levels of *American Headway*.)

Vocabulary Stores and amenities are reviewed and extended. The vocabulary of food and drink is practiced in the context of ordering in a restaurant. The food and drink theme is continued in the *Reading* section with a text on an elderly woman who only eats junk food!

Everyday English This highlights and practices the language used when shopping in a variety of situations.

Workbook *Would like* is practiced in a number of exercises.

There is a pronunciation exercise to practice discrimination in vowel sounds.

The vocabulary of food and drink, and the function of ordering in a restaurant are consolidated in a range of exercises.

Further reading practice is given with a series of short texts on eating habits.

The language of shopping from the *Everyday English* section is practiced.

Notes on the unit

STARTER (SB p. 84)

This *Starter* section reviews and extends the vocabulary of stores and amenities, and also reviews *can*.

1 Focus attention on the example and then get students to continue matching in pairs.

2 Get students to make sentences with the phrases in Exercise 1 using *You can ....*

   T 12.1 Play the recording and get students to check their answers. Explain any individual words that students query. (If you think students need more practice with the pronunciation of *can*, you could have them listen and repeat the sentences.)

> ### Answers and tapescript
> You can buy stamps in a post office.
> You can buy a dictionary in a bookstore.
> You can buy a computer magazine at a newsstand.
> You can change money in a bank.
> You can buy a CD in a music store.
> You can get a cup of coffee in a cafe.
> You can send an e-mail in an Internet cafe.

A TRIP INTO TOWN (SB p. 84)

want and *would like*

1 Focus attention on the "to do" list and check comprehension of the items. (If students ask, you can explain that a "to do" list is a list of shopping and/or other errands that people write for themselves in order to remember what they want to do on a particular day.) Highlight the use of *want* + noun and *want* + to-infinitive in the examples and drill the sentences. Check pronunciation of *wants* /wɑnts/. Check the pronunciation of the other items in the list. Students make sentences with the other items in the list, working in pairs. Monitor and check for correct use of third person *-s* on *wants*.

   Check the answers with the whole class by asking students to read the sentences aloud.

> ### Answers
> He wants Gary Alright's new CD.
> He wants to send an e-mail to Rosa in England.
> He wants a Spanish/English dictionary.
> He wants a *PC Worldwide* computer magazine.

2 This exercise introduces *would like* in different situations. Pre-teach/check *change* (noun) in conversation 1. Make sure students understand that this is a noun form and contrast it with the verb form in *change my money*. Also

pre-teach/check *black coffee* and *milk and sugar* in conversation 2, and *minidictionary* in conversation 3. Highlight the use of *I'd like* and *Would you like ...?* in the example answers in conversations 1 and 2, but do not go into a full grammatical explanation, as this is covered in the *Grammar Spot*.

   T 12.2 Ask students to read and listen to Enrique and complete the conversations. Play the recording through once. With a weaker group, you may need to play it again. Check the answers with the whole class. (If students query the use of *one* in conversation 3, check they understand it stands for *dictionary*, but do not go into a full explanation of the use of *one/ones* at this stage.)

> ### Answers and tapescript
> **E = Enrique**
> 1. **E** Good morning. **I'd like** a stamp for this letter to Venezuela, please.
>   **A** That's 80¢.
>   **E** Here you are.
>   **A** Here's your stamp, and 20¢ change.
>   **E** Thanks a lot. Bye.
> 2. **E** **I'd like** a cup of coffee, please.
>   **B** **Would you like** milk and sugar?
>   **E** No. Black, please.
>   **B** All right. Here you are. A dollar fifty, please.
> 3. **E** Hi. **I'd like** to buy a Spanish/English dictionary.
>   **C** OK. **Would you like** a big dictionary or a minidictionary?
>   **E** Just a minidictionary, please.
>   **C** This one is $6.50
>   **E** That's good. Thank you very much.

3 **T 12.3** Focus attention on the examples in the speech bubbles. Play the recording, pausing at the end of each sentence, and get students to repeat chorally and individually. Encourage them to reproduce *I'd like* correctly and make sure students don't say *I like*. Also encourage accurate intonation:

Would you like milk and sugar?

Would you like a big dictionary or a minidictionary?

Have students practice the conversations in Exercise 2 in closed pairs. If they have problems with pronunciation, drill key sections of the conversations and get them to practice again in closed pairs.

1 Read the notes as a class. Make sure students understand the difference in register between *want* and *would like*, and that *'d like* is the contracted form. Focus attention on the examples and highlight the use of the noun and *to*-infinitive with *would like*.

2 Read the notes as a class. Make sure students understand that *Would you like* is used when we offer things. Focus attention on the examples and highlight the use of the noun and *to*-infinitive in questions with *would like*.

Read Grammar Reference 12.1 on p. 129 together in class, and/or ask students to read it at home. Encourage them to ask you questions about it.

4 **T 12.4** This exercise gives more practice of *would like* in different situations. Explain that students are going to hear Enrique from Exercise 2 in different places in town. Check comprehension of the places in the list by asking *What can you do/buy at a (newsstand)?* Play the first conversation and elicit the correct place from the list *(a music store)*. Get students to write number *1* in the correct box. Play the rest of the recording and get students to number the other boxes.

Ask students to check their answers in pairs. If there is disagreement, play the recording again and get students to check/amend their answers. Check the answers with the whole class.

Answers and tapescript
3. a newsstand
2. an Internet cafe
1. a music store
5. a bank
4. a movie theater

T 12.4
1. **A** Hi. Can I help you?
   E Yes. I'd like the new CD by Gary Alright, please.
   A There you are.
   E How much is that?
   A $17.99.
   E Thank you very much.
2. **E** I'd like to send an e-mail, please.
   B Take computer number ten.
   E Thanks a lot.
3. **E** Hi. I'd like this month's *PC Worldwide* magazine, please.
   C Here you are. That's $4.25, please.
   E Thank you. Bye.
4. **E** Two tickets for James Bond, please.
   D That's $19.50, please.
   E Thanks. What time does the movie start?
   D Seven thirty.
   E Thanks very much.

5. **F** Good afternoon. Can I help you?
   E Yes, please. I'd like to change some traveler's checks, please.
   F Certainly. Are they in American dollars?
   E Yes, they are.
   F OK. That's $150.
   E Thank you very much.

SUGGESTION

If appropriate, you could ask students what were the key words that gave them the correct answer, e.g.:
Conversation 1   *CD*
Conversation 2   *send an e-mail*
Conversation 3   *this month's* PC Worldwide *magazine*
Conversation 4   *James Bond, movie*
Conversation 5   *traveler's checks, American dollars*

Refer students to the tapescript on p. 122. Get students to practice conversation 1 in open pairs. Students continue practicing in closed pairs. If students have problems with pronunciation, drill key sections of the conversations and get students to practice again in closed pairs.

What would you like?

1 This exercise practices question forms with *would like*. Focus attention on the picture and get students to imagine they are at home with a friend. Check comprehension of *feel at home*. Focus attention on the examples in the speech bubbles. Remind students of the use of *would like* + noun and *would like* + *to*-infinitive. Drill the examples chorally and individually. Encourage students to reproduce correct intonation—rising intonation on the Yes/No questions and falling on the *Wh-* question, and a wide voice range on the answers, starting "high."

Check comprehension of the food, drink, and activities on offer. (If students query the use of *some* in *some cake*, explain that we use it when we don't know exactly how much of something is being referred to. Do not go into a full explanation of *some* versus *any* at this stage.) Elicit two or three different exchanges from the students in open pairs. Then get them to continue in closed pairs. Monitor and check for correct use of *would you like* + noun and *to*-infinitive, and pronunciation.

It's my birthday!

2 Tell students they are going to hear three people talking about their birthday. Focus attention on the chart and elicit possible answers to the two questions, e.g.:

What would she/he like? a book, a CD, a picture, a sweater, a camera, etc.

What would she/he like to do in the evening? go to the theater, have a party, go to a restaurant, go shopping, etc.

T 12.5 Play the recording of Suzanne and elicit the answers *(breakfast in bed, to go to the theater)*. Play the rest of the recording and get students to complete the chart.

Get students to check their answers in pairs before checking them with the whole class.

Answers and tapescript

	What would she/he like?	What would she/he like to do in the evening?
Suzanne	breakfast in bed	to go to the theater
Tom	a new computer	to go to a good restaurant
Alice	a cell phone	to go out with her friends

T 12.5

Suzanne

What would I like for my birthday? That's easy. I'd like to have breakfast in bed. With the newspapers. And in the evening, I'd like to go to the theater.

Tom

Well, I'd like a new computer because my computer is so old that the new programs don't work on it. And then in the evening, I'd like to go to a nice restaurant. I don't care if it's Italian, Japanese, Chinese, or Indian—just good food.

Alice

I don't have a cell phone, but all my friends have one, so what I'd really like is my own cell phone. They aren't expensive these days. And in the evening, I'd like to go out with all my friends and have a great time!

---

3   Ask students to imagine it's their birthday soon. Focus attention on the examples in the speech bubbles. Drill the language and check that students say *I'd like* rather than *I like*. Get students to give one or two more examples, working in open pairs. Students continue in closed pairs. Monitor and check for correct use of *would like* + noun and *would like* + *to*-infinitive.

Talking about you

4   Focus attention on the examples in the speech bubbles. Review the difference between *like* and *would like* by asking *General or specific?* about each sentence (*like* = general meaning; *would like* = a specific wish). Also highlight the use of *like* + *-ing* and *would like* + *to*-infinitive. Drill the examples in the speech bubbles. Elicit open question-and-answer exchanges to the questions about traveling and living in another country. Then get students to continue working in closed pairs, asking and answering all the questions in the list. Monitor and check for correct use of *like* + *-ing* and *would like* + *to*-infinitive. Provide feedback on any common errors which might interfere with comprehension, e.g.:

* I like to learning French.

GRAMMAR SPOT (SB p. 87)

1   Read the notes as a class. Make sure students understand that *like* is used to talk about something that is always true. Focus attention on the example sentences and elicit other examples from the class.

2   Read the notes as a class. Make sure students understand that *'d like* is used to talk about something we wish to have or do now or in the future. Focus attention on the example sentences and elicit other examples from the class.

Read Grammar Reference 12.2 on p. 129 together in class and/or ask students to read it at home. Encourage them to ask you questions about it.

Listening and pronunciation

5   **T 12.6** This is a discrimination exercise to help students distinguish *like* and *would like*. Play the first sentence as an example and elicit the sentence that is recorded *(Would you like a soda?)*. Play the rest of the recording and get students to choose the correct sentence. Get them to check their answers in pairs. If there is disagreement on the answers, play the recording again and check the answers with the class.

Answers and tapescript

1. Would you like a soda?
2. I like orange juice.
3. We'd like to go for a walk.
4. What do you like doing on the weekend?
5. We like our new car.

If students need more practice in pronunciation of *like* and *would like*, drill the sentences chorally and individually. Then get students to repeat the task sitting back-to-back—Student A should say a sentence and Student B should say if it is sentence 1 or 2.

Check it

6   Focus attention on the first pair of sentences as an example. Students continue working individually to choose the correct sentence.

Get students to check their answers in pairs before checking them with the whole class.

Answers

1. I'd like to go home now, please.
2. What would you like to do?
3. I like swimming.
4. Would you like a cup of coffee?
5. Do you like listening to music?

Workbook Unit 12

Exercises 1–3 provide further practice of *would like* in a range of exercises.

VOCABULARY AND SPEAKING (SB p. 88)

In a restaurant

This section reviews and extends the lexical set of food and drink, and recycles *would like* and *can* in the context of ordering in a restaurant.

1 Focus attention on the words and photos. Elicit the answer for number 1 *(cheese)*. Students continue matching, working in pairs. Check the answers with the whole class.

T 12.7 Play the recording and get students to repeat chorally and individually. Check students can reproduce the word stress on the following words:

• •
mineral water

•
vegetables

•
tomato

Answers and tapescript
1. cheese
2. fish
3. fruit
4. salad
5. vegetables
6. chicken
7. soup
8. tomato
9. fries
10. mineral water

2 Pre-teach/check the main headings in the menu—*Joe's Diner, To start, Burgers, Meat, Side orders,* and *Desserts*. There are two ways to approach the rest of this exercise—you can either put the students into groups and get them to complete as much of the menu as they can. Alternatively, you can pre-teach the words in the list and then let students complete the menu. Whichever way you choose, check the pronunciation of the food and drink items when students give the answers.

Answers

To start	chicken soup, **tomato juice**
Burgers	hamburger, salad, and fries; **cheeseburger**, salad, and fries
Sandwiches	tuna, chicken, **cheese**
Meat	steak and salad, **roast chicken** and salad

Side orders	fries, **salad**
Desserts	ice cream, chocolate cake, **apple pie**
To drink	soda, orange juice, **coffee**, **mineral water**

3 **T 12.8** Tell students they are going to hear Andrea and Paul ordering a meal. Check that they understand that *Andrea* is a woman's name and *Paul* a man's name. Also check what the letters *W, A,* and *P* stand for. Give students time to read through the sentences. Check comprehension of *How would you like it cooked?* Focus attention on the example and play the first line of the recording. Play the rest of the recording and get students to complete the task.

Ask students to check their answers in pairs. If there is disagreement on the answers, play the recording again and get students to check/amend their answers. Check the answers with the whole class.

Answers and tapescript
P Andrea, what would you like to start?
A Can I have the tomato juice, please?
P And I'd like the chicken soup.
P Can I have the steak, please?
W How would you like it cooked?
W What would you like to drink?
A We'd like a bottle of mineral water, too.
A Delicious, thank you.

T 12.8
W = Waiter   P = Paul   A = Andrea
W Are you ready to order?
P Yes, we are. Andrea, what would you like to start?
A Can I have the tomato juice, please?
P And I'd like the chicken soup.
W And for your main course?
A I would like the uh, ... roast chicken, please.
W OK. And for you?
P Can I have the steak, please?
W Uh-huh ... How would you like it cooked?
P Medium.
W What would you like to drink?
P Can I have a cup of coffee, please?
W Certainly.
A We'd like a bottle of mineral water, too.
W Thank you very much.
    (Pause)
W Is everything OK?
A Delicious, thank you.

4 Refer students to the tapescript on p. 122. Check comprehension of *ready to order, main course,* and *medium* (for a steak). Divide the class into groups of three. Get students to practice the conversation in groups. If students have problems with pronunciation,

drill key sections of the conversation and get them to practice again.

5 Give students time to prepare their roles and what they want to order. Encourage them to rehearse the conversation a few times. Once they are more confident with the language, encourage them not to refer to the text in the Student Book, but to work from memory. (With a weaker group, you could write simple sentence cues on the board to help with the role play.) Monitor and help as necessary. Get students to act out their conversations for the rest of the class.

> **SUGGESTION**
> If you have access to other real menus from American restaurants (or other English-language menus), bring copies of them to class and get students to role-play other conversations, using the different menus. You will need to be careful that the menus you select contain language that is appropriate for the post-beginner level.

ADDITIONAL MATERIAL

Workbook Unit 12

Exercises 4–7 These are a variety of exercises to practice the vocabulary of food and drink, and the language of ordering in a restaurant.

READING (SB p. 90)

She only eats junk food

1 Focus attention on the title of the text and check comprehension of *junk food*. Elicit an example of food from the list that is good for you, e.g., *fruit*. Students decide what other food they think is good for you and then compare answers in pairs. Check students' ideas with the whole class.

2 Tell the students your favorite food and then elicit examples from the class. Be prepared to supply relevant vocabulary if students request it.

3 Pre-teach/check *oldest* (as a lexical item only—don't do a full presentation of superlatives at this stage), *generations*, *popcorn, die, granddaughter, grandmother,* and *hairdresser.* Ask students to read the article. Elicit their reactions to the text and what they find unusual about Mary Alston. Ask them *Who is the oldest person you know? What does he/she eat?*

4 This exercise focuses on the details in the text and also provides question and answer practice. Focus attention on the example and then get students to continue matching and completing the sentences, working individually.

T 12.9 Get students to check their answers in pairs and then play the recording so that they can check against it.

> **Answers and tapescript**
>
> 2. e   5. a   8. b
> 3. h   6. i   9. f
> 4. g   7. j   10. d

T 12.9
1. When was Mary Alston's birthday?
   It **was** yesterday.
2. **Did** she have a party?
   Yes, she did.
3. Does she eat fresh food?
   No, she **doesn't.**
4. What **does** she eat?
   Popcorn, pizza, and burgers.
5. What was her job?
   She was **a** teacher.
6. **Where** was she born?
   On a farm in Pennsylvania.
7. When did she marry?
   She married **in** 1915.
8. What time does she **get** up?
   She gets up at six o'clock.
9. Where does she go every Friday?
   She **goes** to the hairdresser.
10. What did she say to her granddaughter?
    "**I'd like** a cheeseburger and fries!"

Divide the class into pairs and get them to practice the questions and answers. If students have problems with the intonation, drill key questions and answers and get students to repeat in pairs.

> **SUGGESTION**
> The text contains a series of numbers and dates. You could list these on the board and get students to check what they refer to:
> 109   Mary Alston's age
> 6   number of generations at her party
> 85   her daughter's age
> 1915   the year she married James
> 1983   the year James died
> 65   her granddaughter's age
> 6   the time she gets up

ADDITIONAL MATERIAL

Workbook Unit 12

Exercise 10 provides further reading practice on food and eating habits.

Going shopping

1 **T 12.10** Focus attention on the photos. Use them to help you pre-teach/check *film* (for a camera), *meter, shirt, medium* (size), *try on, pair of jeans, size, potatoes, anything else?* Focus attention on the first conversation in the Student Book and on the example. Play the corresponding conversation on the recording and elicit the missing sentences (*Is there a drugstore near here?* and *next to the bank*). Play the rest of the recording, pausing at the end of each conversation, and get students to complete them using the words given.

If necessary, play the recording again to allow students to check/complete their answers. Check the answers with the whole class.

Answers and tapescript

1. **A** Excuse me! **Where can I buy film** for my camera?
   B In a drugstore.
   A **Is there a drugstore near here?**
   B Yes, 200 meters from here, **next to the bank**.
2. **C** Can I help you?
   A **No, thanks.** I'm just looking.
3. **A** Excuse me! **Do you have this shirt** in a medium?
   C No, I'm sorry. That's all we have.
4. **A** **I'd like to try on** a pair of jeans, please.
   C Sure. **What size are you?**
   A I think I'm a 26.
   C OK. The fitting rooms are over there.
5. **D** Yes, miss. **What would you like?**
   A I'd like a kilo of potatoes, please.
   D Anything else?
   A **No, that's all**, thanks. How much is that?
6. **A** Excuse me! **Do you sell Korean** newspapers?
   E **No, I'm sorry**, we don't.
   A Where **can I buy them?**
   E Try the hotel.

---

2 Pre-teach/check *birthday card, phone card, T-shirt, small/medium/large.* Put students into pairs and assign a role, A or B, to each student. Make sure that they understand they have to ask for the things in their list. Check where you can buy a birthday card and a phone card (*at a newsstand*). Choose a pair of students to demonstrate the conversation with Student A asking for a birthday card. Then choose another pair with Student B asking for a phone card. Get students to continue practicing the other conversations, working in closed pairs. Monitor and check for correct pronunciation and intonation. If students have problems, drill key sections of the conversations and get students to practice again in closed pairs.

Refer students to Grammar Reference 12.3 on p. 129.

SUGGESTION

You can give students more practice with the language used when shopping with the photocopiable activity on TB p. 105. Photocopy enough pages for students to work in pairs. Cut up the lines of conversation and keep each set of lines together in an envelope. Hand out a set of lines to each pair of students and explain that they have to put the lines in order to make three shopping conversations. Give students time to do this and then check the answers.

Answers

1. **A** Excuse me! Where can I buy stamps?
   B At a post office.
   A Is there a post office near here?
   B Yes, 200 meters from here, next to the Internet cafe.
2. **A** Excuse me! Do you sell *Le Monde*?
   B No, I'm sorry. We don't.
   A Where can I buy French newspapers?
   B Try the hotel.
3. **A** I'd like to try on this shirt, please.
   B Sure. What size are you?
   A Medium, I think.
   B OK. The fitting rooms are over there.

Elicit where the speakers are in each conversation (*1—in the street, 2—at a newsstand, 3—in a clothing store*). Then get students to practice the conversations in closed pairs.

ADDITIONAL MATERIAL

Workbook Unit 12

Exercise 11 provides further practice of the language used when shopping.

Don't forget!

Workbook Unit 12

Exercise 8 is a pronunciation exercise to practice distinguishing vowel sounds.

Exercise 9 In this exercise, students translate sentences containing the main grammar points presented in the unit.

Word List Ask the students to turn to SB p. 135 and go through the words with them. Ask them to learn the words for homework, and test them on a few in the following class.

EXTRA IDEAS UNITS 9–12

On TB p. 106 there are additional photocopiable activities to review the language from Units 9–12. There is a reading text with tasks, a question formation exercise, and a matching activity on everyday English. You will need to pre-teach/check *wonderful, surprise, nothing, mail carrier, envelope, suitcase,* and *keep a secret* for the reading text.

13

Colors and clothes • Present Continuous

Questions and negatives • What's the matter?

Here and now

Introduction to the unit

The title of this unit is "Here and now" and it introduces the Present Continuous in all forms. Students practice the tense in a variety of contexts and it is contrasted with the Present Simple. The vocabulary of clothes and colors is reviewed and extended, and this is a vehicle for additional practice of the Present Continuous. Students also practice describing people with a focus on clothes, and color of hair and eyes. There is a *Reading and speaking* section talking about what people usually do and what they are doing today. This consolidates the use of the two present tenses. The *Everyday English* section is called *What's the matter?* and it focuses on feelings such as *tired, hungry*, and suggestions with *Why don't you ...?*

Language aims

Grammar—Present Continuous   In *American Headway Starter,* students meet and practice the Present Simple relatively early in the book and it is consolidated throughout the text. This unit introduces the Present Continuous after students have had the opportunity for thorough practice of the Present Simple. The unit contrasts the use of the two tenses and gives students an opportunity to practice them in tandem. Despite presenting the Present Continuous later than the Present Simple, the two tenses can still cause confusion.

POSSIBLE PROBLEMS

Many other languages do not have the equivalent of the Present Continuous and they use a single present tense to express "action which is true for a long time" and "action happening now or around now." This can lead students to use the Present Simple in English when they want to refer to action in progress:

* *You wear a nice suit today.*

Students also confuse the form of the two tenses. They are already familiar with *am/is/are* as parts of the verb *to be*, but they tend to start using them as the auxiliary with Present Simple, and using *do/does* as the auxiliary with Present Continuous.

Common mistakes:

* *She's play tennis.*
* *I'm coming from Thailand.*
* *You're go to work by bus.*
* *What do you doing?*
* *Do they working today?*

The Present Continuous can also be used to refer to the future and this is covered in Unit 14.

Vocabulary   Clothes and colors are reviewed and extended, and students practice describing people's appearance.

Everyday English   This section is called *What's the matter?* and it focuses on feelings, e.g., *tired, hungry*, etc., and suggestions to make people feel better.

POSSIBLE PROBLEMS

English uses *to be* with *hungry, thirsty, tired, cold*, and *hot*, whereas other languages express the same idea with the equivalent of *have*, e.g., Spanish: *tengo sed;* French: *j'ai faim.* This can lead students to use *have* with the adjectives in English and make the following mistakes:

* *I have hunger.*
* *He has cold.*

Workbook Colors are reviewed and consolidated.

The Present Continuous is practiced in all forms in a variety of exercises.

The Present Simple and Present Continuous are reviewed in contrast.

Further reading practice is given with an exercise on a vacation postcard.

The vocabulary of clothes and the function of describing people are consolidated in a number of exercises.

The language of talking about feelings and making suggestions from the *Everyday English* section is further practiced.

Notes on the unit

STARTER (SB p. 92)

1 This *Starter* section reviews and extends the vocabulary of colors and clothes. Focus attention on the colors and get students to find the color black in the pictures as an example. Students continue finding the colors, working in pairs.

2 **T 13.1** Pre-teach/check *jacket, pants, shirt,* and *shoes.* Focus attention on the example and then get students to complete the sentences. Play the recording and get students to check their answers.

> **Answers and tapescript**
> 1. George's jacket is **black**. Sadie's jacket is **red**.
> 2. His pants are **gray**. Her pants are **green**.
> 3. Her shirt is **yellow**. His shirt is **white**.
> 4. Her shoes are **blue**. His shoes are **brown**.

Play the recording again and get students to repeat the sentences. Students then practice the sentences in pairs. Monitor and check for correct pronunciation of the colors and clothes.

3 Demonstrate the activity by talking about the colors of your clothes. Use the model in Exercise 2, e.g., *My shirt is blue,* etc., and do not use *I'm wearing* at this stage. Elicit examples from one or two students and then get them to continue in closed pairs. Monitor and check for correct pronunciation of the colors and clothes.

WORK AND VACATIONS (SB p. 93)

Present Continuous

This section reviews the Present Simple and introduces the affirmative forms of the Present Continuous. Exercise 1 highlights the use of Present Simple for facts and repeated actions.

1 Refer students back to the picture of George in the *Starter* section. Tell students they are going to read about

his job. Pre-teach/check *wear* and *enjoy* and then focus attention on the example. Ask students to complete the rest of the text with the verbs.

Ask students to check their answers in pairs and then check them with the whole class by getting students to read the sentences aloud.

> **Answers**
> George **works** in a bank. He **starts** work at 9:00 and he **leaves** work at 5:00. He always **wears** a black jacket and gray pants. He **has** lunch at 1:00. He sometimes **goes** to the park and **reads** his newspaper. He **enjoys** his job.

2 **T 13.2** This exercise introduces the Present Continuous for actions happening now and around now. Focus attention on the picture of George and his wife. Establish that they are on vacation. Play the recording and get students to read the text. If students query the verb forms, tell them they are in the Present Continuous, but do not go into a full explanation at this stage.

3 **T 13.3** Play the recording and get students to repeat chorally and individually. Encourage students to reproduce the contracted forms and the linking between *-ing* and a vowel:

He's wearing a T-shirt.

Check students understand that *'s* is the contracted form of *is,* and *'re* the contracted form of *are.*

4 Briefly review the use of *is* and *are* by getting students to say which verb can go with which subject (*is—George, His wife; are—We, Four people, Two people,* and *They*). Demonstrate the activity by eliciting the answer for George (*George is reading the menu.*). Students continue making sentences, working individually.

Get students to check their answers in pairs before checking them with the whole class.

> **Answers**
> George is reading the menu.
> His wife is wearing a blue T-shirt.
> Four people are swimming.
> Two people are playing tennis.
> They are having lunch.
> We are enjoying our vacation.

GRAMMAR SPOT (SB p. 93)

1 Focus attention on the examples and read the notes with the whole class. Ask students to underline the Present Continuous forms in the text in Exercise 2. Highlight the full and short forms, e.g., *He's wearing ...,* *His wife is reading ....*

2 Read the notes with the whole class. Remind students of the *-ing* form by giving students the infinitive and

eliciting the -ing form, e.g., go—going, eat—eating, swim—swimming, etc.

3   Focus attention on the sentences. Review the first one with the whole class as an example (am studying). Then ask students to complete the other sentences.

> **Answers**
> You **are wearing** jeans.
> She **is reading** a book.
> We **are working** in class.
> They **are having** lunch.

Highlight that the Present Continuous can be used for actions happening now, e.g., *You're wearing jeans*, and around now, e.g., *I am studying English*.

Read Grammar Reference 13.1 on p. 130 together in class, and/or ask students to read it at home. Encourage them to ask you questions about it.

PRACTICE (SB p. 93)

Speaking

1   This exercise gives practice in the *he*, *she*, and *they* forms of Present Continuous affirmative. Focus attention on the pictures and briefly review the verbs students will need to use (*cook, drive, take a shower, write, ski, eat ice cream, run, dance,* and *play soccer*). With a weaker group, you could write the verbs on the board.

Focus attention on the example and highlight the use of the contracted form. Elicit one or two more examples and then get students to continue making sentences, working in pairs. Monitor and check for correct formation of the Present Continuous.

T 13.4   Play the recording and get students to check their answers. If students had problems doing the task, play the recording again and get students to repeat.

> **Answers and tapescript**
> 1. He's cooking.
> 2. He's driving.
> 3. He's taking a shower.
> 4. She's writing.
> 5. She's skiing.
> 6. She's eating ice cream.
> 7. They're running.
> 8. They're dancing.
> 9. They're playing soccer.

2   Demonstrate the meaning of *mime*. Focus attention on the examples in the speech bubbles and drill the language. Choose an activity that you can mime for the students and get them to guess what you are doing. Encourage them to give sentences in the Present

Continuous rather than just call out the infinitive verb forms. Put students into pairs and get them to continue miming and guessing. Get them to change roles after each mime. Monitor and check for correct formation of the Present Continuous.

> **SUGGESTION**
> You can provide further practice of Present Continuous affirmative forms by getting students to think about what their family and friends are doing. Write the following questions on the board:
> *   *What are you doing now?*
> *   *What are your parents/friends/brothers and sisters/children doing now?*
> Demonstrate the activity by giving your own answers, e.g.:
> *I'm teaching English. I'm working in room ... with Class .... My mother's working at home.*
> Elicit some more examples from one or two students, e.g.:
> *I'm studying English. I'm sitting in room ... next to ... My parents are having dinner.*
> Divide the class into pairs and get students to continue exchanging examples. Monitor and check for correct formation of the Present Continuous. Provide feedback on any common errors with the tense, and if necessary, drill the corrected forms.

ADDITIONAL MATERIAL

Workbook Unit 13
Exercise 1   is a review of colors.
Exercise 2   is an exercise to consolidate the formation of the -ing form.
Exercise 3   is an exercise to consolidate the affirmative form of the Present Continuous.

I'M WORKING (SB p. 94)

Questions and negatives

1   **T 13.5**   This section introduces Present Continuous question forms (*Wh-* and *Yes/No* questions) and negatives. Pre-teach/check *model, fashion show, listener, special,* and *talk* (verb). Focus attention on the photo and ask *What's her name? (Sadie)* and *What's her job? (She's a model.)*. Play the recording and get students to read and listen to the interview. Check that students understand what *it* in *I'm enjoying it very much* refers to (being in New York). Ask students to underline the Present Continuous questions in the interview.

2   This is a transformation exercise to practice Present Continuous questions with *she*. Write the question and answer *What are you doing in New York?* and *I'm working.* on the board, underlining the subject and auxiliary. Elicit the changes needed to make the question and answer about Sadie: *What is she doing in New York? She's working.*

Drill the language in the speech bubbles chorally and individually. Get students to continue asking and answering about Sadie, working in closed pairs. (With a weaker group, you could elicit and drill the questions and answers first, and then get students to work in closed pairs.) Monitor and check for correct formation of Present Continuous third person singular questions and answers.

Check the answers with the whole class.

> **Answers**
> 1. What's she doing in New York?
>   She's working.
> 2. Where is she staying?
>   She's staying with friends.
> 3. Is she having a good time?
>   Yes, she is.
> 4. What is she wearing?
>   She's wearing jeans and a T-shirt.

GRAMMAR SPOT (SB p. 94)

1 Focus attention on the questions and read them with the whole class. Highlight the full and short forms used.

2 Focus attention on the negatives and read them with the whole class. Point out that short forms are usually used in the negative. Ask students to underline the negative form in the interview in Exercise 1.

3 Focus attention on the short answers and read the notes with the whole class. Highlight the full and short forms used. Ask students to underline the short answers in the interview in Exercise 1.

Read Grammar Reference 13.2 and 13.3 on p. 130 together in class, and/or ask students to read it at home. Encourage them to ask you questions about it.

ADDITIONAL MATERIAL

Workbook Unit 13
Exercise 4 is an exercise to consolidate the affirmative and negative forms of the Present Continuous.

PRACTICE (SB p. 95)

Asking questions

1 This exercise reviews *Wh-* question words and practices Present Continuous question formation. Focus attention on the cartoons and check comprehension of all the verbs and answers given. Focus attention on the example and then elicit the question words and nouns that the students need to use:
   2. *what?*
   3. *where?*

4. *why/three sweaters?*
5. *what?*
6. *how many?*
7. *who?*

T 13.6 Get students to write the questions using the verbs in the bubbles, working individually. Play the recording and get students to check their answers.

> **Answers and tapescript**
> 1. **A** **What are you reading?**
>   **B** A love story.
> 2. **A** **What are you watching?**
>   **B** The news.
> 3. **A** **Where are you going?**
>   **B** To my bedroom.
> 4. **A** **Why are you wearing three sweaters?**
>   **B** Because I'm cold.
> 5. **A** **What are you eating?**
>   **B** Chocolate.
> 6. **A** **How many cakes are you making?**
>   **B** Five.
> 7. **A** **Who are you talking to?**
>   **B** My girlfriend.

If you feel students need more question and answer practice, play the recording again and get students to repeat. Encourage them to reproduce the falling intonation of the *Wh-* questions. Students then practice the questions and answers in closed pairs.

2 This exercise practices Yes/No question formation in the Present Continuous. Focus attention on the cues and the example questions and short answers. Point out that the question form is an inversion of the statement form. Get students to write the question forms for the exercise, working individually.

Check the answers with the whole class.

> **Answers**
> 1. Are you wearing a new sweater?
> 2. Are we studying Chinese?
> 3. Are we sitting in our classroom?
> 4. Are you wearing new shoes?
> 5. Is the teacher wearing blue pants?
> 6. Is it raining?
> 7. Are all the students speaking English?
> 8. Are you learning a lot of English?

Model and drill the examples in the speech bubbles. Encourage students to reproduce the rising intonation of the Yes/No questions. Tell students that they have to stand up and ask the questions in a mingle activity and that they should give true short answers. Get students to do the activity and monitor and check for correct question formation, intonation, and short answers.

Check it

3 Focus attention on the first pair of sentences as an example. Students continue working individually to choose the correct sentence.

Get students to check their answers in pairs before checking them with the whole class.

> **Answers**
> 1. I'm wearing a blue shirt today.
> 2. Where are you going?
> 3. Peter isn't working this week.
> 4. That's Peter over there. He's talking to the teacher.
> 5. Michiko is Japanese. She comes from Osaka.

ADDITIONAL MATERIAL

Workbook Unit 13
Exercise 5 is an exercise to consolidate questions and short answers in the Present Continuous.

READING AND SPEAKING (SB p. 96)

Today's different

> **NOTES**
> This is the first "jigsaw" reading in the book. It is a technique that integrates reading and speaking skills. Students read one of four texts; they then work in groups and exchange information about their text in a speaking activity. It's important to remind students to read only their text and to get information about the others via speaking.
> In the lesson before the *A photo of me* stage, ask students to bring in a photograph of themselves to talk about in class. Tell them that the photo needs to be an "action shot" and show:
> - where you are
> - who you're with
> - what you're doing
> - what you're wearing
>
> Get students to look up any useful words they need to talk about the picture. Also bring in a photo of yourself so that you can demonstrate the activity.

This section provides skills practice in reading and speaking, and also highlights the difference between the Present Simple and Present Continuous. Students also review the Past Simple in each reading text and in the questions.

1 Exercise 1 is a warm-up activity for the reading stage. It reviews the use of Present Simple for routines. Pre-teach/check *New Year's*. Give brief examples of what you do on each of the days and then elicit two or three more examples from the class. Students then continue asking and answering in closed pairs. Go around and help.

Monitor and check but do not focus too heavily on errors as the point of this activity is to raise interest in the topic rather than to test accuracy.

2 Pre-teach/check the following new words from the texts: *meet (friends)*, *get married*, *church*, *stand* (verb), *adult* (noun), *have a barbecue*, *bathing suit*, *pack your bags*, and *ski clothes*. Also review the irregular past forms in the texts:

get up	*got up*
get (receive)	*got*
go	*went*
find	*found*

Assign a role and a text to each student and remind them to read only their text:

Student A	Isabel
Student B	Leo
Student C	Mark
Student D	Alissa

Get students to read their text quickly and match the text to the correct photo. Briefly check the answers.

> **Answers**
>
> | Isabel | photo 3 |
> |---|---|
> | Leo | photo 4 |
> | Mark | photo 1 |
> | Alissa | photo 2 |

3 Focus attention on the questions. Pre-teach/check *What happened ...?* in question 4. Get students to work individually and answer the questions about their text. Ask them to write down the answers to their questions. (With a weaker group, you could put all the A, B, C, and D students in separate groups so that they help each other answer the questions.) Go around and help as necessary.

> **SUGGESTION**
> You might want to supply the language students can use for the information exchange, e.g.:
> *Do you want to start?*
> *You next.*
> *Sorry, I don't understand.*
> *Can you repeat that, please?*

4 Divide the class into groups of four. Make sure there is an A, B, C, and D student in each group. Demonstrate the activity by getting a couple of students from one group to talk about their text. Students continue exchanging the information about their text. Monitor and check for correct use of the Present Simple, Present Continuous, and Past Simple. Conduct a short follow-up phase by asking general questions, e.g.:

Who has a similar routine to you?

Who is having the most interesting day?

Who would you most like to be?

Finally, provide feedback on any common errors from the information exchange and review the use of the tenses as necessary.

A photo of me

Demonstrate the activity by talking about a photo of yourself. Then elicit one or two more examples from students in the class. Get students to continue working in pairs and talking about their photo. Monitor and check for correct use of *be* and of the Present Continuous.

ADDITIONAL MATERIAL

Workbook Unit 13
Exercises 6 and 7 These exercises consolidate the Present Simple and Present Continuous.
Exercise 9 provides further reading practice and consolidation of the Present Simple and Present Continuous.

VOCABULARY AND SPEAKING (SB p. 98)

Clothes

This section reviews and extends the vocabulary of clothes, introduces language for describing color of hair and eyes, and recycles the Present Continuous in the context of describing people.

1 Focus attention on the pictures of the models and on the example. Students continue labeling the clothes, working individually. Check the answers with the whole class.

Answers

2. a tie	9. socks	
3. pants	10. a coat	
4. shorts	11. sandals	
5. a shirt	12. shoes	
6. a dress	13. a jacket	
7. sneakers	14. a skirt	
8. a hat	15. boots	

T 13.7 Play the recording and get students to repeat chorally and individually. Check that students can distinguish *shirt* and *skirt*. Elicit which items are for women (*a skirt and a dress*). Highlight the use of *a* with the singular items, e.g., *a sweater*, and that the plural items do not need *a*, e.g., *boots*. Highlight that the word *pants* is plural in English, as this is different in other languages.

2 Briefly review the colors presented in the *Starter* section. Focus attention on the example in the speech bubble. Drill the language chorally and individually. Elicit one or two more examples from the class and then get students to continue in closed pairs. Monitor and check for correct use of clothes, colors, and the Present Continuous.

3 Focus attention on the example in the speech bubbles. Drill the language chorally and individually. Encourage

students to reproduce the rising intonation on the Yes/No questions. Demonstrate the activity by standing back-to-back with a student and asking about his/her clothes. Put students into pairs, asking students to work with a different partner from another part of the room. Monitor and check for correct use of Present Continuous questions and short answers, names of clothes, and colors.

4 This exercise consolidates names of clothes and colors, and also recycles the Present Simple for talking about routines. Get students to ask you the questions and give true answers. Divide the class into pairs and get them to continue asking and answering. Monitor and check for correct use of Present Simple, names of clothes, and colors.

5 **T 13.8** This exercise presents the language used for describing hair and eyes. Play the first line of the recording and elicit the word to complete sentence 1 (*blonde*). Play the rest of the recording and get students to complete the sentences. Check the answers with the whole class.

Answers and tapescript
1. She has long, **blonde** hair.
2. He has **short,** black hair.
3. She has blue **eyes.**
4. He has **brown** eyes.

6 Focus attention on the example in the speech bubble. Demonstrate the activity by describing yourself or a student and getting the others to guess who it is. Elicit one or two more examples from the class and then get students to continue in closed pairs or small groups. Monitor and check for correct use of the Present Continuous, names of clothes, and language of describing people.

SUGGESTION

You can also do a "describe and guess" activity based on pictures from magazines or students' own photographs. Student A describes a person in the picture or photo and Student B guesses who is it. Students then change roles.

Getting information

7 This is an information-gap activity to review the Present Continuous and the language of describing using different pictures. Tell students that they are going to work with a partner and ask questions to find six differences between two similar pictures of a family.

Divide the class into pairs and make sure students know if they are Student A or Student B. Students A should look at page 113, and Students B should look at page 115. Remind them that they shouldn't look at each other's picture. Focus attention on the examples in the speech bubbles and drill the type of questions students can ask:

What is (the father) wearing? Is (the mother) listening to music? etc.

Tell students to circle the part of their picture when they find a difference. Students work in pairs to find all six differences. Monitor and check.

Students compare their pictures to check they have found the differences.

ADDITIONAL MATERIAL

Workbook Unit 13

Exercises 10–12   These are a range of exercises to review clothes and the language of describing people.

EVERYDAY ENGLISH (SB p. 99)

What's the matter?

1   This section presents the language of talking about feelings and offering suggestions. Establish that the people in the cartoons all have problems, and pre-teach/ check the question *What's the matter?* Focus attention on the cartoons and elicit the answer for sentence 1 *(She's cold.)*. Students continue completing the sentences, working individually.

T 13.9   Play the recording through once and get students to check their answers.

Answers and tapescript
1. She's **cold.**
2. He's **hungry.**
3. They're **tired.**
4. He's **thirsty.**
5. They're **hot.**
6. She's **bored.**

Play the recording again and get students to repeat chorally and individually. Make sure they pronounce *tired* and *bored* as one syllable—/taɪrəd/, /bɔrd/ rather than */taɪrɛd/, */bɔrɛd/. Get students to work in pairs. Student A points to a cartoon and Student B says the corresponding sentence.

2   **T 13.10**   Focus attention on the conversation. Play the recording and get students to read and listen. Play the recording again and get students to repeat. Highlight the use of *Why don't you ...?* for making suggestions.

3   Check comprehension of the ideas in the lists. Elicit one or two more conversations from the class and then get students to continue in closed pairs, using the words from Exercise 1. Monitor and check for correct use of the adjectives and *Why don't you ...?*

SUGGESTION
Try to integrate language from the *Everyday English* sections in your lessons and encourage students to do the same. There is a wide range of language that can be used quite naturally in the classroom context to reinforce the communicative value of what the students are learning. This includes:
What's the matter? I'm ...
Why don't you ...?
All right.
Excuse me.
Sorry.
I don't know.
I don't understand.
Please./Thank you.
How do you spell ...?
Can I ...?

ADDITIONAL MATERIAL

Workbook Unit 13

Exercises 13 and 14   provide further practice of the language of feelings and suggestions from the *Everyday English* section.

Don't forget!

Workbook Unit 13

Exercise 8   In this exercise, students translate sentences containing the main grammar points presented in the unit.

Word List   Ask the students to turn to SB p. 136 and go through the words with them. Ask them to learn the words for homework, and test them on a few in the following class.

14

Present Continuous for future

Question word review

Transportation and travel • Sightseeing

It's time to go!

Introduction to the unit

The title of this unit is "It's time to go!" and the theme is travel, transportation, and sightseeing. The use of the Present Continuous for future plans is presented, building on students' knowledge of the form of this tense from Unit 13. *Wh-* question words are reviewed as part of the practice of asking about plans with the Present Continuous. Students also get listening and speaking practice with a section on vacation plans, using the Present Continuous for future. The vocabulary of transportation and travel is reviewed and extended, and there is a *Reading* section about a music-related tour of the United States. The travel theme is continued in the *Everyday English* section with a focus on sightseeing.

Language aims

Grammar—Present Continuous for future plans   Students will be familiar with the form of the Present Continuous, having practiced it for talking about actions happening now or around now in Unit 13. This unit presents and practices its other use—talking about future plans.

> **POSSIBLE PROBLEMS**
> The use of a present tense to refer to future plans may seem strange to students at first, but they soon become accustomed to it with practice. In the presentation and practice, ask a simple concept question—*Now or future?*—about the use of the tense to make sure students are clear about the time reference.

Question words   The questions words students have met in previous units are reviewed as part of the practice of the Present Continuous questions for future plans.

Vocabulary   The lexical set of travel and transportation is reviewed and extended. Students focus on forms of transportation and collocations, e.g., *make a reservation, catch a plane,* etc. The travel theme is continued in the *Reading* section with a text about a tour of musical cities in the United States.

Everyday English   This highlights and practices the language used when talking about places you have visited and also practices conversations in a tourist office.

Workbook   The Present Continuous used for future plans is consolidated in the affirmative and question forms. Students also focus on the time reference in different Present Continuous sentences, and get further practice in understanding plans.

There is a pronunciation exercise to practice shifting sentence stress.

The lexical set of travel and transportation is consolidated.

Further reading practice is given with another text on an eventful trip.

The language of going sightseeing from the *Everyday English* section is also practiced.

Notes on the unit

STARTER (SB p. 100)

1   This *Starter* section reviews the days, months, and years in English. It also establishes the concepts of *now* and *future* as preparation for talking about future plans in the next section. Focus attention on the questions and elicit the answers from the class. Make sure students use *thousand* correctly when

they say the year: *2003—two thousand three*. Also check for correct pronunciation and word stress in the months and days.

2 Get students to say the months around the class. If students have problems remembering the months, or pronouncing them, drill the words chorally and individually and then get students to repeat the task. Repeat the above procedure for the days of the week.

VACATION PLANS (SB p. 100)

Present Continuous for future

1 **T 14.1** Focus attention on the photo and ask *What's her name? (Elena.)*. Focus attention on her diary and explain that it shows her plans for next week. Pre-teach/check *pick up tickets, pack bags*, and *fly* from the diary. (Do not give a detailed explanation of the phrasal verb, *pick up*, at this stage, just explain its meaning to students.) Play the recording and get students to listen and read Elena's diary. Elicit why Elena is excited (*She's going on vacation to Mexico.*).

Tapescript
I'm going on vacation to Mexico next Friday, so next week's very busy. On Monday I'm picking up my tickets from the travel agent's. I'm going on vacation with my friends Grant and Nickie, so on Tuesday I'm meeting them after work and we're going shopping. On Wednesday I'm seeing the doctor at 11 o'clock, then I'm having lunch with mom. On Thursday I'm leaving work early and I'm packing. I'm taking just a bag and a backpack. Then it's Friday. Friday's the big day! At six thirty in the morning, I'm going by taxi to the airport. I'm meeting Grant and Nickie there and at nine thirty we're flying to Mexico City. I'm very excited!

2 This exercise presents the use of the Present Continuous for future plans, but treat it initially as a fill-in-the-blank exercise and leave the explanation of the tense use until you focus on the *Grammar Spot* section. Focus attention on sentence 1 as an example. Also elicit the answer to the second blank in sentence 3 *(having)* to alert students to the need for the *-ing* form in some sentences.

Get students to complete the sentences, working individually. Get them to check their answers in pairs before checking them with the whole class.

Answers
2. On Tuesday she's meeting Grant and Nickie after **work** and they're going **shopping**.
3. On Wednesday she's seeing the **doctor** at 11 o'clock, then she's **having** lunch with her mother.
4. On Thursday she's **leaving** work early and she's **packing** her bags.

5. On Friday at 6:30 in the morning she's going by **taxi** to the airport and she's **meeting** Grant and Nickie there. At 9:30 they're **flying** to Mexico.

GRAMMAR SPOT (SB p. 101)

1 Read the notes as a class. Focus attention on the examples and ask *Now or future?* about each one *(future)*. Establish that the form is the same as the tense students used in Unit 13 to talk about actions happening now, but that these sentences refer to future time.

2 Ask students to underline the examples of the Present Continuous in the sentences in *Grammar Spot* Exercise 1.

Read Grammar Reference 14.1 on p. 130 together in class, and/or ask students to read it at home. Encourage them to ask you questions about it.

ADDITIONAL MATERIAL

Workbook Unit 14
Exercises 1 and 2 are exercises to consolidate the form and concept of the Present Continuous for future.

Questions

3 **T 14.2** This section focuses on *Wh-* questions with the Present Continuous for future plans. Focus attention on the question and answer and refer students back to Elena's diary. Play the recording and get students to repeat chorally and individually. Encourage them to reproduce the falling intonation on the *Wh-* question. Focus attention on the speech bubbles and elicit the answer (*She's meeting Grant and Nickie. They're going shopping.*). Get students to practice the exchange in open pairs. Students then continue in closed pairs, asking and answering the questions about the other days of the week. Monitor and check for correct question formation and intonation.

Check the answers by getting students to ask and answer across the class.

Answers
What's she doing on Wednesday? She's seeing the doctor at 11 o'clock. Then she's having lunch with her mother.
What's she doing on Thursday? She's leaving work early and she's packing her bags.
What's she doing on Friday? She's going by taxi to the airport and she's meeting Grant and Nickie there. They're flying to Mexico at 9:30 A.M.

4 Write your own diary for the next four days on the board. Give true examples if the language generated is within the students' range. If it is not, modify the

examples so that they contain language students will recognize, e.g.:

Tuesday	6:30 P.M. *play tennis with Dave*
Wednesday	7:30 P.M. *meet Helen and Jim at Joe's Diner*
Thursday	*pick up theater tickets*
Friday	*go swimming*

Review *tomorrow* and *on* with days of the week. Elicit the question *What are you doing tomorrow?* from a student and reply with the information in your diary. Ask the question *What are you doing?* and highlight the shift in stress:

●   ●   ●

S: *What are you doing tomorrow?*

●   ●   ●

T: *What are you doing?*

Get students to ask you about the other three days and ask them the question in return, highlighting the stress each time.

Ask students to write notes about their plans for the next four days. Elicit two or three examples of the exchange in open pairs. Then ask students to continue in closed pairs, finding out about each other's plans for the rest of the week. Monitor and check for correct question formation, intonation, and change in stress.

5   This exercise consolidates question formation with the Present Continuous and reviews *Wh-* question words from previous units. Focus attention on the picture of Elena and on the first two lines of the conversation. Ask *Where is Elena?* (*She's at work.*) Ask *What's she doing?* (*She's reading about Mexico and talking to a friend.*)

Pre-teach/check *lucky*. Focus attention on the example and then get students to complete the conversation with the question words.

T 14.3 Get students to check their answers in pairs before playing the recording. Check the answers with the whole class.

> **Answers and tapescript**
> **A What** are you doing?
> **B** I'm reading about Mexico.
> **A Why?**
> **B** Because I'm going there on vacation soon.
> **A** Oh, how nice! **When** are you leaving?
> **B** We're leaving next Friday.
> **A Who** are you going with?
> **B** My friends Grant and Nickie.
> **A How** are you traveling?
> **B** We're traveling by plane to Mexico City, then by bus and train around the country.
> **A Where** are you staying?
> **B** We're staying in small hotels and hostels.
> **A** You're so lucky! Have a good time!
> **B** Thank you very much.

Get students to practice the conversation in closed pairs. If students have problems with pronunciation, drill key sections of the conversation and get students to practice again in closed pairs.

GRAMMAR SPOT (SB p. 101)

1   This exercise highlights the question form in all persons. Focus attention on the examples and then get students to form the question with *When* and *he, she, we,* and *they*. Check the answers by getting students to say the questions aloud. Check for the correct intonation (falling).

> **Answers**
> When is he leaving?
> When is she leaving?
> When are we leaving?
> When are they leaving?

Get students to underline the question forms in the conversation in Exercise 5.

2   This exercise highlights the present and future uses of the Present Continuous. Ask students to answer the questions in pairs and then check the answers with the whole class.

> **Answers**
> I'm reading about Mexico. (now)
> I'm leaving next Friday. (future)

Refer students to Grammar Reference 14.1 on p. 130.

ADDITIONAL MATERIAL

Workbook Unit 14

Exercise 3   is an exercise to practice *Wh-* questions with the Present Continuous for future.

PRACTICE (SB p. 102)

Listening and speaking

This section consolidates the Present Continuous for future with a listening task and information-gap activity on vacation plans. Students are also given the opportunity to personalize the language by talking about their own vacation plans.

Focus attention on the photos of the places and ask students to guess where they are. Tell students they are going to find out about the vacation plans of the people in the photos. Check the pronunciation of the names *Marco* /ˈmɑrkoʊ/, *Rachel* and *Laura*, /ˈreɪtʃl ən ˈlɔrə/, and *Omar* /ˈoʊmɑr/.

1   Exercise 1 consolidates the use of *Wh-* questions with the Present Continuous for future. Briefly review the question words by putting a list of very short answers about your

own vacations on the board and elicit the correct question word, e.g.:

Hawaii (where?)
In August (when?)
For three weeks (how long?)
In a hotel (where?)
By plane (how?)
Because I want to relax on the beach (why?)

Focus attention on the cues in the chart and the example questions. Highlight the use of the Present Continuous by asking *Now or future? (future)*. Then get students to write the other questions, using the cues in the chart.

T 14.4 Tell students they are going to listen to people talking about Marco's vacation plans and they have to check the questions and also complete the missing information. (With a weaker group, you could play the recording through once first and get students to check the questions, and then play it again for students to complete the missing information.) Play the recording and get students to complete the task. If necessary, play the recording again to allow students to complete their answers. Check the answers with the whole class, highlighting the use of ordinals in the date.

Answers and tapescript

A Marco's going on vacation.
B Oh, where's he going?
A To Banff, in Canada.
B Why is he going there?
A Because it's good for skiing and he wants to go skiing.
B When is he leaving?
A Next week—on March third.
B How is he traveling?
A By plane to Vancouver and then by car to Banff.
B Where is he staying?
A In the Banff Springs Hotel.
B And how long is he staying?
A Just ten days.

Chart

Where go?	**Banff, Canada**
Why/go?	**to go skiing**
When/leave?	**March 3**
How/travel?	**by plane and car**
Where/stay?	**Banff Springs Hotel**
How long/stay?	**10 days**

2 Focus attention on the examples in the speech bubbles. Drill the language, highlighting the falling intonation on the *Wh-* question. Then elicit one or two more exchanges in open pairs. Students continue in closed pairs. Monitor and check for correct use of the Present Continuous for future, and for intonation in the questions.

3 This is an information-gap activity based on Rachel and Laura's, and Omar's vacation plans. Pre-teach *uncle* and *tent* from the charts on p. 111 and p. 113 of the Student Book. Check the pronunciation of the places *Whangaparada* /ˌwæŋɡəpəˈradə/, *New Zealand* /nuˈzilənd/, and *Johannesburg* /joʊˈhænɪsbərɡ/. Remind students of the question to ask in order to check spelling (*How do you spell ...?*). Divide the class into pairs and assign a role, Student A or Student B, to each student. Refer all the Students A to p. 111 and all the Students B to p. 113. Explain that they have to ask and answer questions and get the information to complete their chart. Remind them not to show each other their chart but to exchange the information through speaking.

Focus attention on the examples in the speech bubbles and drill the language. Students continue asking and answering in closed pairs. (With a weaker group, you could elicit all the questions from the cues in the chart as a class activity and then get students to do the information exchange.) Monitor and check for correct use of the Present Continuous, intonation on the *Wh-* questions, and use of the alphabet. Get students to check their answers by comparing their completed charts. Provide feedback on any common errors in a brief follow-up session.

4 This exercise gives students the opportunity to talk about their own vacation plans. Focus attention on the examples in the speech bubbles. Drill the language and then get students to ask you the questions. Elicit one or two more exchanges in open pairs and then get students to continue in closed pairs. Monitor and check for correct use of Present Continuous.

The second phase of this exercise practices the third person singular form. Focus attention on the example in the speech bubble and highlight the third person forms in the verbs. Elicit more examples from the class.

ADDITIONAL MATERIAL

Workbook Unit 14
Exercise 4 is a pronunciation exercise to practice sentence stress.

Talking about you

5 This section reviews the Past Simple with both regular and irregular verbs and gives practice of Yes/No questions with the Present Continuous for future plans. It also highlights the intonation of the Yes/No question forms.

Read through the list of sentences about yesterday and ask *Now or past? (past)*. Briefly review the verb forms by eliciting the corresponding infinitive, e.g., *got up—get up, went—go, walked—walk,* etc. Focus attention on the example for number 1 and ask *Now or future? (future)*.

Elicit the questions for numbers 2 and 3 (*Are you going swimming tomorrow? Are you walking to work tomorrow?*). Get students to write the questions, working individually.

T 14.5 Play the recording through once and ask students to check they have formed the questions correctly. Play the recording again and get students to repeat chorally and individually. Encourage them to reproduce the rising intonation on the Yes/No questions.

Review the formation of short answers by getting students to ask you questions 1, 2, 6, and 7. (These are the questions that can apply to all students.) Reply *Yes, I am./ No, I'm not.* And then get students to ask and answer in open pairs. Check for intonation and drill the questions again if necessary. Students then ask and answer in closed pairs.

Answers and tapescript
1. I got up early.
   Are you getting up early tomorrow?
2. I went swimming.
   Are you going swimming tomorrow?
3. I walked to work.
   Are you walking to work tomorrow?
4. I had lunch in my office.
   Are you having lunch in your office tomorrow?
5. I left work late.
   Are you leaving work late tomorrow?
6. I met a friend.
   Are you meeting a friend tomorrow?
7. We had dinner in a restaurant.
   Are you having dinner in a restaurant tomorrow?

6 This exercise gives students the opportunity to use the Past Simple and the Present Continuous for future to talk about themselves. Demonstrate the activity by writing five things that you did yesterday on the board, e.g., *I went to the movies.* Elicit the question about tomorrow and give an answer, e.g., *Are you going to the movies tomorrow? No, I'm not. I'm playing squash.* Drill the examples in the speech bubbles and then get students to continue in closed pairs. Monitor and check for correct use of the Past Simple and the Present Continuous for future, and for correct intonation. Provide feedback on any common errors with the whole class.

SUGGESTION
Try to review the Past Simple and the Present Continuous for future by talking about what students did/are going to do at different times, e.g., last/next weekend, during the last/next vacations, on their last/next birthday, etc. You can set up short pair or group work activities as warm-up stages at the start of a class, or as "fillers" for students who finish a task before the others.

Check it

7 Focus attention on the first pair of sentences as an example. Students continue working individually to choose the correct sentence.

Get students to check their answers in pairs before checking them with the whole class.

Answers
1. I'm leaving tomorrow.
2. We're going to the movies this evening.
3. Where are they going on vacation?
4. What are you doing on Saturday evening?
5. What are you doing tomorrow?

READING AND LISTENING (SB p. 104)

A musical trip around the US

1 This exercise aims to generate interest in the topic of musical cities and to provide motivation for reading the text.

T 14.6 Tell students they are going to hear three different types of music. Play the recording and have students match the pictures with a type of music. Then have them answer the questions in pairs.

Answers
Picture 1 rock 'n roll, Memphis
Picture 2 jazz, New Orleans
Picture 3 country and western, Nashville
The recording contains excerpts of the following music styles:
rock 'n roll
jazz
country and western

2 **T 14.7** Check comprehension of the title of the text *Rocking Around the US!* Pre-teach/check *crazy about, concert, road trip, noisy, visitor, motel, prefer,* and *DJ (disc jockey).* Direct attention to the compass at the lower left of the map, and tell students that the letters *N, E, S, W* stand for the directions *north, east, south,* and *west.* Tell students they are going to read and listen about an interesting vacation in the United States. Play the recording and have students read along. Then have them work in pairs to answer the questions.

Answers
They are from Japan.
The trip is special because they are visiting cities related to the kind of music they like.
Cities:
1. New Orleans, Louisiana
2. Memphis, Tennessee
3. Nashville, Tennessee

4. Cleveland, Ohio
5. New York City

3 Focus attention on the example. Have students work individually to correct the sentences about the text. Let students check their answers in pairs, before going over them with the class. If there are any problems, ask students to find the section in the text with the correct information.

Answers
2. They're going to the US next month.
3. They're traveling from the south to the north.
4. Elvis Presley's house is in Memphis, Tennessee.
5. They are visiting Graceland.
6. Roku prefers rock 'n roll.
7. A DJ in Cleveland named rock 'n roll in 1951.
8. There are a lot of jazz clubs in Harlem.

4 Students work in pairs to discuss the trip. Encourage them to use the cues listed in their discussion to help order their conversation.

NOTE
The next two exercises are based on a song by the famous American singer and songwriter Woody Guthrie (1912–1967). The song was written in 1940 and includes many references to the geography of the United States. Students may have questions about the following:
New York island = Long Island, part of New York state
redwood forest = the giant redwood trees in Northern California
Gulf Stream waters = a current of water that runs along the east coast of North America

5 **T 14.8** Direct attention to the photo of Woody Guthrie and the sheet music. Tell students they are going to listen to a song written by Guthrie. Pre-teach *ribbon*, *highway*, *skyway* (meaning *sky*), *golden*, *valley*, *dust clouds*, and *freedom*. Play the recording and have students just listen. Ask them how much of the song they can remember. Invite students to share with the class and note any phrases from the song on the board.

Have students turn to p. 123 in the Student Book. Play the recording again and have students read the lyrics while the song plays.

Sing about your land!

6 Put students into groups and have them write a song about their own country. If you have a multilingual class, you could group students by country; in a monolingual class, you can have them form groups of three or four. Encourage students to brainstorm ideas before they start writing, asking them what places they want to include in the song. Invite students to sing their songs to the class.

Workbook Unit 14
Exercises 8 and 9   are reading and comprehension exercises that continue the theme of interesting trips.

VOCABULARY AND SPEAKING (SB p. 106)

Transportation and travel

1 This section reviews and extends the lexical set of transportation and travel, and also gives further practice of the Past Simple. Focus attention on the words in the box and the pictures. Elicit the answer for number 1 (*bicycle*) and get students to continue matching, working in pairs. Check the answers with the whole class, making sure students can pronounce the words correctly.

Answers
1. bicycle
2. motorcycle
3. ship
4. the subway

2 Elicit a few more examples of forms of transportation from the class, e.g., car, bus, and then get students to continue working in groups of three. Elicit the answers, checking the spelling and pronunciation, and write them on the board in groups: *by road/rail, by air, by sea*.

Possible answers

By road/rail	By air	By sea
car	plane	ferry
bus	helicopter	boat
truck		
van		
train		
tram		
cable car		

3 This is a collocation exercise with common travel words. Focus attention on the example and then get students to continue matching, working in pairs. Check the answers with the whole class.

Answers
pack your bags
make a reservation
catch a plane
have a great time
arrive in Rome
go sightseeing

4 This exercise consolidates the collocations presented in Exercise 3. Focus attention on the first and last sentences given as examples and then elicit the second sentence (*We made a reservation for the hotel and the flight.*). Get students to write *2* in the correct box. Students continue putting the sentences in order, working individually.

T 14.9 Get students to check their answers in pairs before checking them against the recording.

Answers and tapescript
1. We wanted to go on vacation to Rome.
2. We made a reservation for the hotel and the flight.
3. We picked up our tickets from the travel agent's.
4. We packed our bags.
5. We went to the airport.
6. We caught the plane.
7. We arrived in Rome.
8. We went sightseeing.
9. We had a great time.

---

5 This exercise gives further practice of the Past Simple and the language of transportation and travel. Demonstrate the activity by talking about a trip you took. Say where you went, how you traveled, and how long the trip was. Elicit another example from a confident student and then get students to continue in closed pairs or groups of three, taking turns to ask and answer about a trip in the past. Monitor and check for correct use of the Past Simple and names of transportation.

ADDITIONAL MATERIAL

Workbook Unit 14
Exercises 6 and 7   are exercises to practice the lexical set of travel and transportation.

EVERYDAY ENGLISH (SB p. 107)
Going sightseeing

1 This sections focuses on the topic of sightseeing. Focus attention on the names of the cities and the dates. Elicit sentences by asking *Where* and *when?* (*I went to London in July 2000. I went to Bangkok in January 2002.*) Ask *What did you see?* and *What did you buy?* and elicit possible information about sights and souvenirs, e.g., *We saw Buckingham Palace. We bought some clothes. We saw the Emerald Buddha. We bought some jewelry.*

Review the question *Did you have a good time?* Get students to write down two cities and dates when they were a tourist. Students talk about the cities in closed pairs, using the ideas in the Student Book. Encourage them to ask *Did you have a good time?* about each trip.

2 This section practices typical conversations in a tourist office and reviews *would like* from Unit 12. Focus attention on the photos and ask *Where are the people?* (*On vacation.*) and *What are they asking about?* (*A map, a bus tour.*). Pre-teach/check *take* (verb to show length of time).

T 14.10 Play the first line of the conversation and review the words to fill in the first blanks (*help you*). Play the rest of the recording and get students to complete the conversations. If necessary, play the recording again and allow students to complete any missing answers. Then check the answers with the whole class.

Answers and tapescript
1. A Hi. Can **I help you**?
   B Yes. **I'd like** a map of the city, please.
   A **Here** you are.
   B Thank you.
2. C We'd like **to go on** a bus tour of **the city**.
   A OK. The next **bus leaves** at 10:00. It **takes** an hour.
   C Where does the bus leave from?
   A It **leaves from** the **bus station** on Maple Street.
3. D We'd like to visit the museum. **When is it** open?
   A From nine o'clock to five o'clock **every day**.
   D **How much** is it to get in?
   A Ten dollars for adults and **it's free** for children.

Get students to practice the conversations in closed pairs. If students have problems with pronunciation, drill key sections of the conversation and get them to practice again in closed pairs.

3 This exercise gives students the opportunity to talk about sights in their town or city, and also to role-play conversations in a tourist office. Focus attention on the examples in the speech bubbles. Check comprehension of *market*. Give an example of places to visit in your town and elicit more examples from the class about places where they live. Students continue in closed pairs.

Write key words from the students' examples on the board to help them during the role play, e.g.:

Nouns   *church/temple, museum, art gallery, square, monument, college, theater, palace*

Verbs   *go on a tour, see, visit, buy, go to, take a photo of*

Divide the class into pairs and get them to make up conversations, using the conversations in Exercise 2 as a model. Let students write down their conversations in the initial stage and go around monitoring and helping. Give students time to rehearse their conversations a few times but then encourage them not to refer to the text when they act out the role plays. (With a weaker group, you could draft the conversations as a class activity and write them up on the board. Students rehearse from the text on the board. Then rub off some of the words from the board so that there are just key words left and get students to act out the conversations.)

Workbook Unit 14

Exercises 10 and 11 provide further practice of the language used when sightseeing.

Don't forget!

Workbook Unit 14

Exercise 5 In this exercise, students translate sentences containing the main grammar points presented in the unit.

Word List Ask the students to turn to SB p. 136 and go through the words with them. Ask them to learn the words for homework, and test them on a few in the following class.

EXTRA IDEAS UNITS 13 AND 14

On TB p. 107 there are additional photocopiable activities to review the language from Units 13 and 14. There is a reading text with tasks, a question formation exercise, and a matching activity on everyday English. You will need to pre-teach/check *suit, without, glove, formal/informal, pink, popular, fashionable, designer labels,* and *spend* for the reading text.

EXTRA IDEAS UNITS 8–14

On p. 108 of the Teacher's Book there is a song, "Don't Worry, Be Happy," and suggested activities to exploit it. You will find the song after Unit 14 on the Student Book Cassette/CD. If you have the time and feel that your students would benefit from this activity, photocopy the page and use it in class.

The answers to the activities are on p. 131 of the Teacher's Book.

Stop and Check 4 There is a Stop and Check quiz for Units 11–14 on p. 118 of the Teacher's Book.

Progress Test 3 There is a Progress Test for Units 11–14 on p. 127 of the Teacher's Book.

Photocopiable Material

Unit 2 Suggestion (TB p. 9)

Name	Yoshi 👨	
	Kumiko 👩	
Country	Japan	

Name	Bill 👨	
	Liz 👩	
Country	Canada	

Name	Fernando 👨	
	Marta 👩	
Country	Spain	

Name	Anurak 👨	
	Pim 👩	
Country	Thailand	

Name	Mike 👨	
	Carol 👩	
Country	England	

Name	Sang-woo 👨	
	Soon-hee 👩	
Country	Korea	

Name	Robert 👨	
	Britney 👩	
Country	the United States	

Name	Marco 👨	
	Sara 👩	
Country	Italy	

Name	Li-hong 👨	
	Ya-ping 👩	
Country	Taiwan	

Name	Luis 👨	
	Ana 👩	
Country	Brazil	

Name	Carlos 👨	
	Fatima 👩	
Country	Mexico	

Name	Paul 👨	
	Kim 👩	
Country	Australia	

Extra Ideas Units 1–4 Review

Reading

1 Look at the texts about people in Los Angeles. Read them quickly and answer the questions.

1. Is Cintia from Los Angeles?
2. How old is Jason?
3. Where is Todd from?
4. Who is from Japan?
5. Two people have children. Who?
6. Who isn't married?

Hi! Welcome to Los Angeles ...

My name's **CINTIA CLARK.** I'm from Natal in Brazil. I'm married. My husband's name is Alex. He's from Los Angeles. We have a son, Jason, and a daughter, Daniela. Jason is 12 and Daniela is 8. Alex and I are both teachers at the same school. It isn't in the center of Los Angeles, but it's near our house.

- -

I'm **TODD HASTINGS** from London in England. I'm in Los Angeles with my rock group, The Drivers. We're on tour in the United States, Canada, and Mexico. I'm not married, but I have a girlfriend here in Los Angeles. She's a student and her name is Laura. She's beautiful!

- -

My name's **SUMIO TANAKA.** I'm a businessman from Japan. My company has an office in Tokyo and in Los Angeles, too. I'm married and I have two daughters. They are students at a school in the center of Los Angeles. They are very happy here.

---

2 Read the texts again. Are these sentences true (✓) or false (✗)?

1. Cintia has two daughters.
2. Cintia is a teacher.
3. Alex's school is in the center of Los Angeles.
4. Todd is a taxi driver.
5. Laura is Todd's girlfriend.
6. Sumio's company has two offices.
7. Sumio's children aren't happy in Los Angeles.

Language work

1 Write questions for these answers.

1. **_What's your name?_**
   My name's Niwat Yuvaves.
2. _____ ?
   Y – u – v – a – v – e – s.
3. _____ ?
   I'm from Bangkok in Thailand.
4. _____ ?
   I'm 30.
5. _____ ?
   No, I'm not married.
6. _____ ?
   I'm a bank manager.
7. _____ ?
   It's in the center of town.
8. _____ ?
   My favorite music is jazz.

2 Practice the questions and answers with a partner.

Everyday English

Match the lines (1–5) with the answers (a–e).

1. ☐ What's this in English?
2. ☐ Have a good trip!
3. ☐ Good night.
4. ☐ How are you?
5. ☐ Are you all right?

   a. Fine, thanks.
   b. Good night.
   c. Thank you.
   d. Sorry. I don't know.
   e. Yes, I'm fine.

Adjectives

big	new	awful	cold
great	small	hot	old

Nouns

bag	book	camera	computer
hamburger	sandwich	television	bus
dog	coffee	tea	cell phone
radio	CD player	clock	glass

Extra Ideas Units 1–7

Song

1 Think of someone you like very much—your boyfriend or girlfriend, your husband or wife, your mother, your father, your best friend …

Why do you like them? Use these ideas.

I like _____ because …

He's
She's   friendly   funny   very nice   beautiful   kind

2 Match the verbs with the nouns.

1. sing   a game
2. play   a book
3. read   a video
4. have   a song
5. watch   a dream

3 Complete the list of seasons.

1. spring
2. _____
3. fall
4. winter

4 Listen to the song "You're My Everything." Check if the sentence is true (✔) or false (✗).

1. The singer is in love.
2. His girlfriend is nothing to him.
3. His girlfriend is very important to him.
4. He likes reading books.

5 Work with a partner. Read the song. Some lines are in the wrong order. Put them in the correct order. Listen and check your answers.

You're My Everything

You're my everything

1. sun   underneath   the

_____

You're my everything

2. one   rolled up   into

_____

You're my only dream

3. only   you're   reality   my   real

_____

You're my idea of a perfect personality
You're my everything

4. need   everything   I

_____

5. song   you're   I   the   sing

_____

And the book I read
You're way beyond belief
And just to make it brief
You're my winter, summer, spring

6. everything   you're   my

_____

6 Write your own song. Use some of the words in the box.

| moon | stars | roof | game | video | milk | food | photograph | picture | need |
| want | like | draw | play | drink | take | watch | eat | cook | paint |

You're my everything

Underneath the _____

You're my everything

Everything I _____

You're the _____ I _____

And the _____ I _____

Extra Ideas Units 5–8 Review

Reading

1   Read the text quickly and answer these questions.

   1. What's Toni's job?
   2. Where does she live?
   3. What's her favorite room?
   4. What does she do there?

Writer, **Toni Washington,** *describes her favorite room …*

My house is in the center of Philadelphia and it's about 90 years old. I work from home and my favorite room is my office. It's a beautiful room with big windows and I love **it**! In the office, I have my computer, two comfortable armchairs, a CD player, and a small fridge! There are photos of my three children on the walls. They're at college and I only see **them** on vacation.

I get up at about 7 A.M. every morning and take a shower. I have breakfast in the office and I work on my computer all day. I don't usually go out of the office because it has everything I want —my work, music, food, and coffee! I don't have a telephone but I have e-mail. My mother has a computer and I send messages to **her** every day— **she** loves **them**!

In the evening, I listen to music in the office and eat my dinner. My friends sometimes visit **me** and we have tea. I go to bed at about 11:30 P.M.—but in my bedroom, not in the office!

---

2   Read the text again. Are these sentences true (✓) or false (✗)?

   1. Toni doesn't go out to work.
   2. Toni's office is very big.
   3. Toni's children don't visit her on vacations.
   4. Toni doesn't call her mother.
   5. Toni sleeps in her office.

3   Look at the words in **bold** in the text. What or who do they refer to?

Language work

1   Write questions for these answers.

   1. <u>**Do you live in an apartment?**</u>

      Yes, I do. I live in an apartment downtown.

   2. _____ ?

      My favorite room is the living room.

   3. _____ ?

      No, I work in an office.

   4. _____ ?

      Yes, I sometimes work late.

   5. _____ ?

      No, I don't. I want to be a writer.

   6. _____ ?

      No, but I speak Spanish and Portuguese.

   7. _____ ?

      Because English is important for my job.

   8. _____ ?

      I like coffee and soda.

   9. _____ ?

      I watch TV in the evening.

   10. _____ ?

      I have two sisters and a brother.

2   Practice the questions and answers with a partner.

Everyday English

Match the questions (1–5) with the answers (a–e).

   1. ☐ What time is it, please?

   2. ☐ Can I try on this sweater, please?

   3. ☐ How much is that?

   4. ☐ Is there a bank near here?

   5. ☐ Is it far to the movie theater?

    a. Twelve ninety-nine, please.
    b. About 15 minutes.
    c. Yes. Go down Main Street and turn right.
    d. It's five thirty.
    e. Yes, the fitting rooms are over there.

Unit 9 **Suggestion** (TB p. 58)

Student A *Who was … ?*

1

Name: _____
Job: _____
Born: _____
Country: _____

4

Name: Bob Marley
Job: singer and musician
Born: 1945
Country: Jamaica

2

Name: James Dean
Job: actor
Born: 1931
Country: the United States

5

Name: _____
Job: _____
Born: _____
Country: _____

3

Name: _____
Job: _____
Born: _____
Country: _____

6

Name: Anna Pavlova
Job: dancer
Born: 1881
Country: Russia

Student B *Who was … ?*

1

Name: Albert Einstein
Job: scientist
Born: 1879
Country: Germany

4

Name: _____
Job: _____
Born: _____
Country: _____

2

Name: _____
Job: _____
Born: _____
Country: _____

5

Name: John F. Kennedy
Job: politician
Born: 1917
Country: the United States

3

Name: Agatha Christie
Job: writer
Born: 1890
Country: England

6

Name: _____
Job: _____
Born: _____
Country: _____

Unit 12 Suggestion (TB p. 83)

1 There are three conversations on this page. Put the lines in the correct order.

✂

B At a post office.	**B** OK. The fitting rooms are over there.
A Medium, I think.	**A** Excuse me! Do you sell *Le Monde*?
A Excuse me! Where can I buy stamps?	**B** Sure. What size are you?
B No, I'm sorry. We don't.	**A** Is there a post office near here?
A I'd like to try on this shirt, please.	**A** Where can I buy French newspapers?
B Try the hotel.	**B** Yes, 300 meters from here, next to the Internet cafe.

2 Where are the people in each conversation?

3 Practice the conversations with a partner.

Extra Ideas Units 9–12 Review

Reading

1 Work in groups and answer the questions.
   1. Do you like surprises?
   2. Did you have a surprise on your last birthday?
   3. Did you organize a surprise for a friend's birthday?

.....A wonderful surprise.................

Last Saturday was my fortieth birthday. I got up early but my husband and children stayed in bed. I thought, "That's OK. I can open my birthday cards now." I looked in every room in the house, but nothing—no cards, presents, flowers, or chocolates. I was upset but I thought, "It doesn't matter. I can wait."

An hour later, the mail carrier arrived and gave me a lot of envelopes. "Great—my cards!" I said, and then I saw that the letters were not for me. My husband and children got up and said, "Happy Birthday!" but didn't give me a card or present.

Then at twelve o'clock a taxi arrived at the house. I thought it was a mistake but my husband said, "Get in the taxi. I have your jacket and suitcase." We went to the airport and arrived in New Orleans that afternoon. We went shopping for my birthday present—a beautiful painting of the city. In the evening we had a delicious dinner—salad, steak, and delicious coffee.

On Sunday we had breakfast in the oldest cafe in New Orleans, went on a boat on the Mississippi River, and walked along the famous streets. We arrived home on Sunday evening after a perfect weekend. The next day I asked my husband, "How did you keep the vacation a secret?" "I booked it on the Internet," he answered, "because I know you never use the computer!"

2 Read the text. Are these sentences true (✓) or false (✗)?
   1. The writer didn't receive any presents on the morning of her birthday.
   2. The mail carrier gave the writer some birthday cards.
   3. The writer didn't think the taxi was for her.
   4. The writer and her husband stayed two nights in New Orleans.
   5. The writer didn't know about the vacation because her husband booked it on the Internet.

Language work

1 Write questions about your partner's last vacation.
   1. Where/go?
   Where did you go?
   2. go/in the summer?
   Did you go in the summer?
   3. Who/with?
   _____ ?
   4. travel/by plane?
   _____ ?
   5. Where/stay?
   _____ ?
   6. What/eat?
   _____ ?
   7. weather/good?
   _____ ?
   8. have/a good time?
   _____ ?

2 Ask and answer the questions with a partner.

Everyday English

Match the lines (1–5) with the answers (a–e).
   1. ☐ I'm sorry. I forgot your birthday.
   2. ☐ Can you help me? I'm lost!
   3. ☐ It's time to go to the airport.
   4. ☐ What would you like?
   5. ☐ I can't understand this word.

   a. Where do you want to go?
   b. You can check it in my dictionary.
   c. Black coffee, please.
   d. It doesn't matter.
   e. But I can't find my ticket.

Extra Ideas Units 13–14 Review

Reading

1 Read the text quickly and make a list of the clothes and colors.

Clothes	Colors
suit	blue

What are you wearing?

The world of clothes and fashion is changing. In the 1950s, men wore a suit to work and women never went out without a hat and gloves. Today, people can wear jeans and a T-shirt in the office and young men only wear a suit for interviews or weddings. Colors are also different today. People wear blue, green, yellow, and red as well as more formal colors like black, gray, and brown. My boyfriend works in an office and today he's wearing jeans and a pink shirt!

Sports clothes are very popular today. I'm wearing running pants, a T-shirt, and sneakers today, but I don't go running! I wear them because they are fashionable and comfortable. People sometimes wear ski jackets and walking boots or sneakers when they go to the movies!

Children are also very interested in fashion. In the past, parents chose and bought clothes for children and teenagers. Now, children choose their own clothes and often like to have designer labels. My sister's children are wearing Sean John jeans, Donna Karan T-shirts, and Nike sneakers right now. I think she spends more money on clothes for them than I spend on my clothes!

I like today's fashions because they are more informal and men and women can wear the same things. I often borrow my boyfriend's shirts and T-shirts—but he doesn't borrow my clothes!

2 Read the text again and answer these questions.

1. How are today's fashions different from in the 1950s?
2. What clothes and colors can people wear for work?
3. Does the writer wear sports clothes to go running?
4. Do parents choose clothes for today's teenagers?
5. Why are children's clothes expensive?
6. Why does the writer like today's fashions?

Language work

1 Write questions for your partner.

1. How often/go shopping for clothes?
   How often do you go shopping for clothes?
2. like/today's fashions?
   Do you like today's fashions?
3. What/favorite clothing stores?
   _____ ?
4. buy clothes/on the Internet?
   _____ ?
5. How much/spend on clothes?
   _____ ?
6. buy/designer labels?
   _____ ?
7. What/wear for work/school/college?
   _____ ?
8. What/wear/now?
   _____ ?
9. What/favorite colors?
   _____ ?
10. borrow/other people's clothes?
    _____ ?

2 Ask and answer the questions with a partner.

Everyday English

Match the lines (1–6) with the answers (a–f).

1. ☐ I'm bored.
2. ☐ I'd like to go on a tour of the city.
3. ☐ I'm hungry.
4. ☐ When is the museum open?
5. ☐ How much is it to get in to the museum?
6. ☐ I'm thirsty.

a. Why don't you have a banana?
b. Ten dollars for adults.
c. From ten until five thirty.
d. Why don't you have a glass of water?
e. OK. The next bus leaves at 11:30.
f. Why don't you read a book?

Extra Ideas Units 8–14

Song

1 Match the sentences to the pictures.

a

1. This person worries a lot.

b

2. This person is very happy.

2 Do you worry a lot? Complete the questionnaire. Ask your partner.

	Yes, I do.	No, I don't.
1. Do you worry when you can't do your homework?	❑	❑
2. Do you worry when you are late for school?	❑	❑
3. Do you worry when you travel?	❑	❑
4. Do you worry when you cook dinner for friends?	❑	❑
5. Do you worry when you speak English?	❑	❑

Tell your partner: *You worry a lot!* or *You are relaxed and happy!*

3 Listen to the song "Don't Worry, Be Happy." Does the singer think it's a good idea or a bad idea to worry about things?

4 Look at the chart below. Fill in the missing words.

Infinitive	Past
write	**wrote**
have	
	sang
	worried
get	
lay	
	came
take	

5 Read the song. Fill in the blanks with words from the chart in Exercise 4. Listen and check your answers.

Don't Worry, Be Happy

Here's a little song I (1) _____

You might want to (2) _____ it note for note

Don't (3) _____ , be happy

In every life we (4) _____ some trouble

But when you (5) _____ you make it double

Don't (6) _____ , be happy

(7) _____ no place to (8) _____ your head

Somebody (9) _____ and (10) _____ your bed

Don't (11) _____ , be happy

Now there is this song I wrote

I hope you learned it note for note

Don't worry, be happy

6 Listen to the song again, and sing along. And remember—don't worry, be happy!

Stop and Check 1

Correct the mistakes

Each sentence has a mistake. Find it and correct it.

1. Hi, + John.
   Hi, I'm John.

2. What's you name?
   _____

3. My name are Ana.
   _____

4. This Helen Smith.
   _____

5. Is a book.
   _____

6. Where you are from?
   _____

7. I'm am from Japan.
   _____

8. He's a businessman. Her name's James.
   _____

9. What's she job? She's a doctor.
   _____

10. He no is a teacher. He's a student.
    _____

11. How old you?
    _____

12. Is she from London? Yes, she's.
    _____

13. Is he a sales assistant? No, he not.
    _____

14. Are you from Brazil? No, I amn't.
    _____

15. He's phone number is 555-2541.
    _____

16. My teacher and I is 30.
    _____

| 15 |

my / your, he / she / they, his / her

(Circle) the correct word.

1. (My) / I name's Karen.

2. He's from Japan. _His_ / _Her_ name's Kazu.

3. Helen and Patty are in a pop group. _They_ / _She_ are on tour.

4. What's _you_ / _your_ address?

5. This is Linda. _Her_ / _She_'s from Chicago.

6. Where are the students? _They're_ / _You're_ in Dallas.

7. Mr. Evans is from London. _She's_ / _He's_ a businessman.

| 6 |

Questions and answers

1 Match the questions (1–8) and the answers (a–h).

1. [f] What's your job?
2. ☐ Where's he from?
3. ☐ Is she a sales assistant?
4. ☐ What's his name?
5. ☐ How old are you?
6. ☐ How are you?
7. ☐ Are you married?
8. ☐ What's this in English?

a. No, she isn't.
b. Mr. Brown.
c. Toronto, in Canada.
d. I'm 27.
e. No, we aren't.
f. I'm a student.
g. Fine, thanks.
h. It's a camera.

| 7 |

2 Look at the identity card and write the questions.

NAME:	Keesha Watson
CITY, STATE:	Las Vegas, Nevada
JOB:	Police officer
AGE:	29
PHONE NUMBER:	(702) 555-1396
MARRIED?:	Yes

1. **What's her name?**

   Her name's Keesha Watson.

2. _____

   She's from Las Vegas in Nevada.

3. _____

   She's a police officer.

4. _____

   She's 29.

5. _____

   It's (702) 555-1396.

6. _____

   Yes, she is.

   [10]

Negatives

Write the sentences in the negative.

1. It's from Taiwan.

   It isn't from Taiwan.

2. She's a nurse.

   _____

3. Mike is from Canada.

   _____

4. Julie is 28.

   _____

5. I'm married.

   _____

6. Jim and Sue are students.

   _____

7. They are in New York.

   _____

   [12]

Plurals

Write the sentences in the plural.

1. It's a book.

   They're books.

2. I'm married.

   _____

3. It's a sandwich.

   _____

4. He's a student.

   _____

5. She's from the United States.

   _____

6. I'm not on tour.

   _____

7. Is she a doctor?

   _____

   [12]

Numbers

1 Match the numbers in **A** with the words in **B**.

A	B
6	five
1	two
2	seven
5	six
8	nine
4	eight
9	one
3	four
10	three
7	ten

   [9]

2 Write the numbers in words.

1. 12 _twelve_
2. 11 _____
3. 28 _____
4. 20 _____
5. 14 _____
6. 30 _____
7. 13 _____
8. 15 _____

`7`

Vocabulary

1 Put the words in the correct column.

doctor photograph nurse sandwich student book teacher television businessman sales assistant camera taxi driver bag police officer computer hamburger

Jobs	Everyday things
doctor	photograph
_____	_____
_____	_____
_____	_____
_____	_____
_____	_____
_____	_____

`14`

2 Write the countries.

1. incah   _China_
2. ajpna   _____
3. auitasarl   _____
4. okrae   _____
5. xmecoi   _____
6. lnaegnd   _____
7. aancda   _____
8. het tduine tesats   _____
9. libarz   _____

`8`

TOTAL `100`

TRANSLATE

Translate the sentences into your language. Translate the _ideas_, not word-for-word.

1. What's your name?

   _____

2. How are you?

   _____

3. I'm fine, thanks.

   _____

4. What's this in English?

   _____

5. He's a taxi driver.

   _____

6. His name's John. Her name's Karen.

   _____

7. How old are you?

   _____

8. I'm twenty-six.

   _____

9. They aren't married.

   _____

10. Is she from Japan? Yes, she is.

    _____

Stop and Check 2

Correct the mistakes

Each sentence has a mistake. Find it and correct it.

1. ~~They~~ teacher is from Canada.
   Their teacher is from Canada.

2. My sisters husband is a doctor.
   _____

3. The childrens live in San Diego.
   _____

4. He have a new car.
   _____

5. We car is Japanese.
   _____

6. How old have you?
   _____

7. I am like tennis.
   _____

8. I no speak Italian very well.
   _____

9. She live in Taipei.
   _____

10. We have a house big.
    _____

11. They not like Chinese food.
    _____

12. Where she work?
    _____

13. My husband don't work in an office.
    _____

14. Does they speak Portuguese?
    _____

15. What sports do she like?
    _____

16. We don't never drink tea.
    _____

15

Questions and negatives

1 Write questions.

1. Where / you / live?
   Where do you live?

2. How / you / spell / your name?
   _____

3. How many / sisters / he / have?
   _____

4. What / food / she / like?
   _____

5. Where / you / have lunch?
   _____

6. What / music / you / like?
   _____

7. How many / languages / they / speak?
   _____

8. What time / you / get up?
   _____

9. What / drinks / the children / like?
   _____

10. What time / Helen / go to bed?
    _____

11. Where / your teacher / come from?
    _____

10

2 Write the statements as questions and negatives.

1. Julie is Richard's sister.
   Is Julie Richard's sister?
   Julie isn't Richard's sister.

2. They have a house in the country.
   _____?
   _____.

3. He speaks three languages.

_____?

_____.

4. You get up early.

_____?

_____.

5. Vicky has lunch in her office.

_____?

_____.

6. He goes to bed late.

_____?

_____.

7. We have class at 7:30.

_____?

_____.

8. Your parents drink coffee.

_____?

_____.

9. She speaks English well.

_____?

_____.

10. He cooks lunch.

_____?

_____.

| 18 |

Prepositions

Complete the sentences with the prepositions in the box.

| in   on   by   at |

1. We live __in__ the city center.
2. I go to work _____ 8:30.
3. Do you work _____ the evening?
4. The children go to school _____ bus.
5. He works _____ a hospital.
6. We don't get up early _____ the weekend.
7. My parents eat in a restaurant _____ Friday evening.
8. I don't go to school _____ Saturday.
9. We don't watch TV _____ the afternoon.
10. They have lunch _____ one o'clock.
11. I sometimes go to work _____ taxi.

| 10 |

Times and prices

Write the times and prices.

1.

It's one ten.

2.

It's twenty-nine cents.

3.

_____

4.

_____

5.

_____

6.

_____

7.

_____

8. 95¢

_____

9. $1.35

_____

10. $12.72

_____

11. $68.41

_____

12. $99.99

_____

| 10 |

Vocabulary—countries and nationalities

Complete the chart.

Country	Nationality
England	**English**
China	_____
_____	Spanish
Mexico	_____
_____	Korean
Italy	_____
Brazil	_____
_____	American
Japan	_____

8

Vocabulary—words that go together

Match a line in **A** with a line in **B**.

A	B
watch	late
listen to	coffee
get up	shopping
drink	music
work	the piano
stay	a shower
go	in an office
take	to work
walk	home
play	TV

9

Vocabulary—word groups

Put the words in the correct column. Each column has a different number of words.

good studio beautiful skiing college big office funny classroom favorite tennis nice apartment swimming farm small school great restaurant baseball hospital

Adjectives	Places	Sports
good		

20

TOTAL 100

TRANSLATE

Translate the sentences into your language. Translate the *ideas*, not word-for-word.

1. John is Dina's husband.

   _____

2. What's your friend's address?

   _____

3. My wife has a good job.

   _____

4. We have two children.

   _____

5. I like swimming.

   _____

6. We don't like Chinese food.

   _____

7. "Do you live in the country?" "Yes, I do."

   _____

8. He leaves school at four thirty.

   _____

9. "Does Greg walk to work?" "No, he doesn't."

   _____

10. We never go out in the evening.

    _____

Stop and Check 3

Correct the mistakes

Each sentence has a mistake. Find it and correct it.

1. Do you like dogs? Yes, I love ~~it~~.
   Do you like dogs? Yes, I love them.

2. My son is a student and I don't see her very often.
   _____

3. That's a photo of my children and my.
   _____

4. She lives in a old house.
   _____

5. There is three magazines on the table.
   _____

6. There isn't any good restaurants in this area.
   _____

7. There aren't a computer in the living room.
   _____

8. There are a lot of nice store in the city center.
   _____

9. I am born in 1985.
   _____

10. Where was you born?
    _____

11. The weather isn't very good yesterday.
    _____

12. She play tennis yesterday morning.
    _____

13. She goed on vacation last week.
    _____

14. Where did you go ski?
    _____

15. What did you had for breakfast?
    _____

16. Did you buyed a newspaper yesterday?
    _____

15

Questions and answers

Match the questions (1–11) with the answers (a–k).

1. [b] How are you?
2. [ ] What did you have for lunch?
3. [ ] Where are my keys?
4. [ ] What time did you get up?
5. [ ] How old are your children?
6. [ ] How many children do you have?
7. [ ] How much was your camera?
8. [ ] Why do you want to learn English?
9. [ ] Do you like jazz?
10. [ ] How do you go to work?
11. [ ] Who was John Lennon?

a. At about seven thirty.
b. Fine, thanks.
c. About a hundred dollars.
d. Yes, I love it.
e. By car.
f. They're on the table.
g. He was an English musician.
h. Because I need it for my job.
i. Two—a boy and a girl.
j. Twelve and fifteen.
k. Pizza and salad.

10

there is / are

Complete the sentences with the correct form of *there is/are*.

1. __There__ __is__ a new computer in my school.
2. _____ _____ a Thai restaurant near here.
3. _____ _____ 20 students in my group.
4. There's a TV, but _____ _____ a VCR.
5. _____ _____ a new stove in the kitchen?
6. _____ _____ any pictures on the walls?
7. There are some nice stores, but _____ _____ any supermarkets.

6

Past Simple

Complete the text with the Past Simple form of the verbs in parentheses. There are regular and irregular verbs.

Elvis Presley (1) __was__ (be) born on January 8, 1935. He (2) _____ (live) with his parents in Tupelo, Mississippi, for the first 13 years of his life. In 1948, they (3) _____ (go) to Memphis because his father (4) _____ (want) to find a job. Elvis (5) _____ (not like) his new home or school, but he (6) _____ (love) music. He (7) _____ (leave) school in 1953 and (8) _____ (work) in different jobs. Two years later, Elvis (9) _____ (join) RCA Records and in very little time he (10) _____ (be) famous for his music, dancing, and movies. He (11) _____ (have) hundreds of hits including "Love me Tender," "Hound Dog," "Blue Suede Shoes," and "Jailhouse Rock."

`20`

Irregular verbs

Write the Past Simple form of these irregular verbs.

1. go __went__
2. see _____
3. get _____
4. do _____
5. buy _____
6. take _____
7. say _____
8. eat _____

`7`

was / were / did / didn't

Complete the sentences with the verbs in the box.

was	wasn't	were	weren't	did	didn't

1. I __was__ 25 on my last birthday.
2. The weather _____ cold and wet last week.
3. "_____ you on vacation last week?" "Yes, I was."
4. _____ you get up early yesterday?
5. We _____ at work yesterday. It was a holiday.
6. I love vacations, but I _____ have a good time last year.
7. I went to see my friend, but she _____ at home.
8. "Were they at the party?" "No, they _____."
9. "Did he go swimming yesterday?" "No, he _____."

`8`

Questions and negatives

Write the statements as questions and negatives.

1. He's a doctor.
   __Is he a doctor?__
   __He isn't a doctor.__
2. There's a CD player in the living room.
   _____?
   _____.
3. She was born in 1980.
   _____?
   _____.
4. He was a good student.
   _____?
   _____.
5. We stayed home last weekend.
   _____?
   _____.
6. You went to bed early last night.
   _____?
   _____.

`10`

Vocabulary

Put the words in the correct column.

good sailing painter lamp cheap princess
baseball kitchen new writer hot dancing shower
musician skiing stove singer tennis bed delicious
fast politician armchair cards great

Adjectives	Rooms and furniture	People and jobs	Sports and activities
good			

24

TOTAL 100

TRANSLATE

Translate the sentences into your language. Translate the *ideas*, not word-for-word.

1. "Why do you want to leave your job?" "Because I don't like it."

   _____

2. How many brothers and sisters do you have?

   _____

3. "What's this?" "It's my new English book."

   _____

4. There aren't any Korean restaurants in my town.

   _____

5. Where were you born?

   _____

6. She was a singer.

   _____

7. I went swimming yesterday morning.

   _____

8. We saw our friends last week.

   _____

9. What did you do yesterday?

   _____

10. He didn't have a good time on vacation.

    _____

Stop and Check 4

Correct the mistakes

Each sentence has a mistake. Find it and correct it.

1. He ~~haves~~ lunch at home.
   He has lunch at home.

2. I can speaking Thai.
   _____

3. She want to send an e-mail.
   _____

4. "I like a coffee, please." "Here you are."
   _____

5. "Do you like to come to my party?" "Yes, please."
   _____

6. I'd like shopping.
   _____

7. We learning English.
   _____

8. What do you wearing?
   _____

9. He no working today.
   _____

10. I'm do my homework now.
    _____

11. That's my father over there. He wears a black hat.
    _____

12. Where are you coming from?
    _____

13. We go on vacation next month.
    _____

14. Do you working tomorrow?
    _____

15. We had a good time last weekend.
    _____

16. How much did you stay in Peru?
    _____

| 15 |

Questions and answers

1 Match the questions (1–9) with the answers (a–i).

1. [f] Do you sell computer magazines?
2. ☐ What would you like to start?
3. ☐ Can you tell me the time, please?
4. ☐ Why don't you sit down and relax?
5. ☐ What's the problem?
6. ☐ Where can I buy a phone card?
7. ☐ How long does the bus tour take?
8. ☐ Can I help you?
9. ☐ When is the tourist office open?

a. I'm lost.
b. Try the newsstand.
c. From nine o'clock to seven o'clock every day.
d. It's two fifteen.
e. The soup, please.
f. No, I'm sorry, we don't.
g. I'm just looking, thanks.
h. About an hour.
i. That's a good idea.

| 8 |

2 Complete the questions with a question word or words.

1. **What** 's your name?
   My name's Fadia Kamel.

2. _____ are you doing?
   I'm writing to my friend.

3. _____ are you going on vacation?
   We're going to Thailand.

4. _____ did you travel?
   We traveled by plane and car.

5. _____ did you return early?
   Because the weather was bad.

6. _____ did you go on vacation with?
   I went with my parents.

7. _____ do you get up?
   At seven thirty.

8. _____ did your car cost?
   About $15,000.

9. _____ brothers and sisters do you have?

Two brothers and a sister.

10. _____ is your daughter?

She's 15. Her birthday is in June.

11. _____ is your party?

It's on Saturday, July 20.

| 10 |

can / want / like / would like

(Circle) the correct word.

1. "*Do* / *Would* you want a drink?" "Yes, please."

2. "Do you like Italian food?" "Yes, I *like* / *do*."

3. "*Do* / *Would* you like to watch a video?" "That's a good idea."

4. *I'd like* / *I like* to buy a computer, please.

5. My father *wants* / *want* to learn English.

6. You can *buying* / *buy* stamps in a post office.

7. She *doesn't* / *don't* like dogs.

8. I *cant* / *can't* speak Spanish very well.

9. Do they like *sail* / *sailing*?

10. He *can* / *cans* use a computer.

11. *We like* / *We'd like* our new house.

| 10 |

Present Simple and Continuous

Complete the sentences with the correct form of the verb in parenthesis.

1. He usually __goes__ (go) to work by bus.

2. We __'re having__ (have) lunch right now.

3. She _____ (call) her parents every day.

4. She's on the beach and she _____ (wear) a bathing suit.

5. _____ you usually _____ (get up) late on weekends?

6. John _____ (have) a birthday party every year.

7. Don't talk to Linda. She _____ (do) her homework right now.

8. Where are Mom and Dad? They _____ (sit) in the backyard.

9. The children always _____ (watch) TV in the evening.

10. _____ they _____ (work) at home today?

11. Put your jacket on. It _____ (rain).

12. How often _____ you _____ (go) to the theater?

| 10 |

Present Continuous for future

Complete the sentences with a verb and a noun from the boxes. Use the Present Continuous.

| **Verbs:** |
| ~~stay~~ travel pick up get married meet go have |

| **Nouns:** |
| ~~hotel~~ restaurant movies friends church train tickets |

1. We __'re staying__ in a __hotel__ Bangkok next month.

2. My boyfriend and I _____ in a beautiful _____ next month.

3. _____ you _____ the _____ from the travel agent's tomorrow morning?

4. Tomorrow is Saturday. I _____ my _____ in town.

5. They _____ dinner in a new _____ tomorrow.

6. She _____ to Osaka by _____ next week.

7. We _____ to the _____ next weekend to see the new Brad Pitt movie.

| 12 |

Past, present, and future

Complete the conversation with the correct form of the verbs in parenthesis. Use the Present Simple, Present Continuous, Present Continuous for future, and Past Simple.

A What (1) __are__ you __doing__ (do) tomorrow?

B I (2) _____ (play) tennis with my brother.

A Really? (3) _____ you _____ (play) every week?

B Only in the summer. But my brother (4) _____ (play) two or three times every week—he's very good. He (5) _____ (start) when he was a child, but (6) I _____ (not like) sports very much then. (7) _____ you _____ (interested) in sports?

A Well, I (8) _____ (go) swimming every week, and windsurfing in the summer. I (9) _____ (go) to Australia last year.

B (10) _____ you _____ (have) a good time?

A Yes, it was fantastic. I was with some friends and we (11) _____ (travel) to different places. We (12) _____ (visit) Sydney and Melbourne.

B (13) _____ you _____ (go) to Australia for your next vacation?

A No, we (14) _____ (go) to the US. My sister (15) _____ (live) in Florida, and we (16) _____ (stay) with her for two weeks in August.

B That's great! Have a good time!

A Thank you very much.

☐ 15

Vocabulary—word groups

Put the words in the correct column.

~~hamburger~~ red fish bicycle jeans fries yellow jacket tuna plane gray sweater subway cheese steak train white T-shirt pants brown ship

Food	Clothes	Colors	Transportation
hamburger			

☐ 20

TOTAL ☐ 100

TRANSLATE

Translate the sentences into your language. Translate the *ideas*, not word-for-word.

1. I can't play the guitar.
   _____

2. Can I help you?
   _____

3. "Would you like a sandwich?" "No, thank you."
   _____

4. I'd like to go to the movies this evening.
   _____

5. We're studying English.
   _____

6. What are you reading?
   _____

7. Do you read the newspaper every day?
   _____

8. We're flying to Los Angeles tomorrow.
   _____

9. What are you doing next weekend?
   _____

Progress Test 1

Exercise 1 The present tense of *to be*

Complete the chart with the present tense of *to be*.

	Affirmative	**Negative**
1. I	_am_	_'m not_
2. You	_____	_____
3. He/She/It	_____	_____
4. We	_____	_____
5. They	_____	_____

8

Exercise 2 *to be*—affirmative, negative, and questions

Complete the sentences with the correct form of *to be*.

1. I _'m_ from Cleveland in Ohio.
2. _____ you a student?
3. My sister _____ a doctor.
4. My parents _____ from Portland. They're from Seattle.
5. Are you married? No, I _____ .
6. My sister and I _____ from Japan.
7. _____ your parents from England?
8. Jane _____ a doctor. She's a teacher.
9. Is he a taxi driver? Yes, he _____ .
10. The coffee _____ from Colombia. It's from Brazil.
11. _____ your teacher from Canada?

10

Exercise 3 Questions

Match a line in **A** with a line in **B** to make a question. Then find an answer in **C**.

A	B	C
What	is your daughter?	I'm fine, thanks.
Where	is a sandwich?	Taipei, in Taiwan.
How	is Kayla?	Mr. Brown.
How much	are you from?	She's my daughter.
How old	is his name?	$4.95.
Who	are you?	She's 18.

·5

Exercise 4 Word order

Write the words in the correct order.

1. English / is / What / this / in / ?
   What is this in English?

2. wife / is / This / Sami's / .
   _____

3. phone / is / What / their / number / ?
   _____

4. the / house / have / We / a / in / country / .
   _____

5. your / you / do / How / spell / name / last / ?
   _____

6. you / Do / Chinese / like / tea / ?
   _____

7. well / I / speak / Italian / don't / very / .
   _____

8. car / don't / a / We / have / Japanese / .
   _____

9. Mexican / they / Do / eat / food / ?
   _____

8

Exercise 5 *a* or *an*?

Complete the sentences with *a* or *an*.

1. It's __an__ American city.
2. He's _____ actor.
3. Are you _____ teacher?
4. I have _____ American car.
5. We don't have _____ big house.
6. I have _____ English friend.
7. She's _____ student.
8. They don't have _____ computer.
9. She's _____ Australian doctor.
10. Is he _____ businessman?

9

Exercise 6 *has / have*

Complete the sentences with the correct form of *have*.

1. I __have__ a brother and a sister.
2. He _____ a small farm in Vermont.
3. I like Chinese food but we _____ a Chinese restaurant in town.
4. They _____ an apartment in London.
5. I'm not married, but I _____ a lot of friends.
6. John _____ a new computer.
7. _____ they _____ a big family?
8. My sister _____ a dog and a cat.
9. _____ you _____ a dictionary?

8

Exercise 7 Present Simple

Complete the sentences with the correct form of the verb in parenthesis.

1. My husband and I __live__ (live) in the country.
2. I _____ (not like) swimming.
3. They _____ (drink) tea.
4. What sports _____ your children _____ (like)?
5. We _____ (work) in a hospital.
6. You _____ (not like) hamburgers.

7. How many languages _____ you _____ (speak)?
8. _____ you and your family _____ (speak) Portuguese?
9. Helen and Dave _____ (not work) in Los Angeles.
10. Where _____ you _____ (live)?
11. _____ you _____ (eat) Chinese or Italian food?

10

Exercise 8 Subject pronouns and possessive adjectives

Circle the correct word.

1. *My / I*'m from Thailand.
2. Is this *you / your* dictionary?
3. My brother is a doctor. *His / He's* 27.
4. This is my mother. *He / She*'s a teacher.
5. Do you like *we / our* house?
6. I'm Ana and this is *my / I* husband.
7. Is this your daughter? What's *her / his* name?
8. My father is from Egypt. *His / Her* name's Asad.
9. What are *they / their* names?

8

Exercise 9 Possessive *'s*

Put a check (✓) next to the correct sentence.

1. a. ☐ This is Davids car.
   b. ✓ This is David's car.
2. a. ☐ Peter's wife is Canadian.
   b. ☐ Peter is wife is Canadian.
3. a. ☐ What's your teacher name?
   b. ☐ What's your teacher's name?
4. a. ☐ The children's names are Alaya and Jamal.
   b. ☐ The childrens names are Alaya and Jamal.
5. a. ☐ Mr. Browns car is American.
   b. ☐ Mr. Brown's car is American.
6. a. ☐ Her husband name is Paolo.
   b. ☐ Her husband's name is Paolo.

5

Exercise 10 Numbers

Write the numbers in words.

1. 17 _seventeen_
2. 29 _____
3. 37 _____
4. 43 _____
5. 59 _____
6. 62 _____
7. 74 _____
8. 88 _____
9. 91 _____
10. 100 _____

`| 9 |`

Exercise 11 Word groups

Put the words in the correct column.

| teacher parent sandwich actor water sister hamburger bank manager daughter juice son chocolate sales assistant ice cream police officer coffee orange tea soda husband waiter |

Jobs	Family	Food	Drinks
teacher			

`| 20 |`

TOTAL `| 100 |`

Progress Test 2

Exercise 1 Present Simple and frequency adverbs

Write complete sentences with the words in parenthesis.

1. I / go to bed late (usually)

   I usually go to bed late.

2. He / work late (never)

   _____

3. I / go to work by car (sometimes)

   _____

4. My son / have lunch at school (always)

   _____

5. She / see her friends after school (usually)

   _____

6. I / buy a newspaper (never)

   _____

7. Anela / go windsurfing (sometimes)

   _____

   | 6 |

Exercise 2 Object pronouns

Circle the correct word.

1. My daughter visited _me_ / _my_ last month.

2. My son lives near you. Do you know _he_ / _him_?

3. We bought a video but we didn't watch _it_ / _them_.

4. My daughter is a doctor. This is a photo of _him_ / _her_.

5. Our homework is very difficult. Can you help _we_ / _us_?

6. We called Mom and Dad last week but we didn't see _them_ / _they_.

7. You are very nice. I like _you_ / _your_.

   | 6 |

Exercise 3 _there is/are_ and prepositions of place

Write sentences about the picture.

1. a TV / the room

   There's a TV in the room.

2. two books / the table

   _____

3. a lamp / the sofa

   _____

4. three pictures / the walls

   _____

5. a cat / the table

   _____

6. a magazine / the bag

   _____

   | 10 |

Exercise 4 The past tense of *to be*

Complete the chart with the past tense of *to be*.

	Affirmative	Negative
1. I	was	wasn't
2. You	_____	_____
3. He/She/It	_____	_____
4. We	_____	_____
5. They	_____	_____

8

Exercise 5 *do*, *was*, and *did*

Complete the sentences with the verbs in the box.

do / does	was / were	did

1. Where __*does*__ he work?

2. _____ you like Brazilian food?

3. Where _____ you last night?

4. What _____ you do last weekend?

5. _____ she live in New York now?

6. _____ you go skiing last year?

7. When _____ he born?

8. We _____ home yesterday.

9. How many children _____ they have now?

8

Exercise 6 Past Simple

Complete the sentences with the Past Simple of the verbs in parenthesis. There are regular and irregular verbs.

1. She ___*played*___ (play) tennis yesterday.

2. I _____ (not work) on my computer yesterday.

3. We _____ (buy) a new VCR last month.

4. Where _____ you _____ (go) on vacation last year?

5. They _____ (stay) home last weekend.

6. He _____ (see) his friends last night.

7. You _____ (not take) the painting to an expert.

8. _____ you _____ (eat) in the hotel?

9. The children _____ (do) their homework on their computer.

8

Exercise 7 Negatives

Write the sentences in the negative.

1. I work in an office.
    I don't work in an office.

2. The movie is very good.
    _____

3. There's a CD player in the car.
    _____

4. She goes to work by car.
    _____

5. We go shopping in town.
    _____

6. There are a lot of hotels in this area.
    _____

7. The weather was very hot.
    _____

8. My children were born in Canada.
    _____

9. I was born in 1989.
    _____

10. David played baseball at school.
    _____

11. I had a big lunch.
    _____

10

Exercise 8 Days of the week

Write the days of the week in order.

Days: __Monday__, _____, _____,

_____, _____, _____,

_____

6

Exercise 9 Dates

Write the dates in words.

1. 5 / 5   **May fifth**
2. 1 / 2   _____
3. 6 / 19   _____
4. 8 / 3   _____
5. 12 / 31   _____
6. 10 / 12   _____
7. 4 / 17   _____
8. 5 / 1   _____
9. 7 / 7   _____

8

Exercise 10 Prepositions of time

Write the correct preposition, *in*, *on*, or *at*.

1. **in**_____ the evening
2. _____ Monday
3. _____ seven o'clock
4. _____ Sunday morning
5. _____ the afternoon
6. _____ five thirty
7. _____ the weekend

6

Exercise 11 Words that go together

Match a verb in **A** with a line in **B**.

A	B
get up	in a hotel
go	cards
watch	water
listen to	a good time
play	a CD
stay	in a hospital
work	sailing
cook	dinner
eat	in restaurants
have	early
drink	a video

10

Exercise 12 Which one is different?

Circle the different word.

1. newsstand supermarket (park) drugstore
2. Brazil Chinese Italy Venezuela
3. shower CD player TV VCR
4. ice hockey swimming sailing skiing
5. twenty-second twenty-nine thirteenth ninth
6. writer painter athlete singer
7. watched ate got took
8. swimming windsurfing sailing walking
9. floor kitchen wall window

8

Exercise 13 Adjectives

Match the opposites.

A	B
new	big
early	old
small	awful
expensive	slow
fast	hot
cold	late
great	cheap

6

TOTAL   100

Progress Test 3

UNITS 11–14

Exercise 1 Word order

Put the words in the correct order.

1. fast / you / Can / run / ?

   Can you swim fast?

2. She / long / hair / blonde / has / .

   _____

3. tour / the / long / How / does / bus / take / ?

   _____

4. radio / listen / to / like / you / Would / to / the / ?

   _____

5. Can / tell / please / you / me / the / time / ?

   _____

6. car / want / They / to / a / buy / new / .

   _____

7. like / would / to / What / you / drink / ?

   _____

8. and / a / is / He / wearing / jeans / T-shirt / .

   _____

9. weekend / going / are / Where / you / next / ?

   _____

10. bed / you / Why / don't / go / early / to / ?

    _____

11. agents / picked up / We / our / the / tickets / travel / from / .

    _____

    [10]

Exercise 2 *can* and *can't*

Look at the information in the chart and complete the sentences with *can* or *can't* and a verb.

	use a computer	ride a horse	play the guitar	cook
Jeff	✓	✗	✗	✓
Cathy	✓	✓	✗	✗
Sue	✓	✗	✓	✗

1. Cathy __can ride a horse__ but Jeff and Sue can't.

2. Jeff and Cathy _____ but Sue can.

3. Jeff can use a computer, but he _____ and he _____ .

4. Everybody _____ .

5. _____ Cathy and Sue _____ ?
   No, they can't.

6. Who _____ ? Only Cathy can.

[6]

Exercise 3 *want*, *like*, and *would like*

Put a check (✓) next to the correct sentence.

1. **A** ☑ What would you like for dessert?
      ☐ What do you like for dessert?

   B Ice cream, please.

2. **A** ☐ Would you like a cup of coffee?
      ☐ Do you like coffee?

   B Yes, I love it.

3. **A** ☐ I want to send an e-mail, please.
      ☐ I'd want to send an e-mail, please.

   B OK. Try computer number 3.

4. **A** ☐ Would you like to listen to some music?
      ☐ Do you like listening to music?

   B That's a nice idea.

5. **A** ☐ I like to buy these postcards, please.
      ☐ I'd like to buy these postcards, please.

   B Two fifty, please.

6. **A** ☐ What sports do you like playing?
      ☐ What sports would you like playing?

   B I love soccer and squash.

[5]

Exercise 4 Present Continuous

Complete the sentences with the Present Continuous form of the verbs in the box.

~~read~~ write wear rain take work enjoy leave drive

1. "What __are__ you __reading__ ?" "It's a love story."
2. He can't go to the movies because he _____ late.
3. I _____ work early because I don't feel well.
4. In this photo she _____ shorts and a T-shirt.
5. I can't talk to you now. I _____ the car.
6. _____ it _____ ? No, the weather is great today.
7. "Where's Liz?" "She _____ a shower."
8. "_____ you _____ your vacation?" "Yes, everything is great."
9. The children _____ a letter to their grandparents.

[8]

Exercise 5 Present Simple and Continuous

Complete the sentences with the Present Simple or the Present Continuous form of the verbs in parenthesis.

1. I usually __walk__ (walk) to work but this morning I __'m driving__ (drive) to my office.
2. I _____ (not see) my parents very often but they _____ (stay) with me right now.
3. We usually _____ (have) lunch at home but today we _____ (eat) in a restaurant.
4. Why _____ you _____ (wear) jeans to work today? You usually _____ (wear) more formal clothes.
5. My friends and I _____ (study) Spanish right now. We _____ (like) it a lot.
6. My sister _____ (live) in an apartment in London but she _____ (travel) in Europe right now.

[10]

Exercise 6 Past Simple and Present Continuous for future

Write affirmative and negative sentences, using the verbs.

1. I / get up early
   __I got up early_____ yesterday.
   __I'm not getting up early_____ tomorrow.
2. she / cook dinner
   _____ yesterday.
   _____ tomorrow.
3. we / work late
   _____ yesterday.
   _____ tomorrow.
4. they / leave home early
   _____ yesterday.
   _____ tomorrow.
5. I / go to bed late
   _____ yesterday.
   _____ tomorrow.
6. you / stay home
   _____ yesterday.
   _____ tomorrow.
7. Richard / see his doctor
   _____ yesterday.
   _____ tomorrow.

[12]

Exercise 7 Negatives

1. I can draw well.
   __I can't draw well.__
2. She wants to sell her house.
   _____
3. They like sightseeing.
   _____
4. He can swim.
   _____
5. He works in a bank.
   _____
6. We walk to work every day.
   _____

7. I'm watching this movie.

_____

8. The children are doing their homework.

_____

9. You are playing very well.

_____

10. We're staying in a hotel for a week.

_____

11. We had a nice meal at the restaurant.

_____

12. You picked up the tickets yesterday.

_____

13. Tamika saw her family last week.

_____

| 12 |

Exercise 8 *am/is/are, do/does/did*

Complete the sentences with a verb from the box.

am/'m not	is/isn't	are/aren't
does/doesn't	do/don't	did/didn't

1. I **am** watching TV.
2. My husband _____ going skiing next month.
3. Where _____ the bus tour leave from?
4. How often _____ you travel by plane?
5. They usually go to Florida on vacation but they _____ going there this year.
6. We had lunch in a restaurant but we _____ enjoy it.
7. Why don't we go out? It _____ raining now.
8. "Are you using your computer?" "No, I _____ ."
9. They live in Mexico but they _____ speak Spanish very well.
10. I _____ catching the plane at seven thirty.
11. "Does Paula like skiing?" "No, she _____ ."
12. _____ you have a good weekend?
13. _____ you enjoying the party?

| 12 |

Exercise 9 Which one is different?

(Circle) the different word.

1. (bank) drugstore   newsstand   supermarket
2. soda   coffee   mineral water   cake
3. cheese   tuna   dinner   vegetables
4. soup   chocolate cake   ice cream   apple pie
5. plane   airport   ferry   train
6. farmer   grandmother   interpreter   architect
7. passport   ticket   travel agent   stamp
8. shoes   shorts   jeans   pants
9. T-shirt   dress   jacket   coat
10. black   red   gray   long
11. dessert   waiter   main course   side order
12. film   photo   interview   camera
13. post office   stamp   letter   e-mail

| 12 |

Exercise 10 Words that go together

Match a verb in **A** with a line in **B**.

A	B
listen to	a friend
watch	a plane
read	chess
chat with	in Rome
wear	sightseeing
play	shorts
buy	a good time
catch	a cake
change	your bags
go	a video
have	a CD
pack	a magazine
arrive	money
make	a house

| 13 |

TOTAL | 100 |

Answer Keys

Extra Ideas Units 1–4

Reading

1 1. No, she isn't.
2. He's 12.
3. He's from London, England.
4. Sumio.
5. Cintia and Sumio.
6. Todd.

2 1. ✗ 5. ✔
2. ✔ 6. ✔
3. ✗ 7. ✗
4. ✗

Language work

1 2. How do you spell your last name?
3. Where are you from?
4. How old are you?
5. Are you married?
6. What's your job?
7. Where's your bank?
8. What's your favorite music?

Everyday English

1. d 2. c 3. b 4. a 5. e

Extra Ideas Units 1–7

Song "You're My Everything"

2 1. sing a song
2. play a game
3. read a book
4. have a dream
5. watch a video

3 2. summer

4 1. The singer is in love. ✔
2. His girlfriend is nothing to him. ✗
3. His girlfriend is very important to him. ✔
4. He likes reading books. ✗

5 "You're My Everything"
by Warren, Dixon, Young
1. Underneath the sun
2. Rolled up into one
3. You're my only real reality

4. Everything I need
5. You're the song I sing
6. You're my everything

6 *Sample answer:*
You're my everything
Underneath the moon
You're my everything
Everything I like
You're the photograph I take
And the video I watch

Note

There are some difficult phrases in the song. Ask the students to check them in their dictionaries when they do Exercise 4, before they listen to the song the second time.

Rolled up into one = combined in one person

Way beyond belief = (here) so wonderful I can't believe it

Tapescript

You're my everything
Underneath the sun
You're my everything
Rolled up into one
You're my only dream
You're my only real reality
You're my idea of a perfect personality

You're my everything
Everything I need
You're the song I sing
And the book I read
You're way beyond belief
And just to make it brief
You're my winter, summer, spring
You're my everything

Extra Ideas Units 5–8

Reading

1 1. She's a writer.
2. She lives in Philadelphia.
3. Her favorite room is her office.
4. She has breakfast, works, listens to music, and eats her dinner in her office.

2 1. ✔ 4. ✔
2. ✔ 5. ✗
3. ✗

3 it — Toni's office
them — Toni's children
her — Toni's mother
she — Toni's mother
them — e-mail messages
me — Toni

Language work

1 Possible answers:
2. What's your favorite room?
3. Do you work at home?
4. Do you work late?
5. Do you like your job?
6. Do you speak Chinese?
7. Why do you want to learn English?
8. What drinks do you like?
9. What do you do in the evening?
10. How many brothers and sisters do you have?

Everyday English

1. d 2. e 3. a 4. c 5. b

Extra Ideas Units 9–12

Reading

1 Students' own answers.

2 1. ✔ 4. ✗
2. ✗ 5. ✔
3. ✔

Language work

1 3. Who did you go with?
4. Did you travel by plane?
5. Where did you stay?
6. What did you eat?
7. Was the weather good?
8. Did you have a good time?

Everyday English

1. d 2. a 3. e 4. c 5. b

Reading

1

Clothes	Colors
suit	blue
hat	green
gloves	yellow
jeans	red
T-shirt	black
shirt	gray
sports clothes	brown
running pants	pink
sneakers	
ski jacket	
walking boot	

2   1. People wear informal clothes and colors today.
   2. People can wear jeans and T-shirts for work. They can wear blue, red, yellow, and pink.
   3. No, she doesn't. She wears sports clothes because they are fashionable and comfortable.
   4. No, they don't. Teenagers choose their own clothes.
   5. Children's clothes are expensive because they like to have designer labels.
   6. She likes today's fashions because they are more informal, and men and women can wear the same things.

Language work

   3. What are your favorite clothing stores?
   4. Do you buy clothes on the Internet?
   5. How much do you spend on clothes?
   6. Do you buy designer labels?
   7. What do you wear for work/school/college?
   8. What are you wearing now?
   9. What are your favorite colors?
   10. Do you borrow other people's clothes?

Everyday English

1. f   2. e   3. a   4. c   5. b   6. d

Song "Don't Worry, Be Happy"

1   1. b
    2. a

3   The singer thinks it is a bad idea to worry about things.

4
Infinitive	Past
write	**wrote**
have	**had**
sing	sang
worry	worried
get	**got**
lay	**laid**
come	came
take	**took**

5   **"Don't Worry, Be Happy"**
   by Bobby McFerrin

   Here's a little song I wrote
   You might want to sing it note for note
   Don't worry, be happy

   In every life we have some trouble
   But when you worry, you make it double
   Don't worry, be happy

   Got no place to lay your head
   Somebody came and took your bed
   Don't worry, be happy

   Now there is this song I wrote
   I hope you learned it note for note
   Don't worry, be happy

Note
You may want to pre-teach difficult words in the song before listening the second time.

note = draw a musical note on the board: ♪

trouble = problems

double = x 2

Stop and Check 1

Correct the mistakes

   2. What's your name?
   3. My name is Ana.
   4. This is Helen Smith.
   5. It's a book.
   6. Where are you from?
   7. I'm from Japan. / I am from Japan.
   8. He's a businessman. His name's James.
   9. What's her job? She's a doctor.
   10. He isn't a teacher. He's a student.
   11. How old are you?
   12. Is she from London? Yes, she is.
   13. Is he a sales assistant? No, he isn't.
   14. Are you from Brazil? No, I'm not.
   15. His phone number is 555-2541.
   16. My teacher and I are 30.

my/ your, he/she/they, his/her

   2. His
   3. They
   4. your
   5. She's
   6. They're
   7. He's

Questions and answers

1   2. c   3. a   4. b   5. d   6. g   7. e   8. h

2   2. Where's she from?
   3. What's her job?
   4. How old is she?
   5. What's her phone number?
   6. Is she married?

Negatives

   2. She isn't a nurse.
   3. Mike isn't from Canada.
   4. Julie isn't 28.
   5. I'm not married.
   6. Jim and Sue aren't students.
   7. They aren't in New York.

Plurals

   2. We're married.
   3. They're sandwiches.
   4. They're students.
   5. They're from the United States.
   6. We aren't on tour.
   7. Are they doctors?

Numbers

1   6 six   4 four
   1 one   9 nine
   2 two   3 three
   5 five   10 ten
   8 eight   7 seven

2   2. eleven   6. thirty
   3. twenty-eight   7. thirteen
   4. twenty   8. fifteen
   5. fourteen

Vocabulary

1

Jobs	Everyday things
nurse	sandwich
student	book
teacher	television
businessman	camera
sales assistant	bag
taxi driver	computer
police officer	hamburger

2
2. Japan
3. Australia
4. Korea
5. Mexico
6. England
7. Canada
8. the United States
9. Brazil

Translate

The idea behind this is that students begin to be aware of the similarities and differences between English and L1. Emphasize that they must not translate word for word. Obviously it will only be possible to check their answers in a monolingual class but even in a multilingual class students can discuss their answers in nationality groups.

Stop and Check 2

Correct the mistakes

2. My sister's husband is a doctor.
3. The children live in San Diego.
4. He has a new car.
5. Our car is Japanese.
6. How old are you?
7. I like tennis.
8. I don't speak Italian very well.
9. She lives in Taipei.
10. We have a big house.
11. They don't like Chinese food.
12. Where does she work?
13. My husband doesn't work in an office.
14. Do they speak Portuguese?
15. What sports does she like?
16. We never drink tea.

Questions and negatives

1
2. How do you spell your name?
3. How many sisters does he have?
4. What food does she like?
5. Where do you have lunch?
6. What music do you like?
7. How many languages do they speak?
8. What time do you get up?
9. What drinks do the children like?
10. What time does Helen go to bed?
11. Where does your teacher come from?

2
2. Do they have a house in the country?
   They don't have a house in the country.
3. Does he speak three languages?
   He doesn't speak three languages.
4. Do you get up early?
   You don't get up early.
5. Does Vicky have lunch in her office?
   Vicky doesn't have lunch in her office.
6. Does he go to bed late?
   He doesn't go to bed late.
7. Do we have class at 7:30?
   We don't have class at 7:30.
8. Do your parents drink coffee?
   Your parents don't drink coffee.
9. Does she speak English well?
   She doesn't speak English well.
10. Does he cook lunch?
    He doesn't cook lunch.

Prepositions

2. at
3. in
4. by
5. in
6. on
7. on
8. on
9. in
10. at
11. by

Times and prices

3. It's twelve o'clock.
4. It's eleven thirty.
5. It's nine forty-five.
6. It's two twenty.
7. It's four fifty-five.
8. It's ninety-five cents.
9. It's a dollar thirty-five.
10. It's twelve seventy-two.
11. It's sixty-eight forty-one.
12. It's ninety-nine ninety-nine.

Vocabulary—countries and nationalities

Country	Nationality
England	English
China	Chinese
Spain	Spanish
Mexico	Mexican
Korea	Korean
Italy	Italian
Brazil	Brazilian
the United States	American
Japan	Japanese

Vocabulary—words that go together

listen to music
get up late
drink coffee
work in an office
stay home
go shopping
take a shower
walk to work
play the piano

Vocabulary—word groups

Adjectives	Places	Sports
beautiful	studio	skiing
big	college	tennis
funny	office	swimming
favorite	classroom	baseball
nice	apartment	
small	farm	
great	school	
	restaurant	
	hospital	

Translate

See note about translation above.

Stop and Check 3

Correct the mistakes

2. My son is a student and I don't see him very often.
3. That's a photo of my children and me.
4. She lives in an old house.
5. There are three magazines on the table.
6. There aren't any good restaurants in this area.
7. There isn't a computer in the living room.
8. There are a lot of nice stores in the city center.
9. I was born in 1985.
10. Where were you born?
11. The weather wasn't very good yesterday.
12. She played tennis yesterday morning.
13. She went on vacation last week.
14. Where did you go skiing?
15. What did you have for breakfast?
16. Did you buy a newspaper yesterday?

Questions and answers

2. k 3. f 4. a 5. j 6. i
7. c 8. h 9. d 10. e 11. g

there is/are

2. There is
3. There are
4. there isn't
5. Is there
6. Are there
7. there aren't

Past Simple

2. lived
3. went
4. wanted
5. didn't like
6. loved
7. left
8. worked
9. joined
10. was
11. had

Irregular verbs

2. saw
3. got
4. did
5. bought
6. took
7. said
8. ate

was/were/did/didn't

2. was
3. Were
4. Did
5. weren't
6. didn't
7. wasn't
8. weren't
9. didn't

Questions and negatives

2. Is there a CD player in the living room?
   There isn't a CD player in the living room.
3. Was she born in 1980?
   She wasn't born in 1980.
4. Was he a good student?
   He wasn't a good student.
5. Did we stay home last weekend?
   We didn't stay home last weekend.
6. Did you go to bed early last night?
   You didn't go to bed early last night.

Vocabulary

Adjectives	Rooms and furniture	People and jobs	Sports and activities
cheap	lamp	painter	sailing
new	kitchen	princess	baseball
hot	shower	writer	dancing
delicious	stove	musician	skiing
fast	bed	singer	tennis
great	armchair	politician	cards

Translate

See note about translation on p. 132.

Stop and Check 4

Correct the mistakes

2. I can speak Thai.
3. She wants to send an e-mail.
4. "I'd like a coffee, please." "Here you are."
5. "Would you like to come to my party?" "Yes, please."
6. I like shopping.
7. We are learning English.
8. What are you wearing?
9. He isn't working today.
10. I'm doing my homework now.
11. That's my father over there. He's wearing a black hat.
12. Where do you come from?
13. We're going on vacation next month.
14. Are you working tomorrow?
15. We had a good time last weekend.
16. How long did you stay in Peru?

Questions and answers

1 2. e 3. d 4. i 5. a
   6. b 7. h 8. g 9. c

2 2. What
   3. Where
   4. How
   5. Why
   6. Who
   7. What time
   8. How much
   9. How many
   10. How old
   11. When

can/want/like/would like

2. do
3. Would
4. I'd like
5. wants
6. buy
7. doesn't
8. can't
9. sailing
10. can
11. We like

Present Simple and Continuous

3. calls
4. 's wearing
5. Do…get up
6. has
7. is doing
8. are sitting
9. watch
10. Are … working
11. 's raining
12. do … go

Present Continuous for future

2. are getting married / church
3. Are … picking up / tickets
4. am meeting / friends
5. are having / restaurant
6. is traveling / train
7. are going / movies

Past, present, and future

2. am playing
3. Do … play
4. plays
5. started
6. didn't like
7. Are … interested
8. go
9. went
10. Did … have
11. traveled
12. visited
13. Are … going
14. are going
15. lives
16. are staying

Vocabulary—word groups

Food	Clothes	Colors	Transportation
fish	jeans	red	bicycle
fries	jacket	yellow	plane
tuna	sweater	gray	subway
cheese	T-shirt	white	train
steak	pants	brown	ship

Translate

See note about translation on p. 132.

Progress Test 1

Exercise 1

2. are   aren't
3. is   isn't
4. are   aren't
5. are   aren't

Exercise 2

2. Are
3. is
4. aren't
5. 'm not
6. are
7. Are
8. isn't
9. is
10. isn't
11. Is

Exercise 3

Where are you from? Taipei, in Taiwan.
How are you? I'm fine, thanks.
How much is a sandwich? $4.95.
How old is your daughter? She's 18.
Who is Kayla? She's my daughter.

Exercise 4

2. This is Sami's wife.
3. What is their phone number?
4. We have a house in the country.
5. How do you spell your last name?
6. Do you like Chinese tea?
7. I don't speak Italian very well.
8. We don't have a Japanese car.
9. Do they eat Mexican food?

Exercise 5

2. an	5. a	8. a
3. a	6. an	9. an
4. an	7. a	10. a

Exercise 6

2. has	6. has
3. don't have	7. Do … have
4. have	8. has
5. have	9. Do … have

Exercise 7

2. don't like	7. do … speak
3. drink	8. Do … speak
4. do … like	9. don't work
5. work	10. do … live
6. don't like	11. Do … eat

Exercise 8

2. your	6. my
3. He's	7. her
4. She	8. His
5. our	9. their

Exercise 9

2. a 3. b 4. a 5. b 6. b

Exercise 10

2. twenty-nine	7. seventy-four
3. thirty-seven	8. eighty-eight
4. forty-three	9. ninety-one
5. fifty-nine	10. one hundred
6. sixty-two	

Exercise 11

Jobs	Family	Food	Drinks
actor	parent	sandwich	water
bank	sister	hamburger	juice
manager	daughter	chocolate	coffee
sales	son	ice cream	tea
assistant	husband	orange	soda
police			
officer			
waiter			

Exercise 1

2. He never works late.
3. I sometimes go to work by car.
4. My son always has lunch at school.
5. She usually sees her friends after school.
6. I never buy a newspaper.
7. Anela sometimes goes windsurfing.

Exercise 2

2. him	5. us
3. it	6. them
4. her	7. you

Exercise 3

2. There are two books on the table.
3. There's a lamp next to the sofa.
4. There are three pictures on the walls.
5. There's a cat under the table.
6. There's a magazine in the bag.

Exercise 4

2. were	weren't
3. was	wasn't
4. were	weren't
5. were	weren't

Exercise 5

2. Do	6. Did
3. were	7. was
4. did	8. were
5. Does	9. do

Exercise 6

2. didn't work	6. saw
3. bought	7. didn't take
4. did … go	8. Did … eat
5. stayed	9. did

Exercise 7

2. The movie isn't very good.
3. There isn't a CD player in the car.
4. She doesn't go to work by car.
5. We don't go shopping in town.
6. There aren't a lot of hotels in this area.
7. The weather wasn't very hot.
8. My children weren't born in Canada.
9. I wasn't born in 1989.
10. David didn't play baseball at school.
11. I didn't have a big lunch.

Exercise 8

Tuesday, Wednesday, Thursday, Friday, Saturday, Sunday

Exercise 9

2. January second
3. June nineteenth
4. August third
5. December thirty-first
6. October twelfth
7. April seventeenth
8. May first
9. July seventh

Exercise 10

2. on	4. on	6. at
3. at	5. in	7. on

Exercise 11

go sailing
watch a video
listen to a CD
play cards
stay in a hotel
work in a hospital
cook dinner
eat in restaurants
have a good time
drink water

Exercise 12

2. Chinese (The others are countries.)
3. shower (The others are electrical appliances.)
4. ice hockey (The others go with *go*, not *play*.)
5. twenty-nine (The others are ordinals.)
6. athlete (The others are jobs in the Arts.)
7. watched (The others are irregular.)
8. walking (The others are water sports.)
9. kitchen (The others are parts of a room.)

Exercise 13

early	late
small	big
expensive	cheap
fast	slow
cold	hot
great	awful

Exercise 1

2. She has long, blonde hair.
3. How long does the bus tour take?
4. Would you like to listen to the radio?
5. Can you tell me the time, please?

6. They want to buy a new car.
7. What would you like to drink?
8. He is wearing jeans and a T-shirt. *or* He is wearing a T-shirt and jeans.
9. Where are you going next weekend?
10. Why don't you go to bed early?
11. We picked up our tickets from the travel agent's.

Exercise 2

2. can't play the guitar
3. can't ride a horse; can't play the guitar
4. can use a computer
5. Can … cook
6. can ride a horse

Exercise 3

2. Do you like coffee?
3. I want to send an e-mail, please.
4. Would you like to listen to some music?
5. I'd like to buy these postcards, please.
6. What sports do you like playing?

Exercise 4

2. 's working
3. 'm leaving
4. 's wearing
5. 'm driving
6. Is … raining
7. 's taking
8. Are … enjoying
9. are writing

Exercise 5

2. don't see; are staying
3. have; are eating
4. are … wearing; wear
5. are studying; like
6. lives; 's traveling

Exercise 6

2. She cooked dinner yesterday. She isn't cooking dinner tomorrow.
3. We worked late yesterday. We aren't working late tomorrow.
4. They left home early yesterday. They aren't leaving home early tomorrow.
5. I went to bed late yesterday. I'm not going to bed late tomorrow.
6. You stayed home yesterday. You aren't staying home tomorrow.
7. Richard saw his doctor yesterday. He isn't seeing his doctor tomorrow.

Exercise 7

2. She doesn't want to sell her house.
3. They don't like sightseeing.
4. He can't swim.
5. He doesn't work in a bank.

6. We don't walk to work every day.
7. I'm not watching this movie.
8. The children aren't doing their homework.
9. You aren't playing very well.
10. We aren't staying in a hotel for a week.
11. We didn't have a nice meal at the restaurant.
12. You didn't pick up the tickets yesterday.
13. Tamika didn't see her family last week.

Exercise 8

2. is
3. does
4. do
5. aren't
6. didn't
7. isn't
8. 'm not
9. don't
10. am
11. doesn't
12. Did
13. Are

Exercise 9

2. cake (The others are drinks.)
3. dinner (The others are types of food.)
4. soup (The others are desserts.)
5. airport (The others are forms of transportation.)
6. grandmother (The others are jobs.)
7. stamp (The others are to do with traveling.)
8. shoes (The others are worn on the legs.)
9. dress (The others are items of clothing for both men and women.)
10. long (The others are colors.)
11. waiter (The others are parts of a meal.)
12. interview (The others are to do with taking photos.)
13. e-mail (The others are to do with sending letters.)

Exercise 10

watch a video
read a magazine
chat with a friend
wear shorts
play chess
buy a house
catch a plane
change money
go sightseeing
have a good time
pack your bags
arrive in Rome
make a cake

Workbook Answer Key

1 1. **Ann** Hello. I'm Ann. What's your name?
   Jim My name's Jim.
   Ann Hello, Jim.
   2. **Maria** Hello, Lisa.
   Lisa Hi, Maria. How are you?
   Maria Fine, thanks. And you?
   Lisa I'm OK, thanks.

2 2. OK, thanks. And you?
   3. This is James.
   4. What's your name?
   5. My name's Emi.

3 1. **Ben Jones** Hi. My name's Ben Jones. What's your name?
   Alicia Gonzales Alicia. Alicia Gonzalez.
   2. **Ben** Hi, Alicia. How are you?
   Alicia Fine, / OK, thanks. And you?
   Ben OK, thanks.
   3. **Alicia** Ben, this is Aya Saito. Aya, this is Ben Jones.
   Aya Saito Hello, Ben.
   Ben Hello, Aya.

4 1. **David Smith** Hello. My name's David Smith. What's your name?
   Jane Wilson Jane. Jane Wilson.
   2. **Jane** Hi, David. How are you?
   David Fine, / OK, thanks. And you?
   Jane Fine, / OK, thanks.
   3. **David** Jane, this is Mario Costa. Mario, this is Jane Wilson.
   Mario Costa Hello, Jane.
   Jane Hello, Mario.

5 2. It's a house.
   3. It's a car.
   4. It's a hamburger.
   5. It's a book.
   6. It's a sandwich.
   7. It's a camera.
   8. It's a television.
   9. It's a bag.
   10. It's a computer.

6 See note about translation on p. 132

7 2. five
   3. ten
   4. seven
   5. six
   6. one
   7. two
   8. three
   9. four
   10. nine, one, one

8 2. 5
   3. 9
   4. 1
   5. 2
   6. 8
   7. 6
   8. 4
   9. 7
   10. 10

9 2. s
   3. s
   4. s
   5. es
   6. s
   7. s
   8. s
   9. s
   10. s

10 2. nine books
   3. ten bags
   4. one computer
   5. two televisions
   6. three houses
   7. six photographs
   8. seven sandwiches
   9. eight hamburgers
   10. four cameras

1 2. the United States
   3. Japan
   4. Mexico
   5. Canada
   6. Spain
   7. Australia
   8. Taiwan
   9. England
   10. Korea

2 2. Mexico
   3. Spain
   4. Taiwan
   5. the United States
   6. Japan
   7. Australia
   8. Brazil
   9. Canada
   10. Korea

3 A Spain
   B England
   C Brazil, Japan, Taiwan
   D Mexico, Canada
   E Australia, Korea

4 2. A Where's London?
   B It's in England.
   3. A Where's Taipei?
   B It's in Taiwan.
   4. A Where's Sydney?
   B It's in Australia.
   5. A Where's Boston?
   B It's in the United States.
   6. A Where's Seoul?
   B It's in Korea.
   7. A Where's Tokyo?
   B It's in Japan.
   8. A Where's Toronto?
   B It's in Canada.
   9. A Where's Rio de Janeiro?
   B It's in Brazil.
   10. A Where's Mexico City?
   B It's in Mexico.

5 2. A What's her name?
   B Her name's Amy.
   A Where's she from?
   B She's from the United States.
   3. A What's his name?
   B His name's Luis.
   A Where's he from?
   B He's from Brazil.
   4. A What's her name?
   B Her name's Junko.
   A Where's she from?
   B She's from Japan.
   5. A What's his name?
   B His name's Steven.
   A Where's he from?
   B He's from Australia.
   6. A What's her name?
   B Her name's Eun-joo.
   A Where's she from?
   B She's from Korea.

6 1. **Jaime** Hello. My name's Jaime. What's your name?
   Isabel Isabel.
   Jaime Where are you from, Isabel?
   Isabel Rio de Janeiro, in Brazil. Where are you from?
   Jaime I'm from Barcelona.
   2. **Jaime** Hello, Isabel. How are you?
   Isabel Fine, / OK, thanks. And you?
   Jaime OK, thanks. Isabel, this is Ana. She's from Brazil.
   Isabel Hi, Ana.
   Ana Hello, Isabel. Where are you from?
   Isabel I'm from Rio de Janeiro.
   Ana Oh, I'm from Rio, too!

8 2. Mexico
   3. student
   4. married
   5. Canada
   6. teacher
   7. Adam
   8. Taiwan
   9. doctor
   10. hospital

9 2. her
   3. his
   4. her
   5. her
   6. his

10 11 eleven   21 twenty-one
   12 twelve   22 twenty-two
   13 thirteen   23 twenty-three
   14 fourteen   24 twenty-four
   15 fifteen   25 twenty-five
   16 sixteen   26 twenty-six
   17 seventeen   27 twenty-seven
   18 eighteen   28 twenty-eight
   19 nineteen   29 twenty-nine
   20 twenty   30 thirty

11 2. twenty-nine
   3. twelve
   4. fifteen
   5. twenty
   6. seventeen
   7. eleven
   8. thirty
   9. twenty-seven
   10. twenty-one
   11. fourteen
   12. twenty-eight
   13. nineteen
   14. sixteen

12 See note about translation on p. 132.

UNIT 3

1 2. businessman
   3. doctor
   4. nurse
   5. police officer
   6. sales assistant
   7. student
   8. teacher

2 3. **A** What's his job?
    B He's a taxi driver.
   4. **A** What's her job?
    B She's a teacher.
   5. **A** What's his job?
    B He's a businessman.
   6. **A** What's her job?
    B She's a doctor.
   7. **A** What's his job?
    B He's a sales assistant.
   8. **A** What's her job?
    B She's a student.

3 2. She isn't a doctor.
    She's a nurse.
   3. He isn't a businessman.
    He's a police officer.
   4. She isn't a taxi driver.
    She's a sales assistant.

4 Country
   Address
   Phone number
   Age
   Job
   Married?

5 2. Where's she from?
   3. What's her address?
   4. What's her phone number?
   5. How old is she?
   6. What's her job?
   7. Is she married?

6 3. No, she isn't.
   4. No, she isn't.
   5. Yes, she is.
   6. No, she isn't.
   7. Yes, she is.
   8. Yes, she is.

7 All answers: Yes, I am. / No, I'm not.

8 2. Where are you from?
   3. What's your address?
   4. What's your phone number?
   5. How old are you?
   6. What's your job?
   7. Are you married?

9 Students' own answers

10 See note about translation on p. 132.

11 **A** car, fine, thanks, nurse, Spain
   B doctor, seven, number, sandwich, camera
   C hospital, officer, Mexico, hamburger

12 2. I'm 19
   3. Are you a student
   4. Are you from the United States
   5. 11 Insadong Street
   6. And your phone number
   7. Thank you very much

13 2. No, they aren't. (Michael is from Australia and Carlos is from Brazil.)
   3. They're in Toronto, Canada.
   4. They're 22.
   5. No, he isn't. (He's 24.)

14 2. Good morning.
   3. Good afternoon.
   4. Good night.

15 2. Good night.
   3. Good morning.
   4. Good afternoon.
   5. Good morning.
   6. Good night.
   7. Good afternoon.

16 2. Thank you.
   3. Excuse me?
   4. Sorry!
   5. I don't know.

UNIT 4

1 3. ✔
   4. ✗ Greg is Peter's brother.
   5. ✔
   6. ✗ Sue is Greg's mother.
   7. ✔
   8. ✔
   9. ✗ Tina is Jim's daughter.

2 2. parents
   3. brother
   4. mother
   5. wife
   6. children
   7. sister
   8. father
   9. daughter
   10. husband

3 2. This is Susan's camera.
   3. This is Ana's house.
   4. This is Anita's bag.
   5. This is Dan's computer.
   6. This is Frank's dictionary.
   7. This is Akiko's car.
   8. This is David's dog.

4 3. is
   4. P
   5. P
   6. is
   7. is
   8. P
   9. P
   10. P

5 4. 's
   5. 's
   6. s
   7. 's
   8. 's
   9. ✗
   10. 's

6 you   your
   he   his
   she   her
   we   our
   they   their

7 2. your
   3. their
   4. Her
   5. My
   6. his
   7. Our

8 Students' own answers

9 Students' own answers

10 **Jobs** doctor, nurse, businessman, teacher
   Countries Canada, Korea, Spain
   Numbers nineteen, twelve, six, twenty-three
   Families father, wife, son, sister

11 **A** son, wife, Spain
   B family, children, husband
   C Brazil, hello, Japan
   D businessman, manager

12 Answers will vary.

13 2. have
3. have
4. has
5. has
6. have
7. has

14 See note about translation on p. 132.

15 2. He's 57.
3. Her name's Catherine Zeta-Jones.
4. She's from England.
5. His name's Dylan.
6. He's two.
7. They're in the United States, England, and Spain.

16

1	2	3	4	5	6	7
/eɪ/	/i/	/ɛ/	/aɪ/	/oʊ/	/u/	/ɑ/
a	b	f	i	o	q	r
h	c	l	y		u	
j	d	m			w	
k	e	n				
	g	s				
	p	x				
	t					
	v					
	z					

17 2. Who's calling, please?
3. How do you spell your last name?
4. Thank you. I'm sorry. He isn't in his office. What's your phone number?
5. Thank you for calling. Good-bye.

UNIT 5

1 **Sports**
2. swimming
3. skiing
4. tennis
Food
5. Chinese food
6. hamburgers
7. ice cream
8. Italian food
9. pizza
10. oranges
Drinks
11. tea
12. water
13. coffee
14. juice
15. soda

2 Answers will vary.

3 3. No, I don't.
4. Yes, I do.
5. Yes, I do.
6. No, I don't.
7. No, I don't.
8. Yes, I do.

4 Answers will vary.

5 3. Yes, they do.
4. No, they don't. They speak English and French.
5. Yes, they do.
6. Yes, they do.
7. Yes, they do.
8. No, they don't. They like basketball and skiing.

6 2. Do you like Chinese food?
3. Where do you work?
4. Do you drink coffee?
5. What sports do you like?
6. How many languages do you speak?

7 Students' own answers

8 2. Do they have a dog?
3. Do they play basketball?
4. Do they like soda?
5. Do they live downtown?
6. Do they drink juice?
7. Do they work in a bank?

9 2. is / is
3. Are
4. do
5. are
6. Do / do
7. Is / is
8. do

10 3. are
4. from
5. live
6. do
7. from
8. I'm
9. from
10. in
11. your
12. don't
13. a
14. job
15. work
16. Do

11 2. e
3. f
4. b
5. c
6. g
7. h
8. a

12 See note about translation on p. 132.

13 2. Korean
3. French
4. English
5. Japanese
6. Spanish
7. Chinese

14 Answers will vary.

15
twenty-three	23
thirty-seven	37
forty-eight	48
fifty-one	51
fifty-five	55
sixty-four	64
seventy-nine	79
eighty-six	86
ninety-two	92

16
$26.47	twenty-six forty-seven
$99	ninety-nine dollars
75¢	seventy-five cents
$15.55	fifteen fifty-five
5¢	five cents
17¢	seventeen cents
43¢	forty-three cents
58¢	fifty-eight cents
$3.81	three eighty-one
60¢	sixty cents
$1.68	a dollar sixty-eight
$6.49	six forty-nine
98¢	ninety-eight cents
$5.72	five seventy-two

17 2. **A** How much is the dictionary?
B It's twelve seventy. (It's twelve dollars and seventy cents.)
3. **A** How much is the hamburger?
B It's eighty-nine cents.
4. **A** How much is the bag?
B It's forty-seven fifty. (It's forty-seven dollars and fifty cents.)

UNIT 6

1 2. It's eight fifteen.
3. It's ten thirty.
4. It's four forty-five.
5. It's five fifteen.
6. It's six thirty.
7. It's seven fifteen.
8. It's nine o'clock.

2 2. **A** Do you know what time it is?
B It's eleven o'clock.
3. **A** Do you know what time it is?
B It's ten thirty.
4. **A** Do you know what time it is?
B It's four fourty five.
5. **A** Do you know what time it is?
B It's one fifteen.
6. **A** Do you know what time it is?
B It's three forty-five.

3 2. has
3. leaves / eight thirty
4. goes
5. has
6. gets / six o'clock
7. goes

4 2. Helen never goes to work by bus.
3. She usually has a sandwich in her office.
4. She usually leaves work at 5:30.
5. She never works in the evening.
6. She sometimes goes to a restaurant in the evening.

5 Answers will vary.

6 2. Where does Angeles live?
3. Does she have breakfast?
4. When does she go to the concert hall?
5. Where does she usually have lunch?
6. What does she sometimes do in the afternoon?
7. What time does she cook dinner?
8. Does she usually go out in the evening with friends?

7 2. She lives in an apartment in Manhattan.
3. No, she doesn't.
4. She goes to the concert hall at nine o'clock.
5. She usually has lunch at home.
6. She sometimes goes for a walk in Central Park, and then listens to music.
7. At six o'clock.
8. Yes, she does.

8 2. doesn't live
3. doesn't have
4. doesn't have
5. doesn't drink
6. doesn't listen

9 2. Young-soo doesn't leave work at one forty-five.
3. Raoul doesn't go to work by taxi.
4. Ramiro doesn't eat toast for breakfast.
5. Cheng-li doesn't get home at four thirty.
6. Oliver doesn't speak French.
7. Linda doesn't work in a bank.
8. Tomomi doesn't have three children.

10 **Ai**
2. **A** Does Ai go to work by car?
   B No, she doesn't.
3. **A** Does Ai drink tea?
   B Yes, she does.
4. **A** Does Ai speak English?
   B Yes, she does.
Yoshi
2. **A** Does Yoshi go to work by car?
   B Yes, he does.
3. **A** Does Yoshi drink tea?
   B No, he doesn't.
4. **A** Does Yoshi speak English?
   B No, he doesn't.

11 2. don't
3. Do / don't
4. Do / do
5. Does / does
6. doesn't
7. doesn't

12 See note about translation on p. 132.

13

14 Answers will vary.

15 Students' own answers

16 2. Friday
3. Tuesday
4. Thursday
5. Sunday
6. Wednesday
7. Saturday

17 Monday, Tuesday, Wednesday, Thursday, Friday, Saturday

18 2. at
3. on
4. on
5. in
6. On
7. In
8. At
9. in

UNIT 7

1
you   you
he   him
she   her
it   it
we   us
they   them

2 2. her
3. them
4. me
5. us
6. you

3 2. them
3. him
4. it
5. us
6. you

4 3. **A** What's that?
   B It's a house.
4. **A** What's this?
   B It's a glass.

5. **A** What's that?
   B It's a computer.
6. **A** What's that?
   B It's a car.
7. **A** What's this?
   B It's a cat.
8. **A** What's this?
   B It's a camera.
9. **A** What's that?
   B It's a taxi.

5 3. This is a dictionary.
4. That's a sandwich.
5. That's a television.
6. This is a pizza.
7. That's a bag.

6 2. d
3. b
4. a

7 2. a
3. f
4. c
5. g
6. d
7. b

8 2. How much is that dictionary?
   Answer: d
3. How does Maria go to work?
   Answer: a
4. How many sports do you play?
   Answer: b
5. Why does Ling walk to school?
   Answer: g
6. Where does Sang live?
   Answer: f
7. Who is your best friend?
   Answer: c

9 2. What time do you get up?
3. What do you have for dinner?
4. Who lives in the White House? (Where does the president live?)
5. Why do you drink soda?
6. How many dogs does your brother have? (Who has two dogs?)
7. How does she go to work?

10 Students' own answers

11 2. hot
3. old
4. new
5. big
6. small
7. expensive
8. cheap
9. awful
10. great

12 2. Pilar's coffee is hot.
3. Jim's car is old.
4. Sarah's car is new.
5. Alan's apple is big.
6. Judy's apple is small.
7. Mark's computer is expensive.
8. Wendy's computer is cheap.
9. Keith's hamburger is awful.
10. Yumi's hamburger is great.

13 Answers will vary.

14 See note about translation on p. 132.

15 2. The buildings in San Francisco aren't very old.
3. The food is great.
4. The food is very cheap.
5. The hotel is very new.
6. The hotel is cheap, but it isn't very comfortable.
7. The weather is very hot.
8. They go swimming every day.

16 2. **A** Can I have a ticket to New York, please?
   B Here's your ticket, and $5.00 change.
3. **A** Can I send an e-mail, please?
   A How much is it?
4. **A** Can I help you?
   A How much is it?
5. **A** Can I have a pizza, please?
   B $12.30.

UNIT 8

1 2. bathroom
3. dining room
4. kitchen
5. bedroom

2 A. bedroom
B. bathroom
C. living room
D. dining room
E. kitchen

3 2. magazine
3. lamp
4. picture
5. toilet
6. shower
7. TV
8. sofa
9. CD player
10. armchair
11. VCR
12. table
13. stove

4 (Sample answers)
3. There's a telephone in the living room.
4. There are four chairs in the dining room.
5. There's a TV in the bedroom.
6. There are two pictures in the dining room.
7. There's a cat in the living room.
8. There are two lamps in the bedroom.

5 3. No, there isn't.
4. No, there aren't.
5. Yes, there is.
6. No, there aren't.
7. No, there isn't.
8. Yes, there are.

6 3. **A** Is there a magazine in the living room?
   B No, there isn't.

4. **A** Are there any pictures in the dining room?
   B Yes, there are.
5. **A** Is there a picture in the bathroom?
   B Yes, there is.
6. **A** Is there a TV in the bathroom?
   B No, there isn't.
7. **A** Are there any CDs in the bedroom?
   B No, there aren't.
8. **A** Is there a table in the dining room?
   B Yes, there is.

7 2. d
3. e
4. f
5. a
6. c

8 Students' own answers

9 A armchair, camera, never
B because, Japan, cafe
C hamburger, languages
D computer, Korean, expensive, vacation
E afternoon, engineer, understand

10 2. in
3. on
4. next to

11 2. on
3. in
4. under
5. on / next to
6. on / under

12 Students' own answers

13 2. There are two.
3. Yes, there is.
4. They sit in the living room and watch television or listen to music.
5. On the walls in the dining room.
6. No, it isn't. It's new.
7. They have lunch in the dining room.
8. Yes, there is.
9. Yes, they're very happy.

14 Students' own answers

15 See note about translation on p. 132.

16

¹S	U	P	E	R	¹¹M	A	R	K	E	T	
	²H	O	T	E	L						
³N	E	W	S	S	T	A	N	D			
⁴M	O	V	I	E	T	H	E	A	T	E	R
				⁵B	A	N	K				
			⁶D	R	U	G	S	T	O	R	E
			⁷P	A	R	K					
		⁸T	H	E	A	T	E	R			
⁹I	N	T	E	R	N	E	T	C	A	F	E
	¹⁰P	O	S	T	O	F	F	I	C	E	

17 2. hotel
3. Internet cafe
4. Third Street
5. bank
6. next to

18 (Sample answers)
2. Yes, go down Park Street. Go past Elm Street and Main Street. Turn right on Washington Street. Go past First Street and Second Street. The supermarket is on the right.
3. Yes, go down Second Street. Go past Main Street. Turn left on Washington Street. The Internet cafe is on the right.
4. Yes, go down Elm Street. Go past First Street. Turn right on Park Street. Turn left on Main Street. The train station is at the end of Main Street.

UNIT 9

1 2. two thousand
3. nineteen ninety-nine
4. eighteen forty-eight
5. two thousand two
6. nineteen eighty-seven
7. eighteen fifteen
8. two thousand eight
9. nineteen forty-five

2 Yukie 1930
Tomoko 1955
Kenji 1953
Chieko 1955
Takuya 1978
Emi 1980

3 2. When was Takuya born?
   He was born in 1978.
3. When were Takeshi and Yukie born?
   They were born in 1930.
4. When was Kenji born?
   He was born in 1953.
5. When was Emi born?
   She was born in 1980.
6. When was Tomoko born?
   She was born in 1955.

7. When was Yukie born?
She was born in 1930.
8. When were Chieko and Tomoko born?
They were born in 1955.

4 Students' own answers

5 2. was born
3. 1564
4. was
5. were
6. was born
7. were born

6 Elvis Aron Presley was a musician. He was born in Tupelo, Mississippi, in 1935. His wife's name was Priscilla and his daughter's name is Lisa Marie. She was born in 1968.

7 2. **A** Was Amelia Earhart American?
B Yes, she was.
3. **A** Was she born in Canada?
B No, she wasn't.
4. **A** Was she born in 1887?
B No, she wasn't.
5. **A** Was her plane a Lockheed Electra?
B Yes, it was.

8 2. Mark Twain wasn't a doctor.
He was a writer.
3. Akira Kurosawa wasn't from China.
He was from Japan.
4. John F. Kennedy wasn't president of Canada.
He was president of the United States.
5. Confucius wasn't French.
He was Chinese.
6. Laurel and Hardy weren't Australian.
They were American.
7. Humphrey Bogart and Ingrid Bergman weren't singers.
They were actors.

9 2. Was / wasn't
3. weren't / were
4. were / was
5. Were / weren't
6. Was / wasn't / was

10 2. were
3. bought
4. went
5. said
6. saw
7. took

11 2. saw
3. were
4. went
5. bought
6. said
7. took
8. saw
9. was

12 See note about translation on p. 132.

13 **Food & drink** juice, tea
Jobs nurse, teacher, businessman
Rooms dining room, kitchen, bathroom

Places bank, post office, train station
Family daughter, husband, parents
Days of the week Sunday, Thursday, Wednesday
Furniture armchair, bed, table
Verbs watch, listen, play
Adjectives big, awful, old

14 2. July
3. April
4. December
5. October
6. February
7. September
8. June
9. August
10. March
11. November
12. May

15 February
March
April
May
June
July
August
September
October
November
December

16 2nd   second
3rd   third
4th   fourth
5th   fifth
6th   sixth
7th   seventh
8th   eighth
9th   ninth
10th   tenth
11th   eleventh
12th   twelfth
13th   thirteenth
14th   fourteenth
15th   fifteenth

17 2. July fifteenth
3. February eighth
4. October tenth

18 Answers will vary.

UNIT 10

1 2. cooked
3. stayed
4. worked
5. listened
6. watched

2 **A** cooked, worked
B stayed, listened

3 2. listened
3. watched
4. cooked
5. worked
6. played

4

5 2. had
3. went
4. bought
5. ate
6. saw

6 a. 3
b. 6
c. 1
d. 5
e. 2
f. 7
g. 4

7 Students' own answers

8 3. **A** Did he play basketball?
B No, he didn't.
4. **A** Did he buy a newspaper?
B Yes, he did.
5. **A** Did he do a lot of homework?
B No, he didn't.
6. **A** Did he watch television?
B Yes, he did.
7. **A** Did he go to work?
B No, he didn't.
8. **A** Did he listen to the radio?
B Yes, he did.

9 2. Who did you see last weekend?
3. What time did you get home yesterday evening?
4. How much homework did you do last week?
5. What did you have for breakfast this morning?
6. Where did you have lunch yesterday?

10 Answers will vary.

11 2. We didn't see our friends yesterday.
3. They didn't get up late yesterday morning.
4. You didn't play tennis.
5. I didn't have a big breakfast.
6. He didn't do a lot of housework on the weekend.
7. We didn't watch a movie on TV yesterday evening.
8. Last week I didn't stay in a hotel in Toronto.

12 See note about translation on p. 132.

13 2. play golf
3. go windsurfing
4. go sailing
5. go walking
6. go dancing
7. go ice skating

8. play baseball
9. play soccer
10. play cards
11. play ice hockey
12. go skiing

14 2. They didn't have a terrible time.
They had a very good time.
3. They didn't stay in a hotel.
They stayed in a house with their friends Gary and Rachel.
4. They didn't get up at eleven o'clock.
Every morning they got up at nine o'clock.
5. The weather wasn't awful.
The weather was great—hot and sunny.
6. Hannah and Rachel didn't play golf in the afternoon.
They usually played tennis in the afternoon.
7. They didn't have dinner in a restaurant.
In the evening they cooked a big dinner in the house.
8. They didn't go swimming.
After dinner they went dancing.

15 **Address:** 818 West Iowa Street
Chicago, Illinois
Zip code: 60622
Phone number: (773) 555-4649
Date of birth: September 2, 1980

UNIT 11

1 2. ride a horse
3. use a computer
4. drive a car
5. draw
6. play the guitar
7. run
8. speak Chinese
9. play the piano

2 Answers will vary.

3 3. Bill can use a computer.
4. Bill can't ride a horse.
5. Amanda can't read music.
6. Amanda can ride a horse.
7. Jill and Sam can read music.
8. Jill and Sam can use a computer.
9. Jill and Sam can't ride a horse.

4 3. **A** Can Bill read music?
B Yes, he can.
4. **A** Can Bill ride a horse?
B No, he can't.
5. **A** Can Amanda use a computer?
B No, she can't.
6. **A** Can Amanda ride a horse?
B Yes, she can.
7. **A** Can Jill and Sam read music?
B Yes, they can.
8. **A** Can Jill and Sam use a computer?
B Yes, they can.
9. **A** Can Jill and Sam ride a horse?
B No, they can't.

5 All answers:
Yes, I can. No, I can't.

6 **A** I can draw.
They can ski.
B Yes, we can.
Yes, they can.
C We can't run.
She can't cook.

7 2. Can I help you?
3. Can you tell me the time, please?
4. Can I have a pizza, please?
5. Can you speak more slowly, please?

8 2. Yes, I want to buy this newspaper.
3. It's ten forty-five.
4. Yes, of course. Small, medium, or large?
5. I'm sorry. Can you understand now?

9 See note about translation on p. 132.

10 2. December
3. soccer
4. Tuesday
5. weekend
6. yard

11 2. **A** I can't find my plane ticket.
B You put it on the table.
3. **A** I don't understand this word.
B Check it in your dictionary.
4. **A** This computer doesn't work.
B Did you push this button?
5. **A** I'm lost. Can you help me?
B Where do you want to go?
6. **A** What's the matter?
B The CD player's broken.

UNIT 12

1 2. I'd like to use your dictionary.
3. I'd like to buy her new CD.
4. I'd like a stamp.
5. I'd like to see the new Steven Spielberg movie.
6. I'd like to be a student again!

2 3. I'd like a glass of water, please.
4. I'd like to play cards, please.
5. I'd like to listen to a CD, please.
6. I'd like a stamp, please.
7. I'd like a cup of coffee, please.
8. I'd like to buy a computer, please.

3 3. Would you like to watch TV?
4. Would you like a glass of orange juice?
5. Would you like some cake?
6. Would you like to go skiing?
7. Would you like a pizza?
8. Would you like to play a computer game?

4 2. chicken
3. fish
4. fries
5. fruit
6. mineral water
7. salad
8. soup
9. tomato
10. vegetables

5 3 And what would you like for your main course?

4 Can I have the fish, please?
5 The fish. Very good. And what would you like to drink?
6 Can I have a cup of coffee, please?
7 Certainly. A cup of coffee.
8 And I'd like a bottle of mineral water, too.
9 Yes, of course. Thank you.

6 2. What would you like to start?
3. And for your main course?
4. How would you like it cooked?
5. Can I have the roast chicken
6. I'd like a bottle of mineral water

7 Answers will vary.

8 2. day
3. new
4. sister
5. my
6. shop
7. usually

9 See note about translation on p. 132.

10 2. Mitsuo
3. Kim
4. Serena
5. Kim
6. Jake
7. Serena
8. Mitsuo

11 1. next to
2. No, thanks
3. in a large
4. **A** try on
B The fitting rooms
5. two kilos of / that's all
6. Do you sell

UNIT 13

1 2. red
3. white
4. green
5. brown
6. black
7. blue
8. gray

2 4. studying
5. working
6. making
7. going
8. watching
9. talking
10. eating

3 2. I'm learning English.
3. We're sitting in the living room.
4. She's talking to her sister.
5. They're enjoying the movie.
6. He's dancing.
7. I'm working at home.

4 2. they aren't drinking / They're drinking
3. he isn't sitting / He's sitting
4. I'm not having / I'm having
5. She isn't walking / She's running
6. you aren't wearing / You're wearing

5 3. **A** Is Elisa reading a book?

B No, she isn't.
4. **A** Are Marcos and Mario wearing T-shirts?
  B Yes, they are.
5. **A** Is Rafael sitting on the beach?
  B Yes, he is.
6. **A** Are Rafael and Elisa swimming?
  B No, they aren't.
7. **A** Is Elisa drinking a soda?
  B Yes, she is.
8. **A** Is Rafael reading a magazine?
  B No, he isn't.

6 2. are / am
3. Does
4. do
5. is
6. Does / does

7 2. aren't
3. isn't
4. don't
5. 'm not
6. doesn't

8 See note about translation on p. 132.

9 2. He's reading the newspaper.
3. The sun's great and it's really hot.
4. They usually stay with their friends Chao and Sarai.
5. They're staying in a hotel.
6. They go swimming.

10 3. Maria
4. Maria and Linda
5. Maria and Chris
6. Linda
7. Jane and Chris
8. Chris
9. Jane and Chris
10. Jane

11 (Sample answers)
1. Mike's wearing a jacket, a shirt, pants, and shoes.
2. Carol's wearing a hat, a coat, a sweater, a skirt, and boots.

12 Answers will vary.

13 2. hot
3. hungry
4. cold
5. thirsty
6. bored

14 2. a
3. f
4. b
5. e
6. c

UNIT 14

1 2. On Monday evening he's going to/seeing a movie with Jane.
3. On Tuesday morning he's seeing the doctor.
4. On Tuesday afternoon he's playing soccer.
5. On Wednesday morning he's driving to Los Angeles.
6. On Wednesday afternoon he's visiting Joe.

2 3. F
4. P
5. F
6. P
7. P
8. F

3 2. **A** How's she traveling?
  B She's traveling by train.
3. **A** Who's she meeting?
  B She's meeting Sophie.
4. **A** Where's she meeting her?
  B She's meeting her at Union Station.
5. **A** When's she going to Baltimore?
  B She's going to Baltimore at one o'clock.
6. **A** Why is she going to Baltimore?
  B She's going to Baltimore to see Mike.
7. **A** What's she doing on Friday evening?
  B She's going to bed early.

4 2. **A** <u>What</u>'s your job?
  B I'm a <u>doctor</u>. What's <u>your</u> job?
3. **A** <u>What</u> are you doing <u>tomorrow</u>?
  B I'm <u>working</u>. What are <u>you</u> doing?
4. **A** <u>What</u>'s your <u>name</u>?
  B <u>Mark</u>. What's <u>your</u> name?
5. **A** Where are you <u>from</u>?
  B <u>Boston</u>. Where are <u>you</u> from?

5 See note about translation on p. 132.

6 2. packed
3. picked up
4. caught
5. arrived
6. went
7. had

7 2. subway
3. ship
4. bicycle

8 a. 6
b. 2
c. 5
d. 3
e. 1
f. 4

9 2. They left their car on a street near the city center.
3. They stayed in Los Angeles for five days.
4. No, they didn't.
5. They caught a plane.
6. The police found their car a week later.

10 2. When does the next bus leave?
3. Can I help you?
4. Where is it?
5. when is it open?
6. How much is it to get in?

11 1. The bus leaves at 10:00, 12:00, **1:00**, and 3:00 from 42nd Street. The tour takes **3** hours.
2. Central Park Zoo
  Open from **10:00** to **4:30**
  Adults **$3.50**
  Children **50¢**